Making Reform Work

Making Reform Work

The Case for Transforming American Higher Education

ROBERT ZEMSKY

RUTGERS UNIVERSITY PRESS
New Brunswick, New Jersey, and London

Library of Congress Cataloging-in-Publication Data

Zemsky, Robert, 1940–
Making reform work: the case for transforming American higher education /
Robert Zemsky.
    p. cm.
   Includes bibliographical references and index.
   ISBN 978–0–8135–4591–2 (hardcover : alk. paper)
   1. Education, Higher—United States. 2. Educational change—United
States. I. Title. II. Title: Case for transforming American higher education.
LA227.4.Z45 2009
378.73—dc22

2008048062

A British Cataloging-in-Publication record for this book is available from the
British Library.

Visit our Web site: http://rutgerspress.rutgers.edu

Manufactured in the United States of America

For the TLA Gang—
Ann, Barbara, Bill, Greg, Jim, Joan,
Pam, Rick, Susan, Virginia

Contents

Acknowledgments

This is the first book in more than thirty years that I have not written with a coauthor. It remains the case, however, that in casting and then recasting my sense of how and why American higher education needs to change I have benefited greatly from that extraordinary team that works at the core of The Learning Alliance (now in proper alphabetical order): Virginia Branch, Ann Duffield, Pamela Erney, James Galbally, Barbara Gelhard, Joan Girgus, William Massy, Richard Morgan, Susan Shaman, and Gregory Wegner. Together they were more than the "gang that shot straight"—they are friends, colleagues, critics, and, above all, fellow troopers.

I am also indebted to Jim Duderstadt and David Ward who read key parts of this manuscript as did Bill Massy, Joel Smith, and Bill Tyson. Jody DeMatteo was the editor responsible for cleaning up my prose—no mean achievement given my penchant for dropping words and misspelling those I do include. As before, key chapters appeared first as extended essays. An early version of the chapter on globalization was first published in Luc E. Weber and James J. Duderstadt, eds., *The Globalization of Higher Education*, Economica (London, 2008), under the title "Has Our Reach Exceeded Our Grasp? Taking a Second Look at Higher Education as a Global Enterprise." An early version of the chapter describing some of my experiences as a member of the Spellings Commission first appeared in *The Chronicle Review* (January 26, 2007) under the title of "The Rise and Fall of the Spellings Commission."

My discussion of the rankings was first published in *Academy of Management Perspectives* (February 2008) under the title, "The Rain Man Cometh—Again." I first wrote about how changing American higher education might require a "dislodging event" in *Currents* (July/August 2007) under the title "Was the Discussion the Dog That Didn't Bark?"

Marlie Wasserman of the Rutgers University Press played a major role in the shaping of this book. Deftly she reminded me why we write books—to inform, even to influence others, and that to do so authors need to take account of what their readers want and how they will use what we supply them. Once again, Lisa Nowak Jerry gently but firmly shepherded the manuscript through its final production.

Finally, I owe an incalculable debt to the two people who for so long have been at the center of my adventures: my wife, Ann, who regularly and correctly reminds me that some agenda, starting with family, are more important than others; and Martin Meyerson who, often with a wicked gleam in his eye, took a young historian and made him an expert in higher education. In ways I suspect he only guessed, the writing of this book was for him.

Robert Zemsky
Peach Bottom
August 2008

Making Reform Work

Prologue

The American university, as we regularly remind ourselves, boasts an ancient heritage. We count ourselves the direct descendents of Abelard in Paris, of Oxbridge and a tradition of the college as sanctuary, and finally of the German university with its emphasis on research and codification. As remembrances, these traditions often take on a kind of Lake Wobegon quality, where all are our ancestors were strong, all their students good-looking, and all their claims to virtue way above average.

In truth, however, the modern American university as an institution did not exist a half-century ago—not until the scientific and scholarly revolutions that grew out of the Second World War gathered steam and then, in a cascade of new expectations, all but swept away those who hankered for a simpler, more ordered academy. Somehow a relatively small, frequently isolated set of enterprises has been transformed into an industry of considerable economic heft—in terms of both the monies it spends and the funds it extracts annually from local, state, and national budgets. Today nearly everyone goes to college—people of all ages, ethnicities, economic standing, even academic preparedness—more than fifteen million a year and, at last count, still growing. If the impulse to start new, traditionally configured institutions has waned, then the entrepreneurial push to establish for-profit and electronically configured institutions of postsecondary education is just getting started. None of the icons we celebrate in our remembered history—not

Abelard, not the good dons of Oxford and Cambridge, not those bearded professors of Humboldt, and certainly not Cardinal Newman— would recognize, let alone celebrate, what the American university is in the process of becoming.

The one constant in this history has been the ability of the university to remain a guild of expertise. The one claim, above all others, that faculty can successfully make is that we are experts in our fields— professors, who by scholarship and training know how to separate knowledge's wheat from its speculative chaff.

I begin here because I am often asked, "And just when did you get to be such an expert on higher education?" After all, I was trained as a historian and, by most accounts, was well on my way to a successful career as one of the first to use quantitative techniques to recreate past realities. And then, somehow, I, taking a sharp detour, became something unrecognizable to both those who had trained me and those who had celebrated my early work. Most times when asked, "What happened?" I just mutter something innocuous like "on the job training" or "my interest and training in history led me naturally to an interest in higher education."

I tell my students something else, less well understood by them and me, but nonetheless the statement testifies to how I began accumulating my expertise in higher education. "In the 1970s," I say quietly, "I became apprenticed to Martin Meyerson."

Martin Meyerson was the president of the University of Pennsylvania for a decade following his selection in 1970. For Meyerson, it was a return to Penn, where he had been a faculty member in the 1950s before leaving for Harvard and MIT and then Berkeley. He came to Penn with an impressive resumé, a reputation for having helped save Berkeley while acting chancellor during the student uprisings of 1964, and a habit of surrounding himself with bright young scholars who carried the title of faculty assistant to the president. Meyerson wanted to continue the tradition at Penn, but ultimately he encountered what can only be described as Penn's tradition of faculty skepticism cum crankiness. The president could have a faculty assistant who could even be a younger scholar; however, the assistant would already have to be a tenured member of the faculty. In ruling out an untenured assistant professor, the leaders of the faculty senate pointed out that, at Penn, the president's favor might cut either way; indeed, it was as likely to prejudice the personnel committee against the candidate as it was to provide an unfair advantage.

Meyerson wanted someone younger than thirty. At the time I was told there were only two tenured members of the faculty who met the standard. What I wasn't told, and never asked, was whether I was the president's first or second choice. I took up my duties in the fall of 1971 when the president still resided in Chestnut Hill, occupying the residence of his predecessor Gaylord Harnwell. The president, it turned out, was my neighbor. For those who know that part of the world, his was a big house on the west side of Germantown Avenue and mine a compact twin east of the Avenue. For the next year, I was the frequent victim of what my wife came to see as a Faustian bargain. If I would just stay a little later—attend another meeting, polish another piece of prose, read another report—he would give me a ride home. We would then set off in the Checker limousine Meyerson first used as his official car. Everyone noticed the Checker, it was part of its attraction, and from its high-perched rear seat it was possible to notice everyone noticing you: heady stuff.

But, in the end, only the conversations mattered. Meyerson was the teacher, the man who knew everybody—he really did; the constant traveler with the prodigious memory for names, places, events, books; but most of all the man with a thousand stories, each part of a fabric of understanding. When I knew him better, was less awed and often more impatient with the pattern of discovery he propelled every listener along, I described his way of talking as fundamentally feline, like that of a cat who constantly circles before finally alighting, having exhausted everyone but himself. If you wanted to learn from Meyerson you had to listen carefully to the points he was circling as he invited you to discover for yourself what he was about. This habit of mind reflected both his faith in a market of ideas and his reluctance to proscribe what he would rather induce.

The result was a nearly year-long tutorial on what a university looked like from the top. For Meyerson it proved to be a tough year. His proposal to build the University of Pennsylvania on a program of "Selective Excellence" ran into a faculty buzz saw. He managed to circumvent some of the senate's prerogatives by appointing a development commission, only to have the body itself come to see its principal role as a mediator between the president's vision and the senate's suspicions. To make matters worse, Penn was broke, warned by its bank not to further extend its monthly draws. Through it all, we talked. Part of the process was to make me talk, never a very difficult assignment, so that Meyerson could play off what I knew and didn't know.

Like most presidents I have known, this one loved gossip, as both a diversion and a source of critical intelligence. So he pumped me for what the faculty was thinking, what I was thinking, what he ought to be thinking.

In the conversations about higher education I had with Meyerson, he pushed as well as pulled. Sometimes he would start by asking a very specific question—for example, How many applicants could Penn reasonably expect from the state of Texas?—and then, when I responded with ever more detail, he would push me to see a larger reality. We weren't talking just the admissions game; we confronted the evolving nature of higher education's student markets. Or conversely, when I went off on a speculative tangent, he would pull me down into the details I had so gladly left behind. It was an important but not necessarily complex message. If one was going to study higher education, then one needed to be Janus-like—one eye cocked on the details, the other searching for the larger meaning. Implicit in these discussions was the notion that to know higher education one had to know at least one institution, and preferably a sequence of institutions, intimately. Meyerson was inherently suspicious of what later came to be called policy wonks and their penchant for system-speak and systemic solutions. That message I also imbibed, and I have only come recently to look for my own kind of systemic strategies for effecting change across the wide spectrum of American colleges and universities. By then, of course, I had come to know not just Penn but a host of institutions intimately, so that my understanding of the workings of an American system of higher education was in fact a layering of Meyersonian perspectives.

Working with Meyerson bequeathed to me one final advantage—an ability to see over the horizon just before the contours of the future became obvious and settled. My training as a historian taught me to focus on context, connections, and language. Meyerson helped me to become a listener and facilitator, who, while watching a conversation unfold, came to understand what mattered: not just what people were saying but how and to whom they were saying it. For all my fascination with numbers and models, I most often brought to Meyerson snippets of prose that attempted to capture the conversations swirling about us. This skill has allowed me to label things such that they are remembered differently even by those who said them in the first place.

Through the fall of 1998, that was my understanding of how I became an expert in higher education: Meyerson was the master while

first Penn, and then a widening network of institutions, in which I
served as either a consultant or a convener of roundtables, provided the
necessary laboratory experiences. Then, after more than twenty-five
years, Meyerson and I renewed our conversations. We had spoken
often and frankly in the intervening years—he chaired my Institute's
Board; he was a member of the Board of the National Center on the
Educational Quality of the Workforce (EQW), which I codirected; he
was the one who introduced me to Japan; and he remained my mentor—
but the conversations we began the fall of 1998 had the intensity of our
first meetings, only now we met more as equals trying to remember
what we knew and how we had come to know it.

Meyerson was about the task of writing his memoirs—sort of. He
was too smart and practical to be fooled into thinking many really
cared to revisit his past. But like many leaders of consequence who see
their lives and careers as part of a special history of challenge and
accomplishment, Meyerson wanted his story told. He wanted to set the
record straight and, though he would never admit it, to settle a few
scores while reminding himself and others that what he had done had
in fact mattered.

I told him what he expected. I had little interest in his memoirs,
but I would help him remember if that would spur the process of *his*
writing the book he envisioned. I should have known better. The
remembering hooked me, got me to thinking how I knew what I knew,
on the one hand, and on the other, which lessons were really worth
passing on. The conversations were all-absorbing; they ranged over the
history of Penn, over Meyerson's own career, over the evolution of the
American university following the Second World War. For me these
conversations offered a respite from my real task: completing a set of
analyses and a pair of monographs detailing how market forces had
fundamentally recast the boundary conditions for American higher
education.

Starting in 2005, our conversations included what I was
learning and not learning as a member of the Secretary of Education's
Commission on the Future of Higher Education—the Spellings
Commission. Meyerson was pleased that I had been asked to serve, but
he was more than a little concerned that I would blow it—that I would
talk too much, that I would forget to focus simultaneously on both the
details and the big ideas, or that I would be seduced into joining
the then growing clamor to indict higher education for its perceived
mediocrity. He need only have worried about my loquaciousness, and

even on that score I had proved remarkably well behaved. I shared with him my growing frustration: because the Commission was being led astray, we were losing an opportunity to summon the nation's colleges and universities to do more, be bolder, more willing to take risk, and less self-assured and seemingly complacent.

Toward the end of my service on the Commission, Meyerson asked if I planned to sign the final report. I tried to explain the politics that had engulfed our efforts and the growing suspicion among those of us from the academy that we were being set up as a kind of stand-pat opposition unwilling to face the truth of higher education's declining effectiveness. So I told him I would sign—that the final recommendations did no harm—but I would explain to anyone who was interested that I was a willing member but a reluctant signer.

Meyerson died in the summer of 2007. By then we had already suspended our work on our Penn project as he fought his last battle. I turned instead to the writing of this volume, one that I hoped would prove sufficiently Meyersonesque to deserve his attention. This book is my attempt to answer the question he put to me once it was clear that I would sign but not campaign for the Commission's final report. "One of these days, sooner rather than later, I hope you will write the report the Commission should have submitted. Are you ready for that challenge?" I hope I am. In *Making Reform Work: The Case for Transforming American Higher Education* I attempt to make sense of all that is now swirling about higher education—and to offer what the Spellings Commission did not: a challenge for the future and a strategy for enlisting the very instincts of the academy to do more, to be bolder, to take those risks which the academy, from time to time, since the age of Abelard, has taken.

1 | Prelude to Reform

An invitation from Secretary of Education Margaret Spellings asked me to join her in Denver for a roundtable discussion focusing on American higher education. Nothing seemed right—no list of invited participants, no offer to cover travel costs, no indication, really, of intended purposes or likely outcomes. I had all but decided to decline the invitation by citing family and other responsibilities, when the e-mail from Jim Duderstadt, former president of the University of Michigan, arrived; he hoped I would join him for breakfast in Denver the morning of the secretary's roundtable. I bought my tickets that afternoon.

We all have people in our lives like Jim Duderstadt—mentors, colleagues, friends to whom we have said, "If you ask, I'll be there!" Since 1998 I have done what he has asked and known that his projects and thrusts, if not always successful, are always interesting. In Denver Duderstadt surprised me again; he suggested we arrive early at the session to meet with Charles Miller, who was helping Spellings organize the roundtable.

Miller showed up with a copy of a recent essay I had written for the *Chronicle of Higher Education*. Miller had read the piece—more than that, he had marked up the essay, highlighting what he liked and just as pointedly what he didn't like, all the while using the margins to push an imaginary argument with me about the right way to approach the topic. Miller's copy looked like that of an attentive college student who wanted to make sure he had full control of an argument before launching his critique in class. He need not have worried—he was way ahead of me. What was wrong with higher education, Miller observed, was that no one was really in charge. Rather than the market making American colleges and universities more disciplined, the pursuit of new revenues was making higher education just plain wasteful. "Where's the accountability?" he asked. "Who are the change agents? Why is the academy taking so long to recognize the need for systemic change?"

And that's how I met Charles Miller—like the secretary of education, a Texan and confidant of the president, an investment banker whom then-Governor Bush had appointed to the University of Texas Board of Regents. From the get-go he was larger than life—smart, driven, funny, engaging—not to mention manipulative, controlling, and inherently argumentative. He was, as I later told Jim Duderstadt, "a real piece of work." In Denver, Miller's assignment was to test whether a national commission might successfully launch an extended dialogue on the future of American higher education. Only after the event did I understand that the session Miller chaired was in fact a tryout. Like most other participants, I was being auditioned. In my case Miller wanted to determine whether I was sufficiently independent to judge an enterprise in which I had spent most of my professional life as a prickly and at times just barely tolerated academic gadfly.

The Denver session coincided with the announcement that in the latest round of federal testing of educational outcomes, elementary school students, in particular, had made substantial gains in reading and math. More important, the results indicated that African American youngsters had narrowed the gap between their own and the performance of white elementary students on the standardized tests. Spellings was energized; Miller was in charge, and the discussion that followed was about as good as it gets—focused, forward looking, and decidedly collegial. Most participants came away from the Denver session believing a national dialogue on the future of American higher education just might be possible and just might be a good idea. David Ward, the president of the American Council of Education, later told me that an earlier roundtable Spellings and Miller had convened in Washington had the same character.

The Spellings Commission

In September, the secretary of education's Commission on the Future of Higher Education was officially launched.

Charles Miller would be its chair. Its task, Spellings told a forum at the University of North Carolina Charlotte, was to develop a "comprehensive national strategy" on higher education's future. Echoing Miller's comments in Denver, Spellings claimed, "Now is the time to have a national conversation on our goals for higher education. . . . [and] I'm here to start that discussion."[1]

What surprised everyone, including those of us named to the Commission, was the breadth and standing of those who accepted the secretary's challenge. Among the assembled were Jim Hunt, former Democratic governor of North Carolina and a national champion of higher education, and seven current or former presidents of colleges and universities, including three from major research institutions—Duderstadt of Michigan, Vest of MIT, and Ward of Wisconsin, who at the time headed the American Council of Education. Key executives from Microsoft, IBM, and Boeing joined a former U.S. secretary of health and human services and a scattering of higher education wonks like myself. The lineup gave the Commission instant credibility. At the time one friend told me, "It's a lineup that suggests something serious is about to happen."

The appointment of the Spellings Commission both coincided with and drew upon a quickening debate about the sustainability of American higher education. John Merrow and Richard Hersch had just issued *Declining by Degrees: Higher Education at Risk* as both a PBS documentary and a book of essays that harshly warned that American colleges and universities were becoming decidedly mediocre. In *Measuring Up*, the fifty-state report card on the condition of higher education across the nation, Patrick Callan and his colleagues at the National Center for Public Policy and Higher Education similarly warned that American higher education was already unaffordable, unaccountable, and uninspiring. A host of higher education organizations focusing on reform were joining the chorus; they sensed it was once again time to raise the banner of reform. Thus, when Margaret Spellings stepped before her audience in Charlotte, she had good reason to believe now was the time to put higher education on the national agenda.

Miller had his assignment. For the next year he would hold higher education's center stage—cajoling, criticizing, provoking, where necessary backtracking by suggesting organized higher education was taking him too literally or, as was more often the case, misunderstanding his purpose. Miller above all wanted a real discussion. In his view, really good civic discourse, while always polite, was necessarily pointed as well. One could recognize the substantial achievements of American higher education and still suggest room for improvement—or, as Miller came to increasingly insist, there were real problems out there requiring real, even daring, solutions.

Miller was everywhere spreading the message that this Commission would make a difference. Always charming, always prepared, ever the good listener, he eagerly sought sessions with the leaders of higher education's principal organizations. But his real appeal and power derived from his understanding of the media and his ability to tap into the fourth estate's inherent distrust of higher education, both its pronouncements and its leaders. The press could count on him for a good interview. Like lots of successful politicians he had the ability to distill complex arguments and make them simple; then, for good measure, he wrapped them in the kind of pungent language reporters like to quote and readers end up remembering. He was always on message. Despite higher education's dependence on market income, there was no bottom line, just an endless pursuit of new revenue. No one really knew whether higher education's products were any good. What, if anything, were college students learning? There was no accountability. Accreditation wasn't working. No governmental body—federal, state, or local—could know if it was getting its money's worth. In an era of heightened global competition, business as usual would not suffice.

He talked eagerly and willingly about the need for better tests of educational outcomes and provoked across higher education a renewed interest in standardized testing. There were even bad jokes about Miller's penchant for testing. At the University of Pennsylvania one wag suggested the Commission had as its mandate "No College Left Behind." But there was real give and take as well. In March Derek Bok added his voice to the debate that Miller had provoked. Writing in the *Washington Post*, Bok began by noting that greater accountability on the part of higher education was long overdue, in part at least because a growing body of research indicated that American college students weren't really learning what they needed to. A student, spending four years in college, demonstrated only marginally improved critical thinking. "Tests of writing and of literacy in mathematics, statistics and computer technology suggest that many undergraduates improve these skills only slightly, while some actually regress."[2]

It didn't matter that Bok had made many of these same arguments in his recent book with the provocative title, *Our Underachieving Colleges*, or that he dismissed Miller's call for the development of a national test of learning outcomes as a search for a "standardized test" that could only make matters worse. It did matter that Bok and others were taking Miller and his Commission seriously. They were joining Miller in proclaiming that business as usual was no longer acceptable. They were lending their prestige to the search for a better understanding of learning outcomes and, in the process, were bestowing on Miller's quest a legitimacy it could not have otherwise claimed.

As if to underline this last point, Peter McPherson, newly elected head of the National Association of State Universities and Land Grant Colleges, appeared before Miller and his Commission the month following Bok's commentary; McPherson announced that his organization was prepared to take on the challenge of building a voluntary system of accountability that included the measurement of student outcomes. In a discussion paper he brought with him to the Commission's meeting in Indianapolis, McPherson noted, "We should consider a voluntary system, by type or mission of colleges and universities, based on outcomes. There should be a serious discussion on how to do this within the higher education community and not just in the public policy/ political community. . . . A successful voluntary system would likely contain a small bundle of concepts. It probably would allow for measurement through both student surveys and measures of some key competencies.[3] Miller had what he was looking for—or so it would seem.

Going the Wrong Way on a One-Way Street

As it turned out, the Commission's April meeting in Indianapolis proved to be the apogee of Miller's and the secretary's track across American higher education. With little fanfare and not much notice on the part of the Commission itself, Miller had begun turning increasingly to a hand-picked trio of consultants known to be critical of mainstream higher education. While Miller himself encouraged dialogue rather than combat, the witnesses testifying before the Commission and the papers the Commission's staff and consultants were distributing as official documents had taken on a decidedly negative tone. David Warren, president of the National Association of Independent Colleges and Universities and Miller's most persistent as well as effective critic, voiced the growing concern of many within the academy when he told *Inside Higher Education*'s Doug Lederman that too often the Commission was being treated to a "parade of the disaffected," and so we were.[4]

Miller, who was about to adopt a much less conciliatory public persona, signaled this change in a separate interview with Lederman. Having made the chairman aware of Warren's remarks, Lederman wrote, "Miller suggested that Warren and other college officials might be engaging in a bit of wishful thinking if they believe the Commission isn't still headed toward issuing a 'strong report with strong language,' and turning the general 'goals' agreed to Thursday into a set of tough recommendations that hold institutions much more accountable for their performance."[5] The tone wars had begun.

In May, the Commission, again in open session, drafted a set of basic findings and policy recommendations that most of us felt were largely positive, at times even celebratory. Unbeknownst to the Commission, however, Miller and his trio of consultants, along with the former editor in charge of the rankings issue at US News and World Report, had begun writing a draft report clearly intended to jolt higher education. In June, partly by accident, perhaps partly by intent, a draft of the Preamble and Findings of the Commission's report began circulating, first among some commissioners, then among the whole Commission; shortly thereafter it became a public document.

The draft minced no words: "Our year-long examination of the challenges facing higher education has brought us to the uneasy conclusion that the sector's past attainments have led it to unseemly complacency about the future. It is time to be frank. Among the vast and varied institutions that make up U.S. higher education, we have found equal parts meritocracy and mediocrity."[6] David Warren's warning that a "parade of the disaffected" had taken control of the Commission was proving all too prescient.

The press loved it. Under a headline that proclaimed "Panel's Draft Report Calls for an Overhaul of Higher Education Nationwide," *New York Times*' Karen Arenson summarized the draft: "Nearly every aspect of higher education in America needs fixing." The *Chronicle of Higher Education*'s headline was equally precise, "Draft Report from Federal Panel on Higher Education Takes Aim at Academe." The AP's wire story put the matter in more Millerian terms: "Commission Draft Report Calls for Shake-up in Higher Education."[7]

Miller not only anticipated but also looked forward to the battle that lay ahead. In an interview with the *Austin American-Statesman*, Miller allowed that he "had been advised to say things in moderate terms, to not criticize the academy. . . . It's almost like being censored. Some of the language . . . could be toned down, but the real issue is putting responsibility on the higher education system for things it's not doing well. It has some really bad flaws." And just in case anyone missed the point, he continued, "If you wrap it up in academic language, which is what the academy wants, you get long sentences and footnotes, and it gets put on the shelf. Strong language gets attention."[8]

In Pursuit of Action

After the *Austin American-Statesman* interview there was little prospect that either Miller or Spellings would lead a movement that transformed American higher education. A majority of the Commission did manage to get our final report to be relatively calm rather than pointedly scatological. But the effort exhausted us. Although we won the tone wars, in the process we settled for a final report that was as uncontroversial as it was imprecise. All the changes the Commission recommended became someone else's responsibilities—a to-do list addressed to no one in particular:

1. Every student in the nation should have the opportunity to pursue postsecondary education. We recommend, therefore, that the U.S. commit to an unprecedented effort to expand higher education access and success by improving student preparation and persistence, addressing nonacademic barriers and providing significant increases in aid to low-income students.

2. To address the escalating cost of a college education and the fiscal realities affecting government's ability to finance higher education in the long run, we recommend that the entire student financial aid system be restructured and new incentives put in place to improve the measurement and management of costs and institutional productivity.

3. To meet the challenges of the twenty-first century, higher education must change from a system primarily based on reputation to one based on performance. We urge the creation of a robust culture of accountability and transparency throughout higher education. Every one of our goals, from improving access and affordability to enhancing quality and innovation, will be more easily achieved if higher education institutions embrace and implement serious accountability measures.

4. With too few exceptions, higher education has yet to address the fundamental issues of how academic programs and institutions must be transformed to serve the changing needs of a knowledge economy. We recommend that America's colleges and universities

embrace a culture of continuous innovation and quality improvement by developing new pedagogies, curricula, and technologies to improve learning, particularly in the area of science and mathematical literacy.

5. America must ensure that our citizens have access to high quality and affordable educational, learning, and training opportunities throughout their lives. We recommend the development of a national strategy for lifelong learning that helps all citizens understand the importance of preparing for and participating in higher education throughout their lives.

6. The United States must ensure the capacity of its universities to achieve global leadership in key strategic areas such as science, engineering, medicine, and other knowledge-intensive professions. We recommend increased federal investment in areas critical to our nation's global competitiveness and a renewed commitment to attract the best and brightest minds from across the nation and around the world to lead the next wave of American innovation.[9]

What the Spellings Commission did and did not accomplish will, I suspect, be talked about for years as both policy wonks and graduate students in higher education debate why such a star-studded effort did not spark the transformation of American higher education that its sponsors intended. In part, the problem, as I have already suggested, derives from the fact that the Commission's report reflected an uneasy compromise between Miller and his consultants on one side and those of us from within higher education on the other. Even the wording of the recommendations reflects that tension: the "whereas" clauses contain the remnants of Miller's strong language; the actual recommendations could have been written without holding a single meeting or listening to a single disgruntled witness.

In September 2006, Margaret Spellings spoke before the National Press Club and offered her own "Plan of Action" while acknowledging her Commission's work. The Commission's six recommendations were now reduced to five action items. She began, not with higher education per se, but with the need to expand as well as renew the No Child Left Behind Act that had come to anchor much of the Bush administration's domestic agenda. Next she called for streamlining the process of applying for federal financial aid, to "cut the application time in half and notify students of their eligibility earlier than the spring of their senior year to help families plan." She lobbied for the creation of a national student record database, a proposal, included in the Commission's report but already rejected by Congress. Her fourth action item called for providing matching funds to colleges, universities, and states that collect and publicly report student learning outcomes. Finally, she proposed convening members of the accrediting community in November "to move toward measures that place more emphasis on learning."[10] Organized higher education, along with both the *Chronicle of Higher Education* and *Inside Higher Education*, chose to see in Spellings's presentation a conciliatory invitation to build the kind of consensus that transforming higher education would require. David Ward, who had served on the Commission and was the president of the American Council of Education, told the *Chronicle*, "Many of my deepest anxieties were diminished. . . . The federal role could have been rather aggressive. I didn't get that model at all. She talked about a process, and dialogue."[11]

Even David Warren, the most persistent critic of the Commission, was quoted in *Inside Higher Education* as having said he and his colleagues would look for ways to "move forward where we can work with the department." Under the headline "The Sounds of Conciliation" the same story noted that the "tone that Spellings adopted in her speech—kinder, gentler and less prescriptive than college leaders perceived Miller, as the Commission's strongest voice, as having—seems to have increased the optimism among higher education officials that something productive can come from the process that lies ahead, unclear as it is."[12]

Not everyone was mollified. Charles Miller warned higher education's leaders not to delay in providing the kind of accountability data the secretary was calling for. *New York Times* education editor Sam Dillon wrote an even more pointed story. In near-Millerian language Dillon described a quite different, clearly more combative Margaret Spellings: "Saying she hoped to jolt American higher education out of a dangerous complacency, Secretary of Education Margaret Spellings vowed Tuesday to help finance state universities that administer standardized tests, establish a national database to track students' progress toward a degree and cut the red tape surrounding federal student aid." In her words, the secretary saw the beginning of "a process of long-overdue reform."[13]

As it turned out, Dillon and the *Times* proved the better prognosticators of what the secretary had in mind. She began quietly enough; in March 2007 she convened a summit of nearly three hundred leaders from business, higher education, and philanthropy. Again the tone was conciliatory. She spoke of shared responsibility and joint leadership and avoided the kind of blame game that had come to absorb others within her department. Responding to calls from the Commission in general and from former Governor Hunt of North Carolina in particular to increase Pell Grants, she had promised more money. But she had already seen her new undersecretary and former Commission member Sarah Martinez Tucker pummeled by a congressional committee once it was understood that the so-called new monies would be taken from existing programs.

The secretary's plans for accreditation, however, told those who were watching where Spellings was headed. Accreditation itself is a murky, not very well understood, and too often dysfunctional process that designates those institutions entitled to award degrees. Six regional accrediting agencies are responsible for undergraduate education, and a host of agencies accredit professional programs. Except for these professional accrediting agencies, accreditation itself is a process that brings few benefits to the institutions and satisfies none of those who think colleges and universities need to be held more accountable for what they teach and what their students learn. I pleaded with my fellow commissioners not to see in accreditation a lever for change—I said trying to make sense of accreditation was akin to trying to walk on quicksand—all to no avail. The Commission's Report proclaimed: "Accreditation agencies should make performance outcomes, including completion rates and student learning, the core of their assessment as a priority over inputs or processes. A framework that aligns and expands existing accreditation standards should be established to . . . allow comparisons among institutions regarding learning outcomes and other performance measures."[14]

Somewhere along the line Miller persuaded Spellings that the way to enact her reform agenda was to federalize accreditation. Because only students enrolled in an accredited institution are eligible for federal student aid, if—and it's a big if—the accrediting agencies do their job by denying accreditation and hence access to federal student aid dollars to institutions that do not measure student learning outcomes, then accreditation will become *the* process by which colleges and universities could be compelled to codify what they teach and measure what their students learn. Although it involved a convoluted federal process known as negotiated rule-making, the secretary's plan was relatively simple. Use the negotiated rule-making process to weed out those accrediting agencies unprepared to make the detailed measurement of learning outcomes a necessary condition for accreditation and hence for student eligibility for federal student financial aid.

For nearly a year Spellings and her colleagues in the Department of Education pushed this plan. Whatever the secretary and her undersecretary might have been saying in public, behind closed doors they were playing hardball. But so were the higher education organizations charged with protecting the independence and autonomy of their members.

Spellings next discovered just how adept organized higher education had become at "ropa-dopa"—the art of stalling, dodging, and misdirecting until your opponent is too exhausted to be an effective threat. In this case organized higher education's principal spokesmen were aided by a growing hostility to what Spellings and Miller had in mind, a suddenly pungent payola scandal involving senior financial aid officers at a host of colleges and universities and a growing realization that time had run out on a Bush administration in which Spellings had been an important voice. For a year Spellings and her staff pushed, organized higher education bobbed and weaved, and higher education's trade press, principally the *Chronicle of Higher Education* and its rival *Inside Higher Education*, provided detailed reports on who was winning. Along the way Lamar Alexander, senator from Tennessee and former Republican secretary of education, warned Spellings that Congress would not take kindly to having its powers to decide how higher education would be regulated usurped by a Department of Education that was itself frequently the target of would-be reformers as well as investigative reporters. Lost amidst the political to-ing and fro-ing was Miller's original notion that the imposition of tougher accreditation standards would force colleges and universities to rethink both how and what they taught. Instead, the initial discussion of ideas had morphed into a political contest in which the Department of Education had few, if any, cards to play.

In December 2007, nearly a year after launching her campaign to federalize the accreditation process, Margaret Spellings did what by then she knew she had to—she pulled the plug. A month later, after some unexpected contretemps between the House and Senate and between negotiators representing the accreditors and those representing organized higher education, the Senate inserted into the draft Higher Education Reauthorization Act language that gave colleges and universities mostly what they wanted. Under a headline that summed up the story—"Colleges Emerge the Clear Winner in the Battle Over Accreditation"—the *Chronicle of Higher Education*'s Paul Basken wryly noted, "if the accreditation battles of the past year had been a boxing match, the referees probably would declare American colleges the winner by a technical knockout." Even Miller was ready to concede defeat. Or, as Basken put it, Miller saw "the result as a clear loss for the campaign to improve the quality of American colleges, as the peace agreement is likely to end any remaining hope that Congress might give the Education Department the right to dictate standards." Still, Miller did not want to go quietly. His parting shot: "The governors are going to wake up one day . . . and say, 'What are these people in Atlanta and Chicago and those places doing telling me what my institution should do? We own them.' "[15]

Tallying the Wins and Losses

As I have often observed, I was a willing member of the Spellings Commission but a disappointed signer of its final report. The Commission began as a grand adventure: members were truly extraordinary; a smart, tough secretary of education supported the endeavor; and a dialogue initially promised a discussion that just might lead to a transformed system of higher education. But the Commission had ended with less than a whimper. The time, energy, and political capital invested in and by the Spellings Commission had been exhausted.

It would be wrong, however, to conclude that the Spellings Commission was inconsequential. Through its proceedings and the attention it received, the Commission helped delineate both the strengths and vulnerabilities of American colleges and universities. The Commission provided an important set of clues as to why higher education seems so impervious to change. Indeed, what the Commission presented to the nation, and to every analyst and policy wonk willing to listen, was a moveable feast documenting the current condition of the enterprise and revealing, in ways most unexpected, the roles tribal mores and institutional customs play in determining what can and cannot be done, what should and should not be talked about. Yes, much of the testimony was, as David Warren observed, "a parade of the disaffected." But then again most of us who served on the Commission came either from the heart of higher education or from the enterprise's corporate sponsors and policy advocates. The tension between what was wrong and what was right with American higher education was played out in dozens of confrontations along with endless conversations, both within and without the Commission. Understanding that tension and the limit it places on the would-be reformer turned out to be as important a lesson as any notion of what higher education ought to be doing differently.

The secretary had launched a natural experiment detailing higher education's changing contours and highlighting the fault lines that made reform and transformation so difficult. As a commissioner I was literally flooded with paper and electronic documents. During each of the Commission's public sessions a steady flow of witnesses told us exactly what was wrong with higher education. My e-mail inbox was regularly loaded with communications from fellow commissioners and all those who thought a little extra effort at communication would tip the Commission's deliberations in their favor. On an almost daily basis the Commission staff assembled what the press was writing about the Commission in particular and higher education in general, a truly wonderful thing. The daily "clips" made clear just how important the deliberations of the Commission were to higher education's insiders and just how little attraction higher education stories had for the public at large.

Some of what I was learning I knew about before serving on the Spellings Commission. I had already pretty much concluded that the argument over higher education's affordability was a sham. I had similarly concluded that if the nation wanted to change the demographics and the ethnic composition of its institutions of higher education, all of us needed to talk less about access and more about participation and preparation. I suppose I should have known, but had never focused on, just how dysfunctional federal programs of student financial aid had become or how much federal aid was being awarded using other criteria than financial need. Because Jonathan Grayer, chairman and CEO of Kaplan, Inc., was on the Commission, I got a firsthand glimpse of the growing world of for-profit education—its motivations other than profits, its challenges, and the degree to which it feels disadvantaged by current regulations and accreditation processes.

I was surprised and more than a little disheartened to discover just how unimportant the research and discovery mission had become among higher education's would-be reformers. I was similarly surprised that technology, while often mentioned, was almost never incorporated into our discussions or deliberations. My biggest surprise, however, was the near absence of insights about teaching and learning in either the materials presented to us or in the discussions within the Commission. We talked a lot—perhaps even endlessly—about testing what students knew and didn't know but hardly at all about how students learn and whether different learning modalities would yield better results. It was as if the Carnegie Foundation for the Advancement of Teaching had no voice. To be fair, Jim Duderstadt regularly reminded anyone who would

listen that we now had access to a host of new insights, principally neu-
rological, about how people learn. The problem was that none of us was
really listening.

I also came to understand just how important it was to begin talking, in almost singular terms, about an *American higher education system*—huge, complex, diverse, but nonetheless interconnected by the
workings of the market, by a plethora of federal programs of student
financial aid, and by the machinations of accreditation. Most of my
research and writings had dealt with the workings of individual colleges and universities or, in the case of market segments, with groups or
clusters of institutions. Similarly, much of what currently passes for
public policy focusing on higher education has taken on a disaggre-
gated cast; talk about community colleges is separate from research universities, which in turn are seen as distinct from liberal arts colleges
and comprehensive institutions, both public and private. This mindset
is reflected in the structure of those groups that speak on behalf of
organized higher education—the AAU is not to be confused with
NASULGC, which in turn is seen as distinct from AASCU on the one
hand and CIC and NAICU on the other. The nation's community colleges have their own organization, as do a host of religiously oriented
consortia and advocacy groups. A special and very separate organization—COFHE—speaks on behalf of the nation's wealthiest and most
selective private colleges and universities. In this climate it is easy to
dismiss system solutions as a mistaken search for a one-size-fits-all
answer. Woe to the would-be reformer who would talk broadly and
comprehensively about costs or outcomes or learning—though such
integrating conversations will be needed if higher education is to be
seen as anything other than a diverse set of businesses selling similarly
packaged products. That was my first lesson. A national dialogue that
treated higher education as a whole was really needed. The specific
question surfaced: how do the parts relate to one another?

My second lesson is in many ways more troubling. Too often missing from the reformers' call for change and transformation is any real
strategy for getting large numbers of colleges and universities to do
things differently. Miller would argue that he did in fact have a strategy,
the first step of which was getting higher education's attention. The
way to do that was to use what Miller called "strong language," forcefully identifying the enterprise's many flaws and broken parts—a strategy of jolt and shame that was roughly the educational equivalent of
shock and awe. We tried to tell him otherwise, that changes he sought

would have to come from within higher education. Playing the blame game was not going to produce the surge of creativity that changing higher education required. All to no avail.

A third, related lesson, was the role genuine anger and mounting frustration play in casting the reform agenda—at least the agenda to which the media and at times public officials pay the most attention. The problem, I came to understand, was that higher education really is a Teflon-coated enterprise—a turn of phrase first coined by senior research fellow John Immerwahr of Public Agenda (and author of a number of the organization's studies) to explain why, despite the lamentations of the reformers, the public continued to have faith in an enterprise they have never really understood. As a result most would-be reformers burst upon the scene already angry and frustrated, more than ready to use truly strong language to express their outrage and sense of urgency. Although they almost always begin their lamentations with a quick nod to higher education's importance, past achievements, and future potential, what really matters is simple: a list of things gone wrong and an equally detailed list of how to fix them.

I have spent much of the time since the Commission issued its final report asking myself a basic question: what should have happened? This volume is my best answer to that question. You will not find here the inside story of the Commission. Marlie Wasserman of the Rutgers University Press has persuaded me that little if any real interest exists in an event that is likely to be judged by most to have been a brief, if troubling episode, an event worthy of an extended footnote but not much more.

Instead, I hope that the readers will consider the pages that follow as I intend them—as a narrative of ideas. I begin by describing who is saying what about American higher education—who's angry, who's disappointed, and why. Most pleas for changing higher education from outside the academy are principally lamentations on a theme—as much angst as actual program. The critique from within the academy, more muted to be sure, focuses on a whole different set of issues principally involving money and the power of the market to change colleges and universities. Sandwiched between these perspectives is a public that still has faith in an enterprise that it really doesn't understand. The public, at least as reflected in opinion polls, worries most about the increasing cost of higher education and the fact that colleges and universities, like hospitals, are looking just like the businesses they have become.

2 | The Wine of Our Discontent

Much of the story of reform in higher education has been written by the exhorters who have challenged us to do better while at the same time suggesting they know exactly what "doing better" entails. Often the best known exhorters have been university presidents—Charles Eliot of Harvard, Robert Maynard Hutchins of the University of Chicago, and Clark Kerr of the University of California come readily to mind. More recently, higher education's leading exhorters have come from organizations that promote improvement. Russ Edgerton as president of the American Association for Higher Education (AAHE) and Lee Schulman as president of the Carnegie Foundation for the Advancement of Teaching are good examples. Whether institutional leader or organizational promoter, however, each of these exhorters has led by example as well as precept and in the process has significantly altered the development of the nation's colleges and universities.

When exhortation has failed—and it has failed now—lamentation has inevitably followed. There is a noticeable shift in both the tone and substance of the higher education dialogue. Gone is the sense of challenge and duty, replaced by long litanies of failures along with generalized prescriptions for making right what has gone so horribly wrong. As I have already observed, we are living today in one of those shifts. How do I know? Not because I served on the Spellings Commission, though as I have already testified, that experience certainly confirmed we had entered an era of lamentations. No, I know because in the previous spring, the canary in the mine died in Atlanta. Russ Edgerton's AAHE announced it would close. For nearly four decades, AAHE had been the organization that best exemplified the exhorters' challenge to higher education. To the task of recasting American higher education, AAHE brought an exuberance that was often infectious. The movement promised to climb any mountain and ford any stream if the effort promised better learning or more engaged students and teachers.

Declining membership, however, exacerbated by a shift in the spending priorities of foundations, had left the organization without sufficient resources to continue. The larger problem, however, was that the association had run out of energy. A Japanese visitor to AAHE's last annual meeting in Atlanta told me at the time, "It was all so tired; nothing was really new."

Even before AAHE's demise, the lamenters had assumed center stage. They, with their charge that American colleges and universities had slipped to the point of failing, had come to set the context for nearly every discussion of change and transformation. It was, I am sure, this rising chorus of lament that gave Margaret Spellings and Charles Miller the confidence to argue that higher education was now primed for the same kind of reform they had each helped embed in the No Child Left Behind legislation that became the hallmark of the Bush administration's educational agenda. I want to begin by trying to understand what the lamenters have—and have not—been saying and why.

Declining by Degrees

As if to mark the transition from exhortation to lamentation, Richard Hersh and John Merrow sallied forth with *Declining by Degrees, Higher Education at Risk*, a 2005 PBS documentary on higher education that was accompanied by a companion volume of essays with the same evocative title. Merrow and Hersh were an impressive duo: Merrow was the executive producer and host of *The Merrow Report*, a program on PBS and NPR produced by his nonprofit company, Learning Matters; and Hersh was the former president first of Hobart and William Smith Colleges in New York and then of Trinity College in Connecticut and more recently codirector of the Collegiate Learning Assessment. Their reporting and experiences had taught them—and their interviews with several dozen higher education poohbahs, myself included, seemingly confirmed—that higher education needed a wake-up call, something to convince the nation's colleges and universities that calamity lay just over the horizon.

To save the enterprise, Merrow and Hersh promised to blow higher education's cover. Their avowed model: the 1983 report *A Nation at Risk* that had made fixing elementary and secondary education a national priority. Now it was an "insidious erosion of quality" across higher education that "places this nation at risk." Finding a remedy would necessarily begin with "a national conversation about higher education. No longer can our colleges and universities be allowed to drift in a sea of mediocrity. The stakes are high, but we know that many Americans want the crown jewel of our system restored to its former glory." Like almost all lamenters, Merrow and Hersh believed that starting that conversation required an up-close-and-personal examination of higher education's failures and foibles.[1]

The opening shot in this campaign was to be their two-part *Declining by Degrees* documentary that was, despite Merrow's reputation for innovative TV news reporting, mostly pan shots, interviews, talking heads, and solemn voice-overs. *Declining by Degrees* largely presented a list of what is wrong with American higher education: students who don't learn; faculty who don't teach; escalating prices; the misplaced emphasis on rankings; out-of-control college sports; enormous sums being spent on amenities to attract students; more money going to merit as opposed to need-based student financial aid; and colleges and universities that were getting better and better at "doing it on the cheap" to preserve their bottom lines. The substance of the national conversation Merrow and Hersh sought was laid out in the volume published to accompany their PBS documentary. For that effort, they invited sixteen distinguished commentators to share their own sense of what was wrong with the enterprise and why.

Instead, Merrow and Hersh's accompanying volume made clear just how elusive a task they had set for themselves. Often the distinguished commentators, not on message, left the reader more than a little confused as to what to believe about the nation's colleges and universities. Three of the best essays opened the volume. Gene I. Maeroff, a former national education correspondent for the *New York Times*, dissed not only higher education but also the news media, which had largely "trample[d] over intelligent, informed coverage of higher education." Those assigned to cover education were often inexperienced in covering colleges and universities, found issues involving elementary and secondary education more compelling, and when they did write about higher education, focused on a limited number of old chestnuts rather than on the quality of the learning being delivered.

The result? "Higher education is Teflon-coated, remarkably immune to criticism. It is easier to assume that when students do not succeed at colleges and universities, it is because high schools have not prepared them properly."[2]

Deborah Wadsworth, the retired head of Public Agenda, made the same point, although she began, in an echo of Merrow and Hersh, by noting that the country's opinion leaders, particularly those who cared deeply about higher education, were growing impatient with higher education's reluctance to examine its basic assumptions and modes of operation. The trouble, as Wadsworth knew, having managed Public Agenda while it helped conduct a decade-long set of public opinion surveys on higher education, was that the public believed differently. "Indeed," she wrote, "the public is basically satisfied with higher education pretty much the way it is. And in those rare instances where people begrudgingly acknowledge a potential problem, they exhibit a high degree of tolerance, basically giving the institution of higher education a pass and focusing the blame elsewhere." Like Maeroff, Wadsworth saw colleges and universities as "wrapped in Teflon."[3]

James Fallows, national correspondent for the *Atlantic Monthly*, contributed the third of this set of opening essays. He focused on an admissions process that had become ever more "marketized," in which those most interested in attending a medallion college or university were too often consumed by a competition "for 'positional goods' of . . . evanescent value." But he also knew that such competition, for all the news media's infatuation with it, actually concerns only a small slice of the market for undergraduate education. He concluded that, in general, the process by which students choose colleges and universities—what he called "matchmaking"—in fact "worked very well. Most students end up satisfied with the institutions they attend; most colleges are satisfied with the balance and talents of the student body they attract."[4]

Declining by Degrees's most intriguing essay was contributed by Vartan Gregorian, the president of the Carnegie Corporation of New York (and former president of Brown University and the New York Public Library). The first half is a lamentation verging on jeremiad in which Gregorian lays out the six challenges facing higher education: too much information and not enough learning; a "curriculum crisis"; "the commercialization of research"; the development of a "two-tier" faculty system of full- and part-time instructors; concerns about diminishing quality, "especially in schools of education"; and the challenge of distance education. Then he draws his line in the sand: "Failure to answer these challenges will transform our society and threaten our democratic republic." Neither Merrow nor Hersh could have said it better.[5]

But midway through the essay, the mood and even the language shift as Gregorian, drawing on the work of Jim Duderstadt, becomes inquisitive about the impact technology is likely to have on the American university. Taking seriously Duderstadt's warning that markets and technology in wicked combination can leave the university bereft of both value and tradition, Gregorian demurs. He is an optimist, not a pessimist, he says; he is a believer in the resilience of faculty members and in that unfettered commitment to excellence that will prevent them from becoming "guest workers, so to speak, hanging around the neighborhood waiting for companies to hire them to teach specific courses at specific times and places." No University of Phoenix here, thank you.[6]

Equally central to the argument Hersh and Merrow present in *Declining by Degrees* is the contention that American colleges and universities are no longer teaching the right stuff. In *Declining by Degrees*, responsibility for making that point falls to Carol Schneider, who, as president of the Association of American Colleges and Universities, has taken on the role as higher education's chief exhorter.

In *Declining by Degrees*, however, she too is in Jeremiah mode. The problem, as Schneider presents it, is really twofold. There has been a pernicious downsizing of the academy's commitment to liberal education—to its values, its insights, and the sense that being educated means being broadly curious and hence "well-prepared for an era characterized by greater expectations in every sphere of life." What made it relatively easy to downsize liberal education—which for Schneider is the equivalent of downsizing the academy's commitment to the arts and sciences—was the realization on the part of the faculty that the academy rewarded "scholarship" at the expense of "educational leadership." In this recalibration of roles, the faculty's contributions to the quality of general education have become "simply a form of pro-bono enterprise."[7] "As a result . . . general education is an orphan curriculum, fragmented and incoherent. Frequently, required courses are taught by adjunct faculty or graduate assistants rather than full-time senior faculty. Sensing the lack of strong intellectual purpose in their general studies, many students have come to view general education as an obstacle to surmount rather than a resource for their own lives."[8]

And so it went: a too-often distracting documentary filled with old chestnuts and a volume of essays by interesting and important commentators that didn't hold together. It was not compelling television. Nor was it the ringing indictment of higher education Hersh and Merrow promised in their introduction. As an opening shot in a crusade, *Declining by Degrees* fizzled. As a harbinger of things to come, it was to prove an important artifact.

Measuring Up

A second, somewhat related but more coherent and hence sustaining critique has emerged from the National Center on Public Policy and Higher Education. That effort is being guided by Patrick Callan, a former executive vice president of the Education Commission of the States and before that the State Higher Education Executive Officer (SHEEO) in both Washington and California. Although the National Center on Public Policy and Higher Education has engaged in a wide-ranging set of studies and activities focusing on how states can better improve public higher education, the Center and indeed Callan himself are best known for *Measuring Up*, the biennial report card that grades all fifty states on five key measures reflecting the quality, broadly defined, of the higher education each state provides.

What makes *Measuring Up* both interesting and compelling is its remarkably consistent compilation of data reflecting the current condition of higher education across the fifty states. Nearly everything imaginable has been included—costs, labor market conditions and requirements, the college readiness of high school graduates, college participation and completion rates, and the benefits accruing to both individuals and their states from their college educations. At the same time, the biennial publication of a new *Measuring Up* report card has served as an important opportunity for Callan and his colleagues to assess the shifting quality of the enterprise itself—to say frankly what's working, what's not, and what needs to be fixed immediately. While a wide variety of commentators have lent their voices to this effort, the opening two essays—the forward by the chair of the Center's board, former North Carolina governor and Spellings Commission member Jim Hunt, and Callan's introduction—have carried the brunt of the message.

Measuring Up 2000, the first essay provided Callan the opportunity to specify the two core concepts designed to govern the enterprise. First, higher education had become "virtually the only gateway" to personal economic prosperity. Second, that gateway was the political responsibility of the states rather than of either the federal government or private philanthropy. To drive home this latter point, Callan reminded his readers that nearly four out of every five American college students were enrolled in a public college or university—"institutions created by and financially dependent on state governments." This not so subtle reminder became pronounced in subsequent reports that American higher education was primarily a public as opposed to a private or independent enterprise, more concerned with the many than with the few.[9]

Much of the rest of Callan's initial introduction was devoted to explaining why a state-by-state report card was important, how making comparisons between and among states could lead to improved performance on the part of all states, and how public policy makers might use such measurements to better achieve their stated objectives. In his initial foreword Governor Hunt, employing the same dispassionate tone, noted that, in his gubernatorial experience, when comparisons were made and paid attention to, things got better. He put it simply, "As a governor, I've learned that the things we keep track of, count, and monitor tend to be the ones we improve." Only in passing, or so it seemed, did Hunt question higher education's then current practices and accomplishments. "Despite the accomplishments of American higher education, its benefits are unevenly and often unfairly distributed, and do not reflect the distribution of talent in American society. Geography, wealth, income and ethnicity still play far too great a role in determining the educational opportunities and life chances of Americans."[10]

Two years later Hunt introduced the next report card largely by repeating his basic message. The states were paying attention. The school reform movement was beginning to pay off. But too many Americans were still excluded from the benefits of a good higher education. Callan, however, was more troubled. Particularly irksome was the reputation of American higher education as "the best in the world"—a claim that for Callan reflected the reputations of just "a few elite institutions and . . . the research contributions of a small number of universities." *Measuring Up*, however, examined higher education as it affected "the lives of most Americans, including, but not limited to, the handful of students who attend an elite college or university." When looked at from that perspective, Callan concluded, American higher education's condition was "one of unevenness and even mediocrity."[11] Though the sentence was buried amidst a more general discussion of how the United States was likely to fall behind Europe and the rest of the developed world in the competition for educational capital, Callan was signaling a significant shift in both the spirit and intent of his report card. Careful readers had been warned.

Measuring Up 2004 repeated Callan's barb, though in more muted tones. The operative term was not "mediocre" but rather "underperforming," as cast in the report's foreword: "*Measuring Up 2004* is a 'wake-up call' for our country. We are all justifiably proud of our colleges and universities, but the inescapable fact is that America is underperforming in higher education. Following the path of the past decade will take us to the wrong destinations: diminished opportunities for many Americans and greater economic vulnerability for the country and the states."[12] Callan added that it was time to address those deficiencies before it was truly too late. Two years later, perhaps sensing his argument wasn't making much headway, Callan laid out in considerable detail just how much the U.S. position as the world's leader in higher education had eroded, particularly in terms of participation and completion rates among young adults. The fact that the rest of the world was catching up with the United States was not surprising. What was not predictable was "the 'wall' that the United States hit in the early 1990s and the national failure to make significant progress on key higher education indicators in the last decade and a half, while the rest of the world improved."[13] Then in a special essay on the key affordability measure, Callan summed up his findings and ire.

> As critical as it is, the college affordability problem does not exist in a vacuum. It is one of many symptoms of the underperformance of American higher education that signal the urgent need for a comprehensive and fundamental reexamination of higher education finance. This report card highlights these symptoms: flat college participation rates; lack of progress in extending college opportunity for low-income Americans; poor rates of completion of college programs; escalating costs and prices; and a financial aid system that is less focused on the nation's need to improve college access and attainment. . . . [I]f the nation and the states are to realize improvements commensurate with their investments, they must raise and answer critical questions of fairness, efficiency, effectiveness, incentives, and accountability.[14]

Persistently, carefully, Callan's four national reports had spelled out the key issues that would come to dominate the lamenters' critique of American higher education. Rising prices were pushing a higher education beyond reach of an increasing number of Americans in general and lower-income Americans in particular. In the global competition for economic success, the United States was increasingly at risk, in large measure because too many younger workers lacked the range of skills and knowledge that a college education was expected to supply. Across higher education there was a failure of will to measure what college students were and were not learning. Too much attention and too many kudos lavished on American higher education focused on the achievements and activities of a small number of elite, often private, universities and colleges; however, too often, the experiences of the many were in institutions that offered mediocre as well as incomplete educations. All in all, what American higher education needed was a jolt of sufficient magnitude to make American colleges and universities less complacent, less self-satisfied.

A Familiar Refrain

There is a kind of breathlessness to all these laments, a reflected sense of urgency in the face of an approaching conflagration that, this time, will be of sufficient heat to melt through higher education's Teflon coating. The message is clear: American higher education needs to change, and it needs to change now!

But we have heard it all before. Even the appeal to economic competitiveness and the threat of international competition are not new. Two decades ago the link between educational failure and economic stagnation was the subject of another National Commission and another special report whose title said it all: *America's Choice: High Skills or Low Wages.* Unless the United States radically improved its schools and altered the way it trained young workers, it would find itself surpassed by national economies populated by better educated and hence more productive citizens. The language of *America's Choice* became a key element in Bill Clinton's winning presidential campaign. But when the economy did improve, largely because the United States enjoyed a real spurt in worker productivity, most Americans and most politicians forgot the economic imperatives so vividly spelled out in *America's Choice*; indeed, they forgot about fixing the schools until another successful candidate made improved elementary schooling a key part of his campaign for the presidency.

Nearly all the elements of the laments I have been tracking appeared at least twenty-five years ago. Having first dissed higher education for large classes, binge drinking, students unprepared for collegiate work, courses too often taught by teaching assistants, students who, because they are in college just to have a good time, don't study very much, grade inflation, and professors who have sought a separate peace with their students in order to pursue their own interests untrammeled by the others' concerns, Merrow closed *Declining by Degrees*'s first segment with a lament of what might have been but is not: "A few innovations on the margin won't help higher education regain its special status. As long as Americans believed higher education was serious about teaching and learning, we put it on a pedestal. But in the last 25 or 30 years higher education seems to have become a business ... less [worried] about teaching and learning."[15]

It was a good sentence but bad history. It is as if the 1978 film *Animal House* had never been made, or as if Frederick Rudolph, professor emeritus of history at Williams College, and his compatriots at the Association of American Colleges and Universities had never written *Integrity in the College Curriculum*; indeed *Integrity*, published in 1985, offered a far more reasoned and simultaneously damning critique of what students were then learning in college.

In the PBS documentary version of *Declining by Degrees*, George Kuh, best known for making the National Survey of Student Engagement (NSSE) a standard measure of collegiate outcomes, reveals the fact that some students are allowed to drift through college and still get a degree ought to be "higher education's dirty little secret." Richard Hersh is next heard spelling out Kuh's secret bargain: "You don't bother me, I won't bother you. I won't ask much of you as a faculty member, you don't ask much of me [as a student]."[16]

Nothing new here either. A more eloquent statement of a failed social contract linking faculty members and the institutions that appoint and employ them came from Henry Rosovsky in his 1991 farewell address to the Harvard Faculty of Arts and Sciences (FAS) in which he caustically observed: "FAS has become a society largely without rules, or to put it slightly differently, the tenured members of the faculty—frequently as individuals—make their own rules. Of course, there are a great many rules in any bureaucratic organization, but these largely concern less essential matters. When it concerns our more important obligations—faculty citizenship—neither rule nor custom is any longer compelling."[17]

The frequent references to *A Nation at Risk*, however, best reflect how lamentations cast in the present inevitably repeat the past. The more fervent the call for reform, the more likely the reformer, citing *A Nation at Risk*'s impact on primary and secondary education, will proclaim, "Now it is higher education's turn." Not exactly. *A Nation at Risk* went out of its way to make clear that all of education, including higher education, was being engulfed by "a rising tide of mediocrity that threatens our very future as a Nation and a people." In general, the report laid the same indictment on all "our schools and colleges"—the phrase itself became a constant refrain across its pages. *A Nation at Risk* singled out higher education by calling attention to the fact that "in some colleges maintaining enrollments is of greater day-to-day concern than maintaining rigorous academic standards." That observation anticipated *Declining by Degrees* by more than twenty years.[18]

Modern laments over the declining standing and performance of American higher education have one more quality in common—they are mostly written by outside-insiders—commentators who have spent much if not all of their professional lives associated with higher education without being part of the academy itself. The obvious exceptions are former college presidents, but they too hold their lamentations until they have retired from the fray.

The View from Forty-third Street

The most considered as well as the most sustainable of these inside-outsider laments remains *Measuring Up* and its decidedly Western perspective. Here higher education is seen as a public and hence subsidized endeavor that is expected to be broadly accessible, publicly responsible, and of low cost if not actually free to the citizens of the state. This vision has many of its roots in Clark Kerr's California of the 1960s and the master plan Kerr promoted. He guaranteed all Californians access to one of the state's three systems of public higher education: the University of California for the top 10 percent; a California state college for the next 40 percent; and for everybody else, a local community college.

Traditionally, however, much of higher education has looked eastward, toward that strip of academic heartland running from Cambridge and Boston through to Baltimore and all points in between. Not surprisingly, most of those academics who look eastward are also devotees of the *New York Times*. For them, the *Times* is both a journal of record and a cultural touchstone. A mention in the *Times* is a mark of success. A major story—and even better if that entry is on the front page above the fold—is a major achievement worth scheming for if necessary.

One irony is that the *Times* itself has not been very interested in higher education. Often it covers topics either parochial or precious, and often both. Sometimes, however, those who write for the *Times* are good at catching higher education in a stumble, as reflected in the almost gleeful coverage the *Times* devoted to the payola scandals swirling around the student loan industry—a subject we return to later in this volume. At these moments, there is a kind of incipient populism to the coverage—as though the writers were really outsiders instead of the educational elitists they are. As I have already noted, the *Times*'s coverage of the Spellings Commission came alive only after Charles Miller released his nearly scatological draft report. The fact that the Commission subsequently moved away from Miller's "strong words" in favor of a more reasoned, though certainly blander, set of recommendations went largely unnoticed.

One recurring lament among academics who devote so much of their Sunday mornings to reading that day's edition with its book review and glossy magazine is that higher education never gets its due. Symbolic of the academy's lowly status is the fact that for years the regular newsprint, as opposed to the glossy supplement to the Sunday *Times*, was something called "Education Life," a potpourri of writing about education that was dreary in its presentation and decidedly New York City in its focus. Other parts of the *Times*'s world got glossies, but not higher education.

All that changed on a Sunday morning in September 2007 when higher education got its own glossy, a 180-page, full-color, slick-paper, enticing supplement with a title announcing what it was: the "College Issue." It had all the hallmarks of a *Times* "Sunday Magazine," including lots of advertising, much of it presenting colleges and universities mingled among ads for upscale condos, slick automobiles, and presentable banks (the only traditional ads that are missing are those fold-over, now-you-can-smell-it samples of perfumes and pictures of heavy as well as heavily expensive time pieces). The editorial content was equally faithful to the traditional "Sunday Magazine" format. There were a couple of opening essays by interesting people, a full-page picture of Lloyd Thacker, who was trying to mount a revolution in the college selection process, and his answers to ten biting questions, a series of stories about what it's like to choose, attend, and then begin life in the real world after college. The standard column on ethics written by Randy Cohen sorted out the ethics as well as the legal implications involved when a psychiatrist gave his son Adderal to improve his score on the SAT. William Safire's "On Language" column focused on the lingo of the young. The requisite fashion spread featured interesting-looking students.

The "College Issue" concluded with a last-page remembrance about a life changed by attending college in the 1940s.

The editorial perspective was as consistent as the format. The "College Issue" was written by and for people whose focus on selective institutions helped fuel the admissions arms race. Unlike Callan's interest where higher education is a matter of policy, for these readers, college is a matter of life. They are not so much unhappy with the nation's colleges and universities as they are anxious: will their children get into the right college? And then will they be able to afford what has become an astronomical bill?

The magazine began with three hard-hitting personal perspectives. Under a glowing photo of the Huntsman Tower at Penn's Wharton School, Columbia professor Andrew Delbanco started the issue by asking, "Has the modern university become just another corporation?" In Delbanco's answer, everybody emerged more than a little tarnished. Noting the obvious comparison between hospitals and universities as subsidized agencies intended to benefit the public weal, he asked, given that hospitals are required to provide for indigent patients, "what, exactly, are colleges doing to justify their public subsidies?" He wrote approvingly about the *Wall Street Journal's* exposé of how donors to high-priced, highly selective private colleges and universities "are, in effect, buying slots for their children by giving gifts that are tax-deductible for the giver and tax-free for the recipient." He saved his sharpest barb, however, for the institution writ large when he observed in a near echo of Wadsworth and Immerwahr, "Like hospitals, colleges have generally got the benefit of the doubt on the question of why they cost so much, and many people still regard them as selfless institutions above and beyond the self-serving rules of the marketplace. But their reputation for probity and virtue is deteriorating fast."[19]

Next came an interview with Lloyd Thacker who just the week before had convened a critical meeting at Yale that not only challenged the more than seventy-five institutions in attendance to change the language and values that had dominated the admissions process but also offered a broad-based assault on rankings in general and the *U.S. News*'s rankings in particular. In his personal appearances Thacker is mesmerizing, having the advantage of once being one of *them*—that is, one of that growing army of admissions counselors and consultants who teach youngsters and their parents how to beat the admissions game. He lays out in staggering detail how there are now three separate billion-dollar industries feeding off the admissions process: one industry helps applicants make their best case; a second industry helps institutions fill their classes with the best and the brightest; and the third is the rankings industry itself. In the "College Issue" Thacker had only ten pithy answers to make his case. When asked what was really wrong with the admissions industry Thacker responded: "College admissions has come under the control of commercial interests, at the expense of studenthood." Later he was asked if an institution one year rejected all applicants would it actually rise in the ranking? His response: "Correct. The business model is making a funnel, which means trying to get as many people as possible interested in a product and only selling it to a few."[20]

The third opening essay by Rick Perlstein had originally been published the preceding July in the online version of the magazine, to which college students had been asked to respond; 650 did, and the "College Issue" published the winning entry preceded by Perlstein's. The challenge Perlstein laid on the current generation of college students was summed up in the essay's title, "What's the matter with college?" Perlstein answered that today's colleges were home to a generation that lacks spunk. He began with the story of how Ronald Reagan in his campaign for governor of California ran as much against the University of California, Berkeley, as against his Democratic opponent. Perlstein then asks, is higher education today "important enough to become a national obsession? Controversial enough to fight a gubernatorial campaign over?" Hardly. Students no longer lead the culture. What they do and say they largely do and say in private or at least outside the political arena. Perlstein might not pine for Ronald Reagan, but he certainly is nostalgic about the Berkeley Reagan so successfully railed against.[21]

The winning student response was written by a Yale junior, Nicholas Handler. He pretty much grants Perlstein his basic point: college students today appear to their elders in general and their parents in particular as "a story seemingly without direction or theme, structure or meaning—a generation defined negatively against what came before us." Handler counters by arguing that his parents' generation isn't really listening. Better antennae, less preoccupation with what was important when "we" were in college would teach them that his generation is no less revolutionary—it is just a matter of fighting this round of battles differently—on the Internet in highly focused campaigns that promise to change both the nature of protest and the mechanics of electoral politics. Handler concludes, "perhaps when our parents finally stop pointing out the things that we are not, the stories that we do not write, they will see the threads of our narrative begin to come together. They will see that behind our pastiche, the postgeneration speaks in a language that does make sense. We are writing a revolution. We are just putting it in our own words." It is probably only an accident of bad editing that William Safire's "On Language" feature came next in which he dissected the "Lingo of adultalescence."[22]

Thereafter followed a half dozen more formally journalist articles that elaborated the themes struck in the opening essays of the "College Issue." The first article dealt with the artificiality of the admissions process—or at least the artificiality of the road students seeking admission to a highly selective institution must follow. Some of it is silly, but enough of the stories and their details are sufficiently painful to make one ask whether the selective admissions process, at least as it is currently practiced, still makes sense. An article on the new affirmative action traced the rollback of the commitment to racial and economic diversity that came to elite public higher education in the 1990s. There was a story about forgetting the angst and just being college students— or as the heading in the story put it, "Fear and loathing pave the road to college. But ask recent graduates to reflect on their experience and they advise kids to forget rankings, chill out and be ready to savor the best years of their lives." There were even what I would call counter—or at least unexpected—stories. One dealt with a novel evangelical Christian college in Idaho; a second focuses on learning poetry at West Point; and a third takes a tough look at Teach for America, the volunteer program that has attracted so many elite college grads to temporary positions in elementary and secondary teaching.

The "College Issue" was written for a *Times* constituency that is well-off, well-connected, and well-meaning. The "College Issue" offered an interesting counterpoint to what have come to be the dominant laments over the declining status and quality of American higher education. Where lamenters focus on *them* and *theirs*, the *Times*'s constituency focuses on *me* and *mine*—a near obsession that has made getting a medallion degree at almost any price the sine qua non of upper-middle-class status. These are the parents who have fueled the admissions arms race, spending the sums that Lloyd Thacker decries on admissions consultants and test-prep courses. They are the ones who buy, read, and quote at will the *U.S. News*'s rankings. One day, perhaps, they will ask, "Is all this really worth it?" But not today or even tomorrow. In the meantime their pursuit of the right college education for their children allows organized higher education in general and the nation's elite colleges and universities in particular to shrug off so much of the lamenters' rising critique of higher education's quality and efficiency.

All of which raises an interesting possibility. Had the lamenters not been so defiantly anti-elitist, could they have tapped into the anger that lies just below the surface of so many who see the world of higher education as the *New York Times* sees it? What might have happened if the laments I have been tracing, in addition to focusing on the many and the disadvantaged, had given equal attention to the elite and the empowered? Their collective critique of American higher education would certainly have been taken more seriously by those responsible for managing the enterprise as well as the faculty responsible for what and how students learn. This presents just one more example of a missed opportunity on the road to transformation.

A Cluttered Landscape

That's the sum of it—a chorus of lamenters as confused and contradictory as the object of their affection. Each takes time to point out that American higher education is unique, special, worth preserving. Though their notions of what makes for a successful institution or system of higher education vary, often dramatically, each has derived from his or her own past a clear sense of what success looks like. Merrow and Hersh were bluntest about what they sought: the "crown jewel of our [educational] system restored to its former glory."[23] For Callan, it is a return to a California of yesteryear—largely public, largely free, largely accessible to everyone, though with different portals for people with differing levels of academic preparation. The upscale constituency of the *New York Times* has a similar hankering, but for a Berkeley in which ideas and protests are the dominant icons. More generally, it is a hankering after a time when political activism trumped personal angst.

3 | Commodification and Other Sins

Part snarl, part slogan, part technical term—it is the process by which markets transform educational experiences into educational commodities or products—for many academic insiders, commodification is the other side of the lamenter's coin, the sure sign that the nation's colleges and universities have gone astray. It is the process Andrew Delbanco had in mind when he lamented that the modern university was now dangerously close to becoming "just another corporation." Money matters too much—values hardly at all. Students have been transformed into customers. Faculty have been told to become entrepreneurs, which is just a step above being money-grubbing ambulance chasers. The academy, which was once venerated as a scholarly community, is now little more than a business constantly worried about its bottom line. The image of the professor as bumbling bookworm no longer fits. Instead, as Delbanco reminded the readers of the *New York Times*'s "College Issue," we are more likely to be portrayed as we have become: "jet-setting self-promoters."[1]

Here, the public's discontent with the idea of universities becoming mere businesses and the academic insider's cry against commodification are somewhat similar. It would be misleading, however, to believe the one was really connected to other. As John Immerwahr frequently notes when reporting the results of his higher education public opinion surveys, most respondents confess to not knowing very much about the internal operations of the nation's colleges and universities.

In his surveys, the public's sense of universities as having all the trappings of a business stems largely from the growing concern over rising tuition prices and the attention now being paid to the multibillion-dollar endowments that a handful of major, for the most part private, research universities have amassed.

Within the academy itself commodification as a slogan reflects a growing understanding of just how much market forces have changed the nation's colleges and universities. A growing number of faculty have discovered—to both their discomfort and displeasure—that they really do need to understand not only how their institutions are being funded but also how those funds are being apportioned among competing schools, departments, and programs. Once, not that long ago, higher education finances were governed by two basic principles: first, most funds came to the university centrally in the form of tuitions, the fruits of philanthropy, a few research grants, and, if the university was a public institution, state appropriations; and second, everyone within the university would be treated equally in terms of salary, teaching load, and support for one's graduate students. The academy itself might be a privileged haven, but within those ivied walls no one was to be more privileged than another. Even administrative salaries and stipends were to be kept modest so that those charged with governing the institutions shared the same fate as everyone else. In good times and bad, there was to be a roughly equal sharing of the good and the bad.

Markets, however, are notorious for conferring advantage on some at the expense of others—a lesson nearly everyone in the academy is being taught on a daily basis. Highly selective institutions can both charge higher tuitions and give fewer discounts. In the market for federal research, the universities with established reputations recruit the faculty who can land the big grants. The more success an institution has in recruiting the freshman class it wants at the price it wants to charge and the better its faculty are in garnering the national publicity that accompanies awards of major research contracts, the more success the institution is likely to have persuading its alumni and friends to support its efforts through increasingly targeted donations. In this world the rich have been getting constantly richer.

The same can be said about distributions within the academy—even within the richest colleges and universities. Disciplines, and hence departments supported by the market for research dollars, have seen their fortunes rise, leading to higher salaries, better facilities, summer support, and lower teaching loads. Faculty in prestigious professional schools have won the same advantages, often accompanied by the opportunity to earn substantial extramural income through consulting and practice engagements. Athletic success confers the same market advantages, leading to multimillion-dollar coaching contracts, large staffs, and substantial perks. Perhaps the most dramatic changes, however, have occurred across the ranks of market-successful senior administrators, including those who merely persuade the boards that hire them that they will usher in an era of more students, more research dollars, and greater athletic success. By November 2006, the *Chronicle of Higher Education* could report that the day of the $1,000,000-annual-pay package was at hand. The following year, the number of presidents with million-dollar salaries had increased to three; eight presidents of public research universities earned in excess of $750,000 annually; and perhaps the most astounding statistic of all, "Overall, 81 presidents of private institutions made more than $500,000 in the 2006 fiscal year, up 200 percent from five years earlier." Not included in these figures were the directors' fees most presidents of major universities earned for serving on the boards of private corporations—another subject we return to when we consider the scandals swirling about higher education.[2]

The market laid bare and the denunciations of commodification made clear in almost Orwellian terms that some academics are now more equal than others. On one level these conversations focused on how market forces were changing the American university; at a deeper, more primitive level, these laments were couched in terms of economic winners and losers. The former included professional schools, those sciences supported by federal funding, and those departments with sufficient cachet to be able to raise their own philanthropic funds. The losers included the arts and sciences in general and the humanities in particular, along with specific programs and disciplines that found themselves unable to attract sufficient undergraduate or masters' enrollments to fill their classes. In general, selective private institutions were more advantaged than their public counterparts, while small, nonselective private colleges were the most disadvantaged of all.

Ultimately discussions of commodification evolved into laments about the academy's changing priorities now that colleges and universities were no longer allocating funds on the basis of need but rather on the basis of revenue. Instead of faculty councils working with relatively weak administrative structures to distribute funds and appointments more or less equally, a new class of executive managers was developing elaborate budget systems festooned with detailed calibrations of costs and benefits for rewarding the university's academic entrepreneurs while reducing the subsidies, now made horribly explicit, on which more traditionally organized departments had come to depend.

Not surprisingly, discussions of commodification have taken on political hues as well. Most laments have come from the left; such academics believe commercialism corrupts absolutely, makes the university more common and less rigorous, discourages ideas, and questions the enduring importance of a community of scholars. The most vigorous, perhaps even the most vitriolic, of these laments came from Stanley Aronowitz, a sociologist and old-line CUNY radical; the *Chronicle of Higher Education* in quiet understatement described him as a "long-time combatant in the culture wars." In *Knowledge Factory: Dismantling the Corporate University and Creating True Higher Learning* Aronowitz offered a foot-stomping critique of misplaced priorities and corrupted practices.[3]

On occasion, however, academic voices on the right joined the chorus, as often as not turning the argument about commodification on its head. My favorite among this set of commentaries is Richard Vedder's *Going Broke by Degree: Why College Costs Too Much*. Vedder, who also served on the Spellings Commission, first developed his argument in the pages of the *Wall Street Journal* and then, with the help of a couple of Republican heavyweights, expanded his essay into a book-length treatise. His argument begins with the declaration that higher education is not really subject to market forces. A host of third-party payers—principally the states, the federal government, and subsidized loan programs—have allowed colleges and universities to raise prices at will. Thus shielded from the rigors of a truly competitive market in which productivity and efficiency convey substantial advantage, colleges and universities have grown slothful. Productivity is down, economic discipline is negligible, and far from favoring the entrepreneurial and efficient, universities use their near market monopoly to protect the outdated and outmoded. The result? "While it takes far less time for workers to make a ton of steel, type a letter, or harvest a bushel of corn than it did a generation ago, it takes *more* professors and college administrators to educate a given number of students."[4]

Where the anticommodifiers see a preoccupation with efficiency and productivity making the university less of a magical place, Vedder sees a bloating intended to protect those who cannot change. Vedder dismisses the budget incentives the critics believed spurred commodification as little more than misplaced rules that "work in the direction of reducing productivity and efficiency. Deans, department chairs, and heads of administrative units are always trying to increase their budgets, not minimize them, since bigger budgets mean more power and greater resources to get the job done."[5]

For college and university presidents the established strategy for responding to both the anticommodifiers and the efficiency pundits has been to point out that neither has had much influence over the finances or the operations of their universities. The real meaning of their protests, clever presidents like to point out, is the proof they give to the proposition that universities remain places where anybody can say anything, no matter how wrong or outrageous. Indeed, as most presidents have discovered, there is little to be gained by confronting either set of lamenters directly, whether pointing out that market forces are here to stay or asking the anticommodifiers in particular where the funds to pay their salaries are likely to come from in an age of declining public appropriations for higher education. Taking on Vedder and his compatriots isn't necessary either, though it is fun to point out that those who argue that the universities are inherently wasteful organizations too often focus on expenses like climbing walls and residential amenities that neither the faculty nor the administration has much interest in providing. But even this argument is mostly about scoring debating points. From this perspective, the laments about the internal finances of higher education do not have much more traction than the complaints over binge drinking, wayward professors, and students who just skate by learning little of lasting value.

The lamenters, anticommodifiers, and efficiency pundits, and, even more directly, Richard Hersh and John Merrow have been hoping for something different—something like the perfect rhetorical storm that would result if the various strands of lamentation and protest we have been tracing somehow merged. Suddenly from within the academy there would be a growing cry to better monitor how colleges and universities spend their monies; attacks on the presidency and its perks would become common fare in a new round of culture wars that focuses on money rather than on ideas or values. The public's mounting frustration over rising prices would find a natural echo in the anti-commodifiers' charge that universities are now both amoral and corrupt. Everybody would begin shouting: The market isn't working! The rich and privileged are ever more advantaged, professional education is favored over undergraduate education, and the humanities are becoming shadows of their former selves. Here public officials would add that members of an increasingly isolated senior faculty are teaching less, turning more and more of their responsibilities over to underpaid, overworked adjunct instructors who are often little more than academic gypsies teaching simultaneously at three or more institutions. The final straw would be a wholesale assault on the ability of institutions to amass substantial wealth in the form of tax-free endowments: a perfect storm that resulted in more regulation, caps on tuition increases, a federalized accreditation system, and a really tough look at the tax advantages that both public and private institutions currently enjoy.

I don't think there will be a perfect storm. Higher education will remain largely impervious to forced change—indeed to almost any form of change championed by outsiders, even by outside-insiders, who vilify higher education as a way of explaining why change is necessary. There is, however, a remarkable irony reflected in the arguments of both the anticommodifiers and the efficiency pundits. Change—indeed, fundamental change—has been occurring for nearly four decades, leading to dramatic shifts in institutional priorities along with altered distributions of power and authority. In this respect, the anticommodifiers are right. Throughout the last thirty-five years the financial underpinnings of both public and private higher education have been fundamentally reordered. The rules have changed. Markets have become dominant. Traditional values have been eclipsed. While faculty with direct access to research and entrepreneurial funding now have more freedom and autonomy than ever, the same cannot be said of the faculty as a collective whole. On most campuses faculty organizations have withered; their leadership attracts fewer scholars with external reputations, and they often have trouble mustering the quorum necessary to conduct business. While faculty traditionalists still talk about shared governance, in the day-to-day operations of most universities the cadre of academic managers—deans, department chairs, institute and center directors along with the heads of purely administrative functions—is firmly in charge.

What is spooky about this shift in power and responsibility is that it is a reordering that initially occasioned remarkably little discussion, either within or without the academy. Compared with the public, often impassioned turmoil of the 1960s, the 1970s and 1980s, when the most basic of these changes began, were decades of quiet stagnation. With most academics seeking to protect their own prerogatives within an increasingly fractured institutional setting, the reigning doctrine was often an unspoken version of "don't ask, don't tell."

Then in the late 1980s, academics did begin asking, What happened? For those who found themselves dispossessed, "commodification" became the rallying cry. At about the same time a scattering of economists—for instance, Stanford's Bill Massy and Duke's Charles Clodfelter—turned their analytic skills to the task of making sense of the academy's altered landscape. Michael McPherson and Morton Shapiro, along with Gordon Winston, all of Williams College, while often focusing on student aid and accessibility, contributed both new tools and new metaphors for describing how colleges and universities now functioned. *Policy Perspectives*, the publication of the Pew Higher Education Roundtable and subsequently the Knight Collaborative, similarly contributed a host of new terms and concepts, including the "Lattice and the Ratchet"; this most memorable of our efforts to explain higher education's rising costs described how and why administrative processes were replacing traditional forms of academic governance.

Eventually three quite separate volumes appeared; taken together, they summed up and extended what was known about higher education's reordered finances. The year 2003 brought both Derek Bok's *Universities in the Marketplace: The Commercialization of Higher Education* and David Kirp's *Shakespeare, Einstein, and the Bottom Line: The Marketing of Higher Education*. Two years later Gregory Wegner, Bill Massy, and I wrote *Remaking the American University: Market-Smart and Mission-Centered*. It was no coincidence that each volume made markets and marketing a key element in both title and argument. Each offered an explanation of how and why markets had changed colleges and universities and what the academy could and could not do about it. For the most part their arguments avoided both the sarcasm of the anticommodifiers and the exaggerations of the efficiency pundits. In their stead the volumes collectively described a landscape in which meaningful reforms were possible only if colleges and universities took explicit account of the workings of the market and the fact that for the indefinite future colleges and universities would have to rely on market revenues to fund their ambitions.

These three volumes provide a more realistic platform for change than either the lamenters' warnings of the "fire next time" or the anticommodifiers cries of "shame!" have been able to provide. Both directly and indirectly the three volumes help us understand why, even when the subject is the reform of higher education, talking about money precedes talking about teaching or learning or any other aspect of reform.

Universities in the Marketplace

Twice-president of Harvard—lawyer, law dean, and in the years since leaving the Harvard presidency, a prolific commentator and writer on American higher education—Derek Bok has remained a consummate university insider. A twenty-year presidency of America's first university, both in terms of chronology and standing, taught Bok much about what was right and what was not right across American higher education.

A dozen years after his return to the faculty, Princeton University Press published Bok's *Universities in the Marketplace: The Commercialization of Higher Education*, a relatively slim volume whose title warns the readers that they are about to be launched on an exploration of how money and markets have already changed and will certainly continue to change the academy. Bok deals with all the issues, identifies most, if not all, the foibles and follies, and, without apology, enumerates the substantial benefits commercialization has brought to the American university. In just this way, *Universities in the Marketplace* presents an argument that constantly pushes and pulls on the reader; he warns of the dangers of commercialization while simultaneously noting its importance to an academy constantly in search of new funds.

Like Clark Kerr before him, Bok has understood that the university is forever suspended, to use Kerr's metaphor, between the acropolis and the agora. Kerr, president of the University of California during its growth years, once described the tension between the traditional academy, with its focus on values and mission (the acropolis), and the marketplace (the agora). Arguing that universities always have served the market, Kerr observed: "The cherished academic view that higher education started out on the acropolis and was desecrated by descent into the agora led by ungodly commercial interests and scheming public officials and venal academic leaders is just not true. If anything, higher education started in the agora, the market, at the bottom of the hill and ascended to the acropolis at the top of the hill. . . . Mostly it has lived in tension, at one and the same time at the bottom of the hill, at the top of the hill, and on the many pathways in between."[6]

It is a theme Bok works constantly. He points out that American universities, almost from their inception, have been on the lookout for what we would now call commercial opportunities. The University of Chicago began advertising for students in the early 1900s. Penn established a Bureau of Publicity in 1905. In fact, among the most prized possessions in the Penn Archive are two late eighteenth-century tickets that had been available for purchase to attend the new lectures offered by what would become Penn's School of Medicine. Although commercial interests and practices have been part of higher education for a century or more, the commercialization of the academy today is starkly different: "Throughout the 1980s, deans and professors had brought me one proposition after another to exchange some piece or product of Harvard for money—often quite substantial sums of money. I will admit that I was intrigued by these opportunities, for, contrary to popular opinion, Harvard always seemed to need more resources. Nevertheless, nagging questions kept occurring to me. Was everything in the university for sale if the price was right?"[7]

Is everything for sale if the price is right? Even in a purely commercial enterprise not everything is for sale—just almost. It is not by accident, however, that Bok begins his tale in the 1980s, for in that decade it became clear that big changes were taking place in how universities financed themselves. Once the commercial instinct was confined to the periphery of the campus, but by the 1980s opportunities to make money abounded. Sponsored funding for research kept doubling and then doubling again. Federal legislation in the form of the Bayh-Dole Act effectively required universities receiving federal research grants to commercialize their inventions—products, processes, techniques—that derived from federally funded research. Universities were under similar obligation to share with their faculty inventors a portion of the revenues the university received—the balance was to be used for scientific research and education. It was not hard to fear that the fox had been set loose in the henhouse.

Not only were the scientific products of universities increasingly for sale, there also developed a futures market for research merely contemplated or imagined. Mega firms wanted in on the ground floor—and to get there they began offering proprietary agreements in which they shared in both the cost of the research and the profits that would flow later.

While scientific research led the drive to commercialization, business and other professional schools were not far behind; such schools offered not only their traditional educational programs, but they now built expensive facilities in which to mount profitable programs of professional and executive education. Athletics became even more commercial and, on more than one hundred individual campuses, truly big business. State legislatures, all in the name of local economic development, began rewarding campuses for the commercial activities

they promised to attract to the state. Literally everyone wanted to replicate the success that Stanford had generated across the Silicon Valley
and that Duke, North Carolina State, and the University of North
Carolina, Chapel Hill had spawned in the research triangle.

In telling this tale Bok jokes about universities being like compul-
sive gamblers and deposed royalty ever in search of more revenue.
Here he was simply echoing Howard Bowen's classic theorem that universities will raise all the money they can and spend all the money they
raise. If there is a market for what a university has to sell, then universities will undoubtedly consider entering that market. What pushes as
well as pulls commercialization, in other words, is the constant lure of
new funds with which to accomplish the good ends expected of a right-
thinking and right-behaving university.

En route to describing what a right-thinking, right-behaving university needs to do, Bok takes pains not to be misunderstood.
Commercialization in itself is not bad—it both brings needed funds
and stirs ambition. He explicitly rejects those on the left who have
argued that commercialization is a plot—another example of "the
attempts by the businessmen and lawyers who sit on boards of trustees
to 'commodify' education and research." Nor does he accept the devil-
made-me-do-it argument of those who posit that commercialization
only happened because state governments, in particular, reduced their
support of higher education. He is similarly unimpressed by those who
argue that the weakening of the university's traditional allegiance to an
arts and sciences core opened the door to rampant commercialization.
"Explanations of this kind almost invariably come from philosophers,
literary scholars, and other humanists," Bok notes, the very "fields of
study most widely accused of having lost their intellectual moorings."
Thus it is not surprising "that their professors see a similar aimlessness
as the cause of other ills that have overtaken the academy."[8]

Indeed, commercialization is no enemy of purpose; nor is purpose or
mission, in itself, a barrier to commercialization. Within the traditional
disciples, no faculty members feel a stronger sense of mission than the scientists, yet it is there—not in the humanities—that commercialization has
taken hold most firmly. Among the several faculties, none has a clearer
sense of purpose than schools of business and medicine, yet their
professors—not their colleagues in literature and philosophy—are the
most deeply involved in lucrative consulting and entrepreneurial activity.

The problem with commercialization is not aimlessness but rather
an "intellectual confusion" that has much more to do with means than

with ends. The challenge, given the constant lure of revenue in a market economy, is how to keep commercialism within bounds; that is, how do we know when some opportunities are simply inappropriate. Bok's answer is almost deceptively simple: universities must have real articulated values that are clear to all members of the community. "When the values become blurred and begin to lose their hold, the urge to make money quickly spreads throughout the institution." Or, to put the matter differently, Bok is arguing for reform that does not seek a less business-like academy but rather an academy recommited to values as a key part of its business.[9]

What would Bok do? He offers several lists, beginning with gaining a real understanding of the threats—he calls them the "costs"—commercialization poses for higher education. First and foremost is the threat to academic standards. Big-time athletics are now an inherent risk: just how much should an athlete's prowess and hence potential profitability count in the admissions process? Purely vocational courses pose a risk to educational purpose, though often they can yield substantial revenue. Vocationalism poses the further risk of devaluing the liberal arts by making a job the be-all-end-all of a college education. Corporate contracts that can often involve the proprietary distribution of knowledge, along with substantial secrecy, pose risks of their own.

In this litany Bok is presenting many of the same arguments that the anticommodifiers press; he suggests, as they argue, that commercialization can corrupt as well as contaminate the academy. In an academic community, commercialization carries with it the danger of introducing unwanted distinctions—between winners and losers, between those who can earn their own way and those who require the material support of the institution as a whole, between those who thrive on competition and those who believe the academy is primarily a collaborative undertaking. Here Bok joins Stanley Katz in worrying about what happens to the humanities in a pure market economy for higher education. "Professors who work hard at their traditional academic tasks will resent the extra income earned by [entrepreneurial] colleagues. . . . Humanists will feel devalued. Conflicts will arise between faculty and administration over the proper division" of market-generated rewards.[10]

Finally there is an incipient risk or threat to the university's reputation as an objective pursuer of ideas as well as scientific knowledge. Universities have come to play a central role in the venting of new ideas, a testing bed whose validity depends on them being seen as an institution ready and willing to offer disinterested advice as well as disinterested research. If one ties a university too closely to its corporate sponsors and benefactors, then its voice becomes lost in the chorus of celebratory spin.

But unlike the anticommodifiers, Bok has no intention of crying in his beer. Commercialization is here to stay. Long ago universities made what Bok calls a "Faustian bargain," which has brought them perilously close to compromising "their basic values—and thereby risk[ing] their very souls—in order to enjoy the rewards of the market place." Thus, a true value proposition lies at the heart of Bok's argument.[11]

Universities need to know fundamentally what they believe and value in the old-fashioned sense of that word. They actually have to draw a line in the sand defining in advance what they will and will not do. They cannot rely on a kind of ersatz cost-benefit analysis to situationally determine what is permissible and what is not. If not everyone will agree with this drawing of the line, then most will concede it is an argument that identifies the key do's and don'ts. Fight the corporations and their insistence on keeping their sponsored research secret. Define clearly and precisely what constitutes conflict of interest—and then don't compromise, don't recognize the so-called special circumstances. Avoid "excessive reliance on industry support." For example, the bargain the University of California, Berkeley (UC Berkeley) made with the healthcare giant Novartis was truly Faustian; the agreement gave the company prior rights to research not yet conducted and a significant voice in the kind of research the faculty in the sponsoring department was expected to conduct. While the Novartis contract, in itself, was not a significant threat to academic freedom, to the extent it becomes *the* model for future arrangements it becomes an ever-present danger. Finally, don't go into business with your faculty; there is almost no way of untangling either interests or alliances. In sum, universities need to be more than careful as they navigate the often murky waters of corporate relationships, tech transfer, and entrepreneurial investments. "It is unhealthy for universities to have their integrity questioned repeatedly by reports of excessive secrecy, conflicts of interest, and corporate efforts to manipulate and suppress research. Surely the time is ripe to set appropriate limits and see to it that they are vigorously enforced."[12] "Bok's list of necessary academic values is not very long—but heeding both the spirit and the letter of his do's and don'ts is an arduous task. As a former president of Harvard he has the good sense to acknowledge that heeding his call for drawing the line will be easier for some than others."[13] The idea of a value-constrained commercialism is exactly what Bok has in mind. If it advantages Harvard—whose endowment as of this writing is $35 billion—so be it. The line needs to be drawn. Accept commercialization. Prize its rewards but know that without a restatement of basic values and a corresponding commitment to their enforcement, commercialization will consume us all. Bok's call to reform may seem oblique, but at its core it tells us that reform is ultimately about how values and money mix. You can have the latter without the former—but not for long—and remain a university in the best sense of the word.

Shakespeare, Einstein, and the Bottom Line

Bok is too careful, too concerned with illustration and documentation, to have couched his arguments in terms of either villains or heroes. David L. Kirp and his colleagues Elizabeth Popp Berman, Jeffrey T. Holman, Patrick Roberts, Debra Solomon, and Jonathan VanAntwerpen have no such compunction. Their *Shakespeare, Einstein, and the Bottom Line: The Marketing of Higher Education* is a romp full of heroes and villains all relating to the market's often perverse impact on colleges and universities. *Shakespeare, Einstein, and the Bottom Line* is like an illustrative appendix to Bok's *Universities in the Marketplace*.

And they tell stories with the verve and gusto usually reserved for more sensational subject matter! There is the remaking of New York University, arguably the institution that proved the most adept at harnessing the discipline of making targeted investments in pursuit of enhanced visibility. Dickinson College, with its embrace of a president plucked from the for-profit world, provides the canvas for exploring the clash between old ideas and new realities in a world made harsh by the pursuit of prestige and tuition revenue. The transformation of the University of Southern California into a mega force by rewarding entrepreneurial *chutzpah* is offered as proof of what can be accomplished when the rewards are real and the means are at hand. The University of Michigan is served up as an example of the other side of the coin—as an institution full of professors and at least one dean who knew that the market's siren song was not for them.

There are stories about the false lure of the market for e-learning—and just as important, how and why MIT turned that market on its head largely by giving away what others wanted to charge so much for.

Kirp tells the Novartis story in considerable detail, documenting how his own campus, UC Berkeley, came to understand why a commitment to public science and openness is more in keeping with the traditions of a great public university—Bayh-Dole not withstanding. All these stories and more are told without sneer and with only the hint of reproach. Unlike so many who decry the commercialization of the university but never ask where the money should come from to support them in comfort and isolation, Kirp knows better; he knows, like Bok, that the search for revenue with which to do good things and the necessity of earning those funds in an increasingly raucous market place underlies the transformation of the American university.

Readers of *Shakespeare, Einstein, and the Bottom Line* easily draw two key lessons from Kirp's analysis. First, higher education's focus on funds and funding is not new. From the beginning, first colleges and later universities knew their futures depended on securing the funds to do what they thought best, even if at the time of pursuit that funding involved unfortunate compromises. No, it is not the pursuit of money that is new, but rather "the raw power that money directly exerts over so many aspects of higher education. Even as public attention has been riveted on matters of principle such as affirmative action and diversions like the theatre-of-the-absurd canon wars, the American university has been busily reinventing itself in response to intensified competitive pressures. Entrepreneurial ambition, which used to be regarded in academe as a necessary evil, has become a virtue."[14]

But "opting out" is not an option either. There is no turning back—higher education is now a market enterprise and its constituent colleges and universities are in fact businesses; as provost of Kirp's UC Berkeley put it, "We are businesses," and we "mean business." There can be no Thoreau-like search for the sanctuary of a Walden Pond. To retreat would be "courting self destruction." Kirp continues, "Even—perhaps especially—the elite schools are ever vigilant, lest a rival steal an edge (or a professor or a major donor). Prestige is the coin of the realm among the leading research universities and liberal arts colleges; and since prestige is a scarce commodity, the losers will far outnumber the winners."[15] In this world-gone-mad, survival requires a balancing act if the faculty are to remain academics amidst the very markets that provide the funds that let them be academics in the first place. To make this point both real and poignant, Kirp leads the reader through a series of stories—each with its own moral, each with its own set of winners and losers. He begins with the now-fecund field of consulting. Here he introduces us to Jack Maguire—once a physicist, once Boston College's dean of admissions, and now on nearly every institution's short list of experts to call to beef up admissions or develop a market-smart discount policy, and often both. Maguire is precisely the kind of person Lloyd Thacker has in mind when he decries the amount of time, attention, and money the new educational consultants have come to command. Still, Maguire's business success demonstrates how financial desperation has revolutionized the care and feeding of prospective students. If Maguire is the doer, the theoretician is the marketing guru and Northwestern business school professor, Phillip Kotler, who would persuade his faculty colleagues that the marketing of a college or university is not materially different from the marketing necessary to boost tourism and church attendance. "Explicitly and unapologetically" the enrollment managers Maguire has trained and Kotler inspired have come to regard "students as customers and see a college education as the product students consume."[16]

Hence, it is but a short step to regard the annual setting of tuition rates and accompanying financial aid policies as an exercise in strategic pricing. The goal is not to level the playing field so that all students, regardless of personal means, have an equal chance at enrolling. Rather, the goal of strategic pricing is to distribute the price discounts the financial aid budget pays for in such a way that the institution matriculates the most competitive class possible.

From there—as Kirp points out in his discussion of what Michel Benke has learned in his peripatetic journey as an admissions professional moving from Amherst to Tufts to MIT to the University of Chicago—it is just another short step to defining the job of the dean of admissions as getting the right professionals in the admissions office to do the right kind of job. Did it work? Yes. Despite the grumping of Chicago's faculty traditionalists, Behnke's new admissions strategies have yielded a 22-percent increase in applicants, a number that allowed the University "for the first time in its history" to admit "fewer than half of those who applied."[17]

Like many academics, Kirp has a soft spot for the University of Chicago—its history, verve, and gritty presence. For him, Chicago is "more self-absorbed—more precisely, self-obsessed—than any other institution of higher learning in America." He notes with bemusement how a passing remark made by the philosopher Alfred North Whitehead—"I think the one place where I have been that is most like ancient Athens is the University of Chicago"—has been "recycled as if it were gospel." It is a place of ideas, of brains as opposed to brawn or beauty, of iconic heroes such as the likes of Mortimer Adler, Saul Bellow, and, of course, Alan Bloom, whose *Closing of the American Mind* made him rich and famous and reinforced his university's image as a haven for intellectually combative, occasionally fuzzy-thinking professors. "While Harvard preens, Chicago navel-gazes, turning out bookshelves'-worth of histories and biographies, faculty committee reports, student newspapers, broadsheets, and websites devoted to itself."[18]

And then there is that other Hyde Park tradition, an often money-grubbing search for the funds necessary to keep the university in business. Athens it may have aspired to, but when it came time to pay its bills the University of Chicago could not afford to be too choosy. Among the various schemes its illustrious presidents, including both Robert Maynard Hutchins and William Raney Harper, have pursued are a community college, the nation's biggest correspondence school, and, in 1998, an attachment to Unext.com's for-profit business school.

This juxtaposition of the sacred and profane makes what happened at the University of Chicago during the presidency of Hugo Sonnenschein an important object lesson in the ongoing war being waged over market forces and academic values. Sonnenschein came to the University of Chicago in 1993 following a two-year stint as Princeton's provost and a term as Penn's dean of Arts and Sciences. He was viewed as a catch in the best Chicago tradition—urbane, gracious, and above all, both an experienced administrator and a world-class scholar, an econometrician, theorist, and member of the National Academy of Sciences. In Kirp's hands, what Sonnenschein discovered about the University of Chicago and what the University learned about him becomes a morality tale in itself.

Like many new presidents, Sonnenschein had been misled about the state of Chicago's finances. For a decade, the university had maintained its financial balance largely by cutting budgets and postponing needed expenses. After the fact, Sonnenschein told Kirp and a colleague, "In every place the budget for staff was stripped to the bone. Services were poor and students and faculty complained." More troubling to someone who saw in his presidency the chance to make Chicago great again were the academic deficits. The university needed a massive infusion of funds for new laboratories, expanded libraries, competitive salaries, and new student facilities, including new dorms. Chicago also needed to refurbish its standing as an undergraduate institution of the first rank. Chicago was admitting an embarrassing portion of its applicant pool, and Chicago enrolled most of the top students it admitted because it offered a merit scholarship package that was beyond rich.[19]

Sonnenschein and his provost's answer to what ailed Chicago was better, more forceful, indeed, more incisive management. One way to raise more revenues was to admit more undergraduates—1,200 in all—and to have more senior faculty time devoted to teaching them. One peculiar quirk of Chicago is that its faculty traditionalists wax eloquent on the importance of general education, a common core, and truly rigorous standards; they want even more, however, to teach their graduate students and then not very many of them. Hence Sonnenschein's observation, "If you put every straining dollar into maintaining an arts and sciences faculty that's larger than Harvard's, with half as many students . . . that's a tough way to run a ship."[20]

Sonnenschein excelled at running the ship—as long as running the ship did not mean building political consensus among the Chicago faculty that change was necessary. He raised funds. He built new buildings. He made the management of the university more rational and the budget more transparent. And he fixed the admission problem largely by bringing in Behnke as dean of admissions.

None of these accomplishments made him a hero in Hyde Park; in fact, to the faculty traditionalists who viewed each proposal with growing skepticism, his successes only confirmed their belief that he was ruining their University of Chicago. By making the undergraduate college bigger, he was making the university subject to market fads that seldom if ever favored Chicago. There was a sense that he was really after bright, rich kids from good private schools who were not Chicago quirky. Some went so far as to suggest that Sonnenschein sought freshmen who were both better looking and better athletes than Chicago's standard undergraduates.

But the battle over the budget marked just how great a chasm had come to exist between the president and the faculty traditionalists. Like many an economist turned university administrator, Sonnenschein made the mistake of assuming that the argument over money was a contest among and between rational actors. To the traditionalists who opposed his remaking of their university, this game could not be neatly summed up in an elegant model; rather, it became a fundamental quarrel, a war, really, over definitions and values: what is the university supposed to be? Sonnenschein's provost and comrade in arms Geoffrey Stone apparently noted that "to focus on finances was to see the university as something other than a 'pure' institution whose sole value was academic excellence."[21]

Because it was a war waged over values, it swiftly turned nasty. Across campus Sonnenschein was taxed for his use of stock phrases— "Hugospeak"—while his missteps quickly became "Hugoisms." The students parodied Sonnenschein, mocking him as a modern "Darth Vader." His goal, they suggested, was to create a "University of Chicago Lite . . . specially brewed by the freshest consultants and coerced into its refreshing taste." The flier for a student event designed to roast the administration proclaimed its purpose as "a critique of an administration that thinks it needs to sacrifice some of our intellectual greatness in order to survive financially and attract more paying customers to campus." They were student voices, but the vitriol originated in the faculty.[22]

Financially, even managerially, Sonnenschein saved the University of Chicago; he made it more prosperous, more attractive to more students, more deserving of alumni and other philanthropic support. Chicago, was, however, a changed university; not only did more undergraduates compete for the faculty's time and attention, but also more law and MBA students gave Chicago a decidedly more professional caste. Kirp's summation said it all: "Hugo Sonnenschein may someday be hailed in Hyde Park as a hero, the leader who saved an institution by dragging it into modern times. The ultimate question, though, is whether what the traditionalists refer to as the soul of the institution, its singularity, can withstand this transformation."[23]

Market-Smart and Mission-Centered

In *Universities in the Marketplace*, Derek Bok asked the ultimate question. What happens if universities do not compete, do not price their products at market rates, do not watch their expenses and husband their resources as good businesses ought to? Then Bok answered his queries: "If universities do not enter the field, refusing to cater to consumer and vocational tastes, other providers, such as the University of Phoenix, will do the job for them, with even more blatantly commercial results. On the other hand, if universities compete, any profits they earn can presumably go to finance precisely those precious forms of teaching and research that cannot be supported by the marketplace alone."[24]

Gregory Wegner, Bill Massy, and I asked that same question in our 2005 volume, *Remaking the American University: Market-Smart and*

Mission-Centered. Our answer then and my answer now are the same: given the reality of the market and the lessened probability that either private philanthropy or public appropriation will provide sufficient funds to shelter all but a handful of institutions from the forces of the market, making money in the market will increasingly become the only way to invest in what David Kirp would define as the soul of the institution. Being market-smart and mission-centered does not lessen the conflicts that occur between values and markets, but the attitude does provide key operating principles for letting the academy proceed in the face of those conflicts—make your money honestly and spend it wisely in pursuit of the values you deem most important.

Hence my response to both the anticommodifiers and the efficiency pundits is similar. I forcefully remind the former that it does no good to cry over spilt milk in a world in which monies are always bestowed with strings attached. In turn, I remind the latter that the best way to get colleges and universities to control their expenses is to insist that they fund their discretionary investments, including investments in programs without sustainable markets, out of the revenues they save from being efficient. To these dictums Bok would no doubt add one more: also required is a willingness to talk explicitly about the values colleges and universities ought to promote even as they respond to the lure of an expanding marketplace for education and research. Kirp would go further by cautioning that values almost always involve passions that at times are barely controllable. It is not so easy to follow Bok's advice—witness the conflicting perceptions of what Hugo Sonnenschein was really about.

I have one further question, one that lies at the heart of my exploration of the reform impulse. Does being market-smart and mission-centered also point the way toward achieving the kinds of changes and transformations American higher education needs to be better? The anti-commodifiers, answering in the negative, will chide me in the process for not understanding that values and decidedly not money need our concern. The efficiency pundits will lament that I am once again letting colleges and universities off the hook and that once again I am not being tough enough on higher education's wasteful practices. The lamenters, however, will hardly know what I am talking about.

4 | The Way We Are

It is as good a time as any to ask, Is American higher education really as bad as the lamenters, efficiency pundits, and anti-commodifiers would have us believe? Have the nation's colleges and universities truly lost their way, and do they require strong words to put them back on course? Who is really angry and who is merely disappointed with American higher education? Is there now—or likely to be in the near future—a groundswell of discontent sufficient to burn through higher education's Teflon coating? All of which is to ask, Who beyond those who would remake higher education in their own image are ready to heed their calls for reform?

One way to answer those questions is to focus on public opinion, drawing from a growing number of public opinion surveys a collective portrait of what Americans outside of higher education think about the nation's colleges and universities. What do the polls tells us? Are most Americans as disenchanted with the nation's colleges and universities as the lamenters want them to be? And if not, why not?

The Polling Game

As a nation, Americans are genuinely poll happy. We may claim to not believe the polls, but we follow them assiduously. What we buy, what we believe, who we trust, who we intend to vote for—even our sexual preferences—are more than fair game for the pollsters. Even higher education is no longer immune. Starting in California in the early

1990s, Patrick Callan, with the help of Public Agenda and others, began charting what parents and opinion leaders, along with ordinary citizens, thought about the quality of the higher education enterprise. To those who expected a public scolding of higher education, the results were both surprising and disappointing. On the one hand, members of the public reported they were generally satisfied with the colleges and universities they knew about, while, on the other hand, they readily confessed to not knowing that much about what went on inside the academy. The exceptions to this generalization were the opinion leaders, who knew more and were less satisfied.

Today, there are hosts of polls tracking higher education's successes and foibles. Nearly every call for changing the higher education landscape—for improving quality or making a college education more affordable or making certain that all Americans have unfettered access to a college education—now references a public opinion survey of some kind. What those who would reform higher education repeatedly discover, however, is that their polls document concerns and irritants without ever supporting their calls for change. The reformers' laments notwithstanding, Americans continue to express satisfaction with the colleges and universities they know about while still confessing they do not know all that much about how colleges and universities operate. To make sense of this paradox, to understand why American colleges and universities today face so many calls for their reformation from so many quarters, it helps to begin with the surveys themselves and what they may—and, then again may not—be telling us about how the American public feels about the nation's colleges and universities.

In the Beginning

The report was called *Great Expectations*—an apt title for a study summarizing the results of a 1999 national survey of public opinion detailing what most Americans thought of the nation's colleges and universities. The public opinion survey was principally the work of Public Agenda's John Immerwahr and was conducted at the behest of the National Center for Public Policy and Higher Education, the National Center for Postsecondary Improvement at Stanford University, and Penn's Institute for Research on Higher Education.

What Immerwahr, who would go on to become the most credible designer of public opinion surveys focusing on higher education, produced was a remarkably detailed portrait of just how comfortable most Americans were with the collective efforts of the nation's colleges and universities. The questions the Public Agenda pollsters asked were as reasonable as they were straightforward. How are colleges and universities performing as institutions? What kinds of primary goals should they pursue? On what concerns should they expend organizational energies?

The upshot was that in 1999 most Americans thought most colleges and universities had it just about right. Higher education's stakeholders viewed academic goals as being paramount. Then the public's collective advice was that colleges and universities should continue to focus on what they did best: attracting the best possible teachers and researchers to their colleges and ensuring that students work hard to achieve high academic standards.

The need for colleges and universities to control their costs and be efficient was thought, by nearly three out of every four respondents, to be higher education's top priority. Limiting tuition increases was important too, but in 1999 slightly less so than achieving academic goals. By and large, the public regarded institutional goals concerning services and support to students as being less important than academic standards and pursuits. This finding provided a first hint of a conviction that runs throughout public opinion: namely, that students themselves bear a considerable share of responsibility for meeting the challenges of attaining a higher education.

Not surprisingly, education level affected the degree to which the public believed academic goals are at or near the top of the public's list of the most important functions of colleges and universities. The more education respondents had attained, the greater importance they attached to attracting the best faculty and ensuring high academic standards.

What is the one aspect that the public would change in order to improve the colleges and universities in their communities? Would it be to make these institutions more efficient, to lower prices, to eliminate tenure, or to raise entrance standards? In a sense, this question invited respondents to consider whether the primary issue for improvement was one of quality on the one hand, or of cost and efficiency on the other.

The answers suggested a public then feeling pretty confident about the quality of the nation's colleges and universities. Even tenure was an issue that quietly simmered rather than boiled. Less than 20 percent indicated they would eliminate tenure, and an even smaller proportion indicated they would raise entrance standards. One in four respondents with an advanced degree, however, chose the elimination of tenure as the single item they believed would most improve colleges and universities—suggesting that the more familiar respondents were with colleges and universities, the stronger the perception that faculty should not be exempt from the pressures of job security and accountability roiling other professional classes.

Of more immediate concern to the public was higher education's efficiency and price. One out of three respondents reported they would make colleges and universities more efficient, and a quarter said they would lower prices. However, when asked directly about how colleges and universities spent their funds and managed their operations, half the respondents said they did not know enough about higher education's internal practices to offer a comment, a quarter of the respondents said higher education was inefficient and wasteful, and the remaining quarter considered colleges and universities to be careful and efficient. Here, however, familiarity with higher education increased one's confidence. Except among those who had not completed high school, the number of those who thought higher education was efficient consistently exceeded the number who believed it to be wasteful.

A Report to Stakeholders

Immerwahr's *Great Expectations* survey also anchored the National Center for Postsecondary Improvement's tri-part *Report to Stakeholders on the Condition and Effectiveness of Postsecondary Education* that I drafted for *Change* magazine in 2001. The principal assumption underlying that effort was that higher education's stakeholders needed to have reliable information about the condition and effectiveness of the enterprise. Students and parents needed to know if they were getting their money's worth. Employers needed to know whether or not U.S. colleges and universities were producing graduates ready for tomorrow's jobs. Among the nation's lawmakers, accountability had already become both a slogan and a practice, as government officials sought assurances that institutions of higher education were pursuing missions and achieving results consonant with their public purposes. Though the language often reflected private agendas, the same basic question was being asked by everyone: Do the nation's colleges and universities meet, exceed, or fall short of our expectations?

Published in three installments over the 2001–2002 academic year, the National Center's *Stakeholder Report* focused separately on the general public, on recent graduates, and on employers. The data for the installment focusing on public opinion was drawn from the *Great Expectations* survey whose results I have just summarized.

The next installment focused on recent college graduates—the men and women who completed requirements for a baccalaureate degree from an accredited institution of higher education between 1991 and 1994. In the broadest sense, the question asked of these alumni was simply: What do you know? Or perhaps more elegantly, What did you learn, and was it helpful? Or again, in terms amenable to a direct answer, How confident do you feel about doing the things a college education is supposed to prepare you to do?

The *Stakeholder Report's* ability to report cogent answers to these questions derived from a special survey instrument Penn's Institute for Research on Higher Education had developed and later dubbed the Collegiate Results Instrument (CRI). Administered primarily as a paper instrument mailed directly to respondents' homes beginning in the fall of 1999, the CRI collected data from the graduates of eighty baccalaureate-granting colleges and universities across the United States. While these colleges and universities did not compose a random sample of higher education institutions (each campus belonged to the Knight Higher Education Collaborative and chose to participate in this National Center on Postsecondary Improvement [NCPI] research project), collectively they did provide a cross-section of four-year institutions—large and small, public and private, as well as from all parts of the country, all major Carnegie classifications, and most segments of the market.

In all, the CRI yielded a rich database of 34,000 alumni who had graduated between 1991 and 1994, with most having graduated in 1992–93. In their choices of occupations in particular, the alumni responding to the CRI represented a sample mirroring the distribution of occupations for college graduates aged twenty-seven to thirty years as reported by the U.S. Bureau of Labor Statistics. While their undergraduate experiences were still relatively fresh in their minds, they were far enough beyond the baccalaureate degree to have made choices and identified goals that would likely shape the rest of their lives. Within this context, the CRI asked alumni to report on their occupations, skills used in the workplace, educational activities since graduation, personal values, and current activities. They were also asked to self-evaluate their ability to perform a variety of tasks derived from real-life scenarios.

It was their answer to this last set of questions that allowed the gauging of how well the nation's colleges and universities were meeting the expectations of their students. Two out of three felt they could confidently organize information and communicate its meaning to others;

nearly as many felt confident in their ability to perform quantitative tasks and analyses. But less than half felt confident in their ability to find information—essentially, in the skills a person would employ to research a topic.

The overall portrait of recent college graduates that emerged from the CRI was one of important achievements and troubling lacunae. The good news—for higher education, for individual graduates, and for the nation at large—was that, overall, most recent college graduates were confident, liked to learn, and were likely to keep informed about current events. Just as important, nearly half of these graduates had already pursued additional schooling in search of advanced degrees either on a part-time or full-time basis.

The other values and attributes tracked by the CRI tell a more uncertain story. Only half of these recent graduates were strongly committed to keeping physically fit; only 50 percent indicated they were active politically or engaged in the civic life of their communities; just between one third and one half of these alumni were strongly interested in the arts and culture; and just about one third were strongly religious.

Where much of higher education was once segregated by gender, by 1999, the year the CRI was administered, the nation's colleges and universities were broadly co-educational. Still, important gender differences remained, some of which affirmed old stereotypes. On the average, women graduates were more engaged in arts and culture, and as well in religious activities. Men, on the other hand, were more physically active and more confident in performing quantitative tasks and analyses. The intriguing finding was that women were substantially more engaged in civic pursuits, while more men reported they kept up with current events. There was parity between the genders in their confidence in communication and organization as well as in their commitment to lifelong learning.

Older stereotypes were also reflected in the distribution of respondent occupations. Men predominated in science/engineering/technology; women predominated in teaching/counseling and health and social services. It was the areas of parity that deserved particular note—near parity in business, law, creative arts/design, and medicine/dentistry/veterinary.

The responses of these 34,000-plus recent college graduates also provided important clues for understanding the factors associated with specific skills, abilities, and values. Two qualities were generally associated with a graduate's increased confidence in tasks involving communication and organizational abilities: having completed or attempted an advanced degree and/or having entered a career in either business or law.

Confidence in one's quantitative abilities required a more complex explanation. Seven attributes were positively associated with a strong confidence in the ability to perform quantitative tasks: being a business major; being employed in a business occupation; being a math, computer science, or engineering major; attending an engineering school; and/or being in a science or engineering occupation. The other two factors in the set—graduating from a medallion institution and seeking further education—reflect one of the basic aspects of the structure of the market for postsecondary education. In all, three out of four graduates with at least two of the seven factors listed here were likely to see themselves as being confident of their quantitative abilities.

The ability to find information, however, yielded a radically different picture. Only the basic market markers—graduating from a medallion institution and seeking an advanced degree—were repeat entries on the list of significant factors. The other significant factors included being a woman, having a liberal arts or creative arts major, and pursuing a law or creative arts occupation. Those recent graduates without any of these factors had a less than one-in-three chance of being confident of their ability to find information.

The third installment of our *Stakeholders Report* focused on employers. Beginning in 1994 a new National Employer Survey (NES), first administered under the auspices of the National Center on the Educational Quality of the Workforce (EQW) and subsequently by the NCPI, surveyed nationally representative private establishments with twenty or more employees. Designed and administered by the U.S. Bureau of the Census, the NES asked employers in 1994, 1997, and 2000 about their perceptions of both secondary and postsecondary education, institutional quality, and the work preparedness of graduates from across the educational spectrum.

The NES was conceived by Peter Cappelli, then chair of the Management Department at the Wharton School and codirector of EQW. The surveys he superintended were the first to use a national sample of businesses to capture the interaction of education and employment from an establishment perspective. When it was first administered in 1994, the NES documented that, when making hiring decisions nearly all employers discounted educational credentials of every stripe and their measures of student performance. Ironically, perhaps, the 1994 NES also documented that in the long run, those establishments that hired more educated workers reported that they were more productive workplaces.

The 1997 NES specifically asked employers to rate how well four-year colleges and universities prepared their graduates for the workforce—10 percent rated the performance of colleges and universities in providing skilled employees as outstanding, 46 percent said their performance was more than adequate, and 40 percent said their performance was adequate to satisfy current skill requirements. In the estimation of the managers of these private establishments, more than half of the nation's four-year institutions deserved an "A-minus," while nearly another half deserved a "B-plus." Through most of the decade of the 1990s, employers appeared to take for granted that a college graduate was inherently employable, only in passing commenting on the nature of the education that colleges and universities actually delivered.

The 2000 NES focused primary attention on the nature and extent of employer involvement with secondary schools and community colleges across the United States. Because the 2000 survey was also the third administration of the NES, it allowed us to tease out how employer strategies for finding skilled workers changed over the course of the 1990s, and when and why they engaged with schools and colleges in pursuit of skilled workforces.

As employment levels in their establishments started to expand in the mid-1990s, employers began commenting more readily on the strengths and weaknesses of American secondary schools and community colleges and their capacity for supplying front-line workers with the basic skills and aptitudes they required. When asked in 2000, "Based on your experience with hiring their graduates over the past three years, how would you rate local community colleges' overall performance in preparing students for work in your establishment?" Only 4 percent of employers reported that graduates of these institutions were very poorly or poorly prepared. Just over half reported that community college graduates were relatively prepared for their entry-level front-line and production jobs. More important, the remaining 41 percent found the community college graduates they hired to be either well prepared or very well prepared. Employers' impressions of community colleges had changed little from those recorded in 1997—granting these two-year institutions a solid, consistent "B" in both the 1997 and 2000 administrations of the NES.

These employers' assessments of high schools, however, were decidedly less cordial. While roughly the same percentage of employers (60 percent) rated high school graduates as being relatively prepared, one in four considered the high school graduates they encountered to be poorly prepared for work—a rate nearly six times that of community college graduates. On the eve of a new century, a generous grade for America's high schools from the nation's employers would be, at best, a "C."

On the other hand, employers, like the general public, were inclined to let four-year colleges and universities off the hook. In fact, the perceived value of the nation's educational providers was remarkably monotonic. A four-year baccalaureate degree was becoming the necessary credential for entry into the world of work—a credential largely accepted without reservation, examination, or criticism. The certificates and degrees of two-year institutions, particularly community colleges, were less well regarded than those granted by four-year institutions, but were still considered valuable signals of work preparedness for new hires. High schools, at the lower rungs, received the brunt of the criticism. And while the nature of employers' complaints had less to do with the academic skills of recent high school graduates, employers' concerns were now more directly work related, focusing on a potential hire's comportment, motivation, attitude, and occupation-specific skills.

Those of us responsible for launching the National Employer Survey were aware then, as now, that the Survey's findings were at variance with the sense of educational under-preparedness that was coming to dominate the business press and the public pronouncements of industry leaders. It was possible that the NES was simply wrong, though the U.S. Bureau of the Census, which was responsible for testing and administering the survey, brought to the assignment the best frame for sampling American establishments with twenty or more employees. Perhaps the surveys asked the wrong questions, though the consistency of results across three administrations of the NES suggested otherwise. In the end, we concluded that the NES provided contrary results because it queried local managers and hiring professionals. We had purposefully chosen to focus on establishments, rather than firms, in order to insure our results captured the opinions of those middle managers most responsible for bringing recent graduates into the labor force. Their perceptions were different from the perceptions of those who held senior executive positions in the kinds of large firms that so often supply the public spokesmen and industry leaders that the press is fond of quoting. The truth of the matter was that the local managers who were the focus of the NES were more familiar with the actual supply of prepared and under-prepared workers.

The Rainbow Sign

Looking back at the three installments that constituted the National Center's *Report to Stakeholders on the Condition and Effectiveness of Postsecondary Education*, one basic theme emerges: perceptions of the U.S. educational system were shifting with economic winds. As conditions and labor market requirements changed, so did the perceived value of the education provided at various levels in the system. For the general public, things were OK—as long as students were finding gainful employment that maintained or improved their socioeconomic status and covered the borrowed cost of attendance. For employers in particular, economic conditions dictated the pool of applicants from which they can hire, placing a higher premium on baccalaureate and advanced degrees and even driving the nature and extent of their participation with colleges and schools.

The 2001 summary I wrote for *Change* magazine of how the American public felt about the nation's colleges and universities began by noting that

> The clear message from the American public is that the nation's colleges and universities are in good shape. When recently asked, "Overall, how good a job are the colleges in your state doing?" among a random sample of 1,000 adults who felt they knew their state's institutions of higher education well enough to make an assessment, 20 percent rated higher general performance as excellent, 59 percent thought it good, and 21 percent considered it just fair or poor. . . . If an "A" is excellent, "B" is good, "C" is fair, and "D–F" is poor, then colleges and universities today are earning a respectable "B" in the public's perception.[1]

The Great Expectations Survey on which much of the *Report to Stakeholders* was based was jointly sponsored by the NCPI and Patrick Callan's newly formed National Center for Public Policy and Higher Education. Callan and I shared responsibility for securing the funding as well as providing the survey's overall content. Eventually, however, we came to interpret the results of these and related polls differently. My take was that those of us who argue that reforming higher education was a good thing to do could not expect public displeasure with higher education to drive or even necessarily support any substantial remaking of the American higher education system. Rather, reform would have to come from within higher education, driven either by the need or the desire to do better because doing so was the right thing to do.

Callan and his colleagues at the National Center for Public Policy and Higher Education believed higher education could only be reformed by external forces. Colleges and universities in general, and their faculties in particular, were too complacent, too smug really to consider changing much of anything. Hence, even the good news reflected in *Great Expectations* needed to be tempered, as in the line from the folk song, "God gave Noah the rainbow sign, no more water, fire next time." In her afterword that concluded the *Great Expectations* report, Deborah Wadsworth, then Public Agenda's president, echoed this sentiment when she noted: "For now, for most Americans, higher education is a public policy success story. It is not too difficult, however, to envision events that might cloud the public's current rosy outlook." Those events might include "problems with affordability," the "potential for increased frustration from minorities," and "scalebacks in quality." Were any or all of those events to happen it would likely feed "an uncomfortable, sometimes fractious, still emerging debate about higher education among leaders."[2]

In 2003 the National Center for Public Policy and Higher Education and Public Agenda conducted a new poll charting public attitudes toward higher education. John Immerwahr again led the effort. In his introduction to the report presenting the survey's findings, Immerwahr reminded readers of Wadsworth's predictions and then went on to note, "the country has, in fact, experienced tough economic times in the years since . . . [our 1999 survey]. Many state governments are in a state of economic crisis, and public higher education is competing with other services (such as K–12, highways, and prisons) for scarce public resources. The tough times have taken their toll on higher education in terms of cutbacks and sharp increases in tuition and fees."[3]

The problem was that general public attitudes toward higher education had hardly changed. On the one hand, a college education was essential, though on the other, most people continued to report knowing relatively little about the inner workings of higher education while higher education as a political or policy issue continued to attract little attention. "This is not surprising," Immerwahr pointed out, "since there is often a lag between objective changes and public opinion, particularly when it comes to subjects that are not at the top of the public's agenda." Again, however, there were signs "that public attitudes toward higher education have become more troubled, especially for those groups most affected, including parents of high school students, African Americans, and Hispanics."[4]

Immerwahr then summarized the survey's findings, noting that the percentage of the public who viewed that "getting a college education had become more difficult than it was 10 years ago" had increased from 43 percent to 47 percent and that minorities among the parents of high school students were significantly more worried about their prospects. But on the question of higher education's waste and inefficiency—a subject that had drawn increasing attention in Washington and elsewhere—Immerwahr concluded, "our studies do not suggest that the public is especially concerned about this issue at the moment."[5]

In May 2007, the National Center on Public Policy and Higher Education, this time in partnership with the Lumina Foundation's Making Opportunity Affordable initiative, released a new Immewahr tracking of public attitudes on higher education. By then, the Spellings Commission had spoken, and the Center's most recent *Measuring Up* had concluded that an affordable college education was unavailable in all but three of the nation's fifty states. And yet, once again, higher education got what Immerwahr and company viewed as "high grades" from the public. More than half (51 percent) reported four-year colleges were doing a good to excellent job; two out of three indicated that "college is worth the money despite the high cost"; and most surprising of all given the increased focus of whether colleges and universities were still places of quality, the proportion of Americans who believed higher education was "teaching students what they need to know" increased from just over half in 1998 to two thirds in 2007. Even on the question of affordability, two thirds of the public strongly agreed with the proposition that "anyone who really wants to go to college can find a way to do so, if they are willing to sacrifice." Another 19 percent somewhat agreed, while just 13 percent disagreed.[6]

As in his earlier work, Immerwahr also pointed to what he called "warning signs for the future." Most prominent among those indicators was the growing proportion of Americans who believed there were qualified as well as motivated students who wanted to go to college but did not have the opportunity to do so. The proportion agreeing with this proposition increased from 45 percent in 1998 to 62 percent in 2007. But he also observed that his initial 1993 survey for Callan had reported that 60 percent of the population had agreed with the proposition that there were significant numbers of qualified and motivated students who did not have the opportunity to attend college. It is also worth noting that over this same period, both the number of young people attending college and the proportion of high school graduates who started college had actually increased.[7]

Where's the Beef?

So where's the beef? Why are so many important people calling for the reform of American higher education? Who is really angry and why? And why, outside of a concern for prices and a nagging suspicion that the door of opportunity that a college education represented was about to be closed, has the public remained relatively untroubled in their support of American colleges and universities? Are Immerwahr, Callan, and Wadsworth right to warn about a fire next time? Or is there another explanation for the eddies in public opinion Immerwahr so carefully tracked?

In his 2007 *Squeeze Play* report, Immerwahr provided one set of clues. In addition to the survey Public Agenda conducted, Immerwahr had at his disposal twenty-six one-on-one interviews with men and women who were considered important leaders. If the public in general was more than satisfied with American higher education, this leadership sample was decidedly unhappy. The quotes included in *Squeeze Play* were scathing. The lead quote said it all: "Higher education is a disaster. We will not, as a country, be competitive, our standard of living will not be maintained and our society will not continue to function if we are unable to educate our population." The catalog of laments was nearly endless. The liberal arts have been diminished. But students "aren't getting a practical education either." Higher education's costs are "out of control." And, in case anyone missed the message, colleges and universities are not likely to change themselves:

> I liken higher education to the auto industry. Many of the compa-
> nies are losing market share by not embracing how much things
> have changed. They are arrogant, complacent or in denial. It is the
> same in higher education. The rate of change in higher education
> is inadequate compared to the rate of change in the world around
> higher education. We are going to have problems. Can the system
> change? I'm not sure.[8]

Did the National Center only choose leaders who had strong opinions about higher education? Probably—but I too have spent too much time in that arena not to know that most leaders with strong opinions about higher education are far from satisfied. They may not all believe in a "fire next time," but they are convinced that higher education today is not good enough to meet the challenges of tomorrow.

To state the obvious, however, does not explain why such a wide gap exists between opinion leaders and the public whose opinions they are helping to form. Here a pair of surveys conducted by the *Chronicle of Higher Education* in 2003 and 2004 suggests an intriguing answer. The surveys included most of the standard questions then being asked about higher education: if higher education is valued (yes), what role should colleges and universities play (prepare undergraduates students for a career was the number one answer), which type of institutions provide high-quality educations (the number one answer was private four-year colleges and universities, which 80 percent believed provide a good quality education).

Near the end of each poll was a different kind of question, essentially asking, Who do you trust? or, more precisely, "In which institutions do you have great confidence?" Here the number one answer was the military—68 percent said they had a great deal of confidence in the military. Then, in rank order, the *Chronicle* reported the following results: 48 percent of the weighted sample said they had a great deal of confidence in four-year private colleges and universities; 44 percent said they had a great deal of confidence in churches and religious organizations; 41 percent had the same level of confidence in community colleges; 40 percent said they had a great deal of confidence in four-year public, state-supported colleges and universities. Colleges and universities of different stripes occupied three of the top five categories.

The bottom six categories also tell an interesting story. Just 16 percent said they had a great deal of confidence in local news media, 12 percent in the U.S. Congress, 11 percent in state government, 10 percent in national news media, and just 9 percent said they had a great deal of confidence in lawyers and large corporations. What the *Chronicle* poll reflects is a general lessening of confidence in institutions of every kind. Everybody is in trouble, with politicians, national news media, and large corporations at the bottom of the pile.[9]

Perhaps the way to read the polling data then is to suggest that in the first decade of the new century the American public was just plain edgy—not knowing who to trust, more ready to focus on weaknesses than strengths. American leaders had particular reason to be edgy knowing full well they were among the least trusted. The more educated the respondent, the more responsible for what happens to others, the more likely to be critical of—not just higher education—but of everything and everyone. Was—or rather is—higher education in trouble? You bet, but actually less in trouble than most other American institutions.

Squeeze Play, the 2007 Public Agenda survey, offers one additional clue. One of the questions that survey asked was, "Do you believe that colleges today mainly care about education and making sure students have a good educational experience, or colleges today are like most businesses and mainly care about the bottom line?" More than half (52 percent) said colleges and universities are mainly businesses that care principally about the bottom line.[10] In the first decade of the twenty-first century, it was not a good thing to be like a business in general or a large corporation in particular.

The easy linking of colleges and universities on the one hand, and, on the other, business, also suggests something else about higher education today. Immerwahr titled this section of his report, "The Bloom Is Off the Rose," suggesting perhaps that the nation's colleges and universities are no longer so special.[11] Higher education had really done little that was wrong and, in general, was still more valued than most other American institutions. That is what the polls are telling us. But being just like everybody else is not good enough.

Is there really a fire next time that American higher education needs to fear? Perhaps, but it will more likely be a general conflagration involving every American institution. What the reform movement needs is a strategy—or better yet, a collection of strategies and tactics— for confronting that possibility. The answer, I think, lies in making certain that American higher education recaptures its sense of being special. American colleges and universities need to be both in and yet somehow above the fray.

Recapturing that sense of being special will require learning to live with—perhaps even learning to take much better advantage of—the tension between the ideas of the acropolis and the practices of the agora, that is, between the sanctity of the temple and the necessity of the market place. Once accepted and explored, this path to meaningful reform and transformation becomes better illuminated. Making that case is what this book is about. Before I can proceed, however, I have to work through what has become an increasingly cluttered landscape of unresolved issues: globalization, the specter of scandal, the dreaded rankings, the four horsemen of reform (affordability, accountability, access, and quality), technology's disappointments, and finally, why to date learning hasn't really mattered. I hope you stick with me. If I get it right, at the end of the trail is a national agenda and a process for changing American higher education that is reasonable, doable, and important.

5

The Rain Man Cometh—Again

For colleges and universities October has tradition-ally been a tough month—growing darkness, impending rain and cold, the creeping realization that the football team won't win that many games, and, to make matters worse, an opportunity for really bad news. It was on an October day in 1987 that the stock mar-ket experimented with free-fall, jangling the nerves of every institution whose endowment included equity holdings. Two years later, on Friday the 13th of October, the market flirted with a similar decline. For resi-dents of the San Francisco Bay area, October is now marked as the month of the "Little Big One," the seismographic event that shook all of our foundations. And it was October 2007 when fires scorched Southern California. In October 2008 colleges and universities were reminded again that the stock market taketh as well as giveth.

In the 1980s and 1990s, October was also the month of reckoning for higher education. October 16, 1989—Black Monday—which that year came neatly book-ended by the market plunge and the earthquake—marked the publication by *U.S. News and World Report* of its annual rankings of institutions. Under the soft-sell title, "America's Best Colleges" and in the breathless prose of a Sunday supplement, *U.S. News* again offered up a collegiate telling of who's in, who's out, who's hot, and who's not.

A True Phenom

Now the rankings are an American icon. Though, as it turned out, there were myriad schemes for comparing and judging American colleges and universities, all you have to say today is the "rankings" word or, as is often the case, the "dreaded rankings," and everyone immediately understands you mean the *U.S. News* rankings. By the time the *U.S. News* collegiate rankings had celebrated its twenty-fifth anniversary in 2007, the enterprise had spawned a veritable tribe of rankings that told Americans about the best law schools and graduate schools and medical schools and more.

Not surprisingly the rankings have become the subject of extended analyses, most of which are designed either to discredit them or to discover what they truly measure. As every right-thinking academic knows, the rankings cannot possibly measure what they propose to measure—that immeasurable quantity, academic quality. Then, as now, there were three basic ways to attack the rankings. The easiest was to point out that the rankings were silly; the numbers were arithmetically precise but largely without meaning.

U.S. News had started with a clever idea: ask college and university presidents to list what they thought were the best institutions for an undergraduate education. Even if the results of what became known as the beauty contest reflected a bias in the magazine's choice of presidents, then most knowledgeable observers were still intrigued by the outcome. Although there were some notable as well as curious omissions, few readers doubted that those at the top of the presidents' list belonged there. It may have been gossip, but good gossip sold a lot of magazines.

The problem was that the losers in these early polls wouldn't accept the result. With unexpected force—after all, *U.S. News and World Report* was a not particularly important magazine—those slighted by the poll argued that the rankings were too simplistic, too much a product of fading reputations and old-school networks. *U.S. News* responded with science. Starting in 1989, the annual rankings issue included, in addition to the results of the beauty contest, a variety of statistics the editors presented as objective measures of institutional quality. At this point, things really got murky. Most measures reflected educational inputs rather than outputs. How selective was the institution? What was the average SAT/ACT of the freshmen class? What was the student/faculty ratio? How much money did the institution have to spend on undergraduate education? Many within and a few without higher education asked what had happened to that old-fashioned notion that education quality meant good teaching, engaged faculty, and industrious students.

There were also problems with the statistics themselves. Some numbers, it turned out, counted for more than others, though the reader was never told exactly how much more or why. Some institutional resources were counted twice, first as revenue and then as expense. Other revenues did not count at all—tuitions, for example, which for most private institutions are the financial equivalent of the public appropriations, which did count. Federal research funds were factored out, even though they helped create the research climate that bright undergraduates said they found attractive.

The titles of categories did not mean what they seemed. The category *faculty reputation* was not about faculty standing but rather faculty/student ratios. Initially, at least, transcription and data errors abounded. Vassar College complained to the magazine that a simple data-entry error cost it four places in the rankings. Obvious errors originating in an institution's federal Integrated Postsecondary Education Data System (IPEDS) report, which *U.S. News* used to construct the rankings, were allowed to stand without further checking. In the beginning apparently little or no checking of the admissions data submitted by institutions occurred; in recent years, *U.S. News* has both checked and deducted penalty points when its algorithms detected an implausible submission.

Like the calculations of the autistic savant Dustin Hoffman played in the Hollywood epic *Rain Man*, the rankings were invested with arithmetic precision, but the numbers themselves were largely devoid of meaning.

The second way to attack the rankings has been to declare them wrong-headed, a confusion of ends with means. Seemingly the editors responsible for the rankings issues did not understand what their statistical staff and consultants were doing, or why. One of the earliest essays that introduced the rankings began with a sensible, at times eloquent, statement of the need for a new sense of financial limits in higher education. "In the end," the editors declared, "bidding for limited resources will intensify, and colleges will have to make ever more-Draconian decisions about what is truly essential to their mission."[1]

It would have been difficult, but not impossible, for the rankings to reflect this new sense of limits. *U.S. News* might have rewarded those institutions that had demonstrated their quality and efficiency by in fact doing more with less. Instead, the numbers imbedded in the ranking's methodology rewarded profligacy.

What the financial information used in the analysis reflected was not efficient expenditures, but rather gross revenues. The winter of 1990 brought "The Rain Man Cometh," which Bill Massy and I contributed to this growing discourse on the rankings. There we argued that the rankings, at best, were sending mixed singles. To make our point we used the case of Carleton College in Minnesota. The college had participated in our study of the cost of an undergraduate education, and we had come away with an appreciation of Carleton's efficiency, the work ethic of its faculty, and the structure and leanness of its curriculum. We were not alone in our admiration. In the beauty contest section of the rankings issue, Carleton placed sixth among national liberal arts colleges. In overall ranking, however, the college was only fourteenth. Why? Because the college ranked forty-first in faculty quality (a slightly higher faculty/student ratio than most of its peers) and twenty-sixth in financial resources (slightly lower endowment income and almost no public appropriation). "How could," we asked, "a college judged to have a 'statistically' mediocre faculty in fact have a national reputation that puts it among the top ten liberal-arts colleges year after year?"[2]

The answer was simple. The measures were nonsensical.

The third and, by now, the most damning attack on the rankings holds that the exercise itself is inherently dangerous. The rankings have become the scorecard of an admissions arms race that has encouraged a spiraling competition for students and faculty that, over the last twenty-five years, has dramatically escalated the cost of an undergraduate education. I sat in horror one afternoon at a board of trustees meeting of a nationally ranked liberal arts college as its members berated the president because the college had once again failed to crack the top twenty-five national liberal arts colleges—a category that makes up half the "nifty-fifty" that are featured each year in the *U.S. News* annual rankings issue. On this day the president had had enough. Forgetting who and where he was, he snapped. In a voice barely distinguished from a snarl he responded, "You let me run a hundred million dollar deficit, and I will guarantee you a top ten finish!" He was wrong, of course; at that time it would probably have taken little more than an annual increase of expenditures in the $10- to $15-million range.

There was, we pointed out in our original "The Rain Man Cometh," a secondary danger as well. More than one trustee, we suggested, would be tempted to take charge of the problem themselves. Drawing on their business experiences, particularly their successes at having their own companies included among America's Best Corporations, some trustees and regents would likely argue for an immediate investment in creative public relations. The result would be more business for high-priced consultants who promise to polish the institution's image.

Alas, that is pretty much what has happened. Preparing an institution's annual submission to *U.S. News* has become presidential business. With so much at stake the president wants to make sure the numbers submitted allow the institution to put its best foot forward. Presidents are ever watchful for the opportunity to tout the excellence of their institutions—and if those opportunities coincide with the distribution of the institutional rating forms, so much the better. Talk about the rankings and the importance of becoming a top-ranked institution now permeates an ever-increasing number of strategic plans along with promises to be increasingly student-centered and civically engaged.

Colin Diver, former dean of the Law School at the University of Pennsylvania, and now the president of Reed College, recently captured this aspect of the problem for the *Atlantic Monthly*. Diver, an educational insider, who by his own testimony now feels liberated from the rankings madness, restated Reed's policy of not cooperating with the rankings and in the process summed up what many believe but only few act upon.

> A somewhat more important consequence of Reed's rebellious stance is the freedom from temptation to game the ratings formula (or, assuming that we would resist that temptation, from the nagging suspicion that we were competing in a rigged competition). Since the mid-1990s numerous stories in the popular press have documented how various schools distort their standard operating procedures, creatively interpret survey instructions, or boldly misreport information in order to raise their rankings. . . . I was struck . . . in reading a recent *New York Times* article, by how the art of gaming has evolved in my former world of legal education, where ranking pressure is particularly intense. The *Times* reported that some law schools inflate their graduate-employment rates by hiring unemployed graduates for "short-term legal research positions." Some law schools have found that they can raise their "student selectivity" (based in part on LSAT scores and

GPAs for entering students) by admitting fewer full-time first-year students and more part-time and transfer students (two categories for which data do not have to be reported). At least one creative law school reportedly inflated its "expenditures per student" by using an imputed "fair market value," rather than the actual rate, to calculate the cost of computerized research services (provided by LexisNexis and Westlaw). The "fair market value" (which a law firm would have paid) differed from what the law school actually paid (at the providers' educational rate) by a factor of eighty!

He then drives the point home by quoting a presidential colleague who, when asked why he didn't refuse to participate in the *U.S. News* process, responded, "The rankings are merely intolerable; unilateral disarmament is suicide."[3]

Diver's critique reflects the often private anger of presidents who feel helpless to do anything but play the game. More recently, however, a number of presidents of selective private liberal arts colleges have started taking on the rankings on educational grounds. Often the leading voice is Lloyd Thacker, the former admissions counselor who the *New York Times* made a poster boy for the case against the madness of an admissions arms race. What alarms Thacker and those who share his concerns is that the rankings have so corrupted the college choice process that students, particularly the best, brightest, and most affluent, make decisions that are all but devoid of educational content and value. Students don't ask the right questions and don't draw the right conclusions; they simply buy the implication of the rankings that somewhere out there is *the* very best college. The reality, as most presidents know, though in their public pronouncement often deny, is that most colleges competing for the same students are pretty much the same—or as Larry Litten, an institutional researcher for some of the United States' best and priciest colleges and now a consultant to Thacker's Educational Conservancy, told a meeting of anti-ranking activists called by Thacker:

> The message that needs to be delivered by colleges (both by what they say and how they market, recruit, and admit) is that most institutions seek similar goals, at least within broad groupings of institutions with similar resources and programs, and that each institution is sufficiently complex so that a given student can find a situation that is comfortably challenging and rewarding. As long as individual institutions are implying otherwise in their own marketing and competitive behavior, however, students will turn

to the mechanism that most efficiently and plausibly differentiates and ranks institutions.[4]

The ultimate danger inherent in any ranking scheme is that by enshrining the language of competition and uniqueness, the rankings themselves corrupt both student and college. The former arrives for his or her freshman year with the wrong expectations. The latter engages in a process that devalues education. Nobody wins in the rankings game.

The Flip Side

Not everyone and certainly not every president of an American college or university would agree. Competition is not necessarily bad, and in some cases it has actually proved beneficial. When Judith Rodin became president of the University of Pennsylvania in 1993 she found an institution that had grown progressively stronger without ever quite losing its inferiority complex. Indeed, that internal sense of not being quite as good as its competition had already led Penn in the 1920s and then again in the 1950s to commission an Educational Survey designed to help the university understand its place within American higher education. Each exercise yielded the roughly the same result—Penn, when all its strengths and weaknesses were taken into account, ranked about fifteenth among the nation's principal universities. Not coincidently, fifteenth is about where Penn consistently placed in the *U.S. News* rankings prior to Rodin's arrival.

Rodin instead wanted Penn's strengths to be recognized and celebrated both within and without the university. Her message to her deans, including Colin Diver, was simple. She expected them to secure for their schools a top-ten ranking. She did not care which rankings were used as long was they were comprehensive and garnered wide attention. She did not insist that each school use the *U.S. News* ranking, but, absent another recommendation, that is the ranking she would pay attention to.

The results were spectacular. Penn rose in the overall rankings, achieving top-ten and occasionally top-five status among national research universities. Its professional schools—Wharton, Medicine, Law, even Nursing and Education—solidified their positions as top-ten institutions. Were the rankings directly responsible for these schools' or the university's achievements writ large?

Of course not—but the presence of the rankings and the fact that here was a president who took them seriously certainly helped focus people's attention.

Northeastern University presents an even more dramatic example of how paying attention to the rankings was essential for institutions seeking to reposition themselves in an increasingly competitive market for students, faculty, and research dollars. In the 1980s, Northeastern had floundered. Once a blue-collar university whose co-op programs had particular appeal for Boston's working-class students, Northeastern was losing its markets for both full- and part-time students to a newly invigorated and very public University of Massachusetts system. The university's first response was to expand its offerings, making up in volume what it was necessarily losing in price as it tried to at least come close to matching UMass-Boston's lower tuitions. When that strategy failed, Northeastern underwent a dramatic down-sizing; the university shed programs, faculty, and staff and bet on its ability to reposition itself as a selective institution worth the higher price it found itself necessarily charging.

The president responsible for steering Northeastern through the shoals of repositioning was Richard Freeland, something of a surprise choice who nonetheless had a remarkably surefooted instinct for what had to be done. The challenge facing Northeastern, he said not just once but over and over again, was to become a top-100 university. At that moment Northeastern was ranked 162nd. Freeland believed the rankings methodology actually told him and his colleagues what they had to do: improve selectivity, improve retention, increase the propor-tion of students graduating within six years, garner more sponsored research, and increase Northeastern's media visibility. At the same time, Freeland believed that focusing on the rankings would actually animate the Northeastern community. To track progress Freeland established an annual score card with specific targets to be met each year in each category. And year-by-year and inch-by-inch Northeastern improved its metrics—and each year that progress culminated in a higher *U.S. News* ranking. In the year Freeland stepped down as presi-dent, Northeastern ranked ninety-eighth among national research uni-versities.

Was Northeastern really that much better a university? Most would agree that it was and, more importantly, that it was worth the increased tuitions it now charged. Were the rankings really that important an ele-ment in Freeland's march to reposition Northeastern? Skeptics point out that what really transformed Northeastern was the trustees' willingness to authorize more than $400 million in construction debt, which made Northeastern a more residential as well as a more attractive campus—again, worth the price. But as in Penn's case, Freeland's score-card focused the campuses' attention on what had to be done and why. The nay-sayers—and there were some who decried Northeastern's abandoning its traditional mission to become a Boston University look-alike—never had a chance as long the rankings improved and Northeastern looked both more solid and more successful.

In the Eye of the Beholder

The differences in perspective between Thacker, Litten, and the liberal arts presidents who champion the Educational Conservancy, on the one hand, and on the other, presidents like Rodin and Freeland, who have used the rankings to move their institutions up the rankings ladder, are important for what they reveal about the kind of strategies each group wants higher education to pursue. The former see in the rankings a world in which competition and conflict have replaced collaboration and cooperation. Because rankings reward the wrong behavior, they diminish the importance as well as the uniqueness of the American educational experience.

The latter group is much more accepting of competition as a way of life in a market economy. If handled right, competition brings out the best in people, makes them reach inside themselves to do better. Only by asking, How is the other guy doing? can an institution know for sure that it is making the most of its assets and opportunities.

These differences in perspective also highlight the importance of determining just exactly what the rankings measure. It is a question we—that is, Susan Shaman, Dan Shapiro, and me—stumbled into when working as part of the National Center on Postsecondary Improvement (NCPI) based at Stanford. As before, we were interested in the structure of the market for undergraduate education, only this time we wanted to build a model that explained the various prices charged by institutions. The result was a market taxonomy—many remember its initial publication that used a paper-airplane-like sketch to present the typology—that distributed colleges and universities across a continuum that began with the high-priced, highly selective institutions on one end and ended at the other with institutions designed for students more likely to earn their higher education by taking one course at a time—often from several institutions. The former we dubbed *medallion* institutions; the latter we labeled *user-friendly* or *convenience* institutions; in between, we found *name brand, good-opportunity*, and *good-buy* institutions.

Impressive about the taxonomy was both its ability to actually predict the prices institutions charged and its link to commonsense definitions of market attractiveness. One parlor game we liked to play was to ask a group of educators to list, preferably in rank order, the two dozen or so *medallion* institutions that resided at the top of the market. It was a test almost no one failed.

The statistical model underlying our market taxonomy had the additional advantage of being remarkably simple. Just five variables were needed to predict price: the percentage of an institution's freshman class that graduated with a baccalaureate degree within six years of initial enrollment; the proportion of applicants an institution admitted and the proportion of those admitted applicants who actually enrolled; the geographic region of the country in which the institution was located; and its designation as either a public or a private institution. The most powerful variable was the six-year graduation rate. An advanced graduate student at the University of Pennsylvania, who in a previous life had been a Wall Street trader, offered probably the best explanation of what made that variable so important in predicting an institution's potential tuition: "Think how the best fund traders hedge their bets." The extra tuition a medallion can charge was a premium against the risk of not graduating and thus losing the value of the money the student had already invested. The fact that the country's most selective students were attracted to as well as sought out by these medallions made enrollment there that much more of a bargain.

Inevitably, we were asked how well our market taxonomy tracked with the *U.S. News* rankings. The answer we quickly learned was unnervingly well. Both the market taxonomy and the *U.S. News* rankings produced roughly the same list in roughly the same order. But then again, we should not have been surprised because both analyses use the six-year graduation rate as a key variable. What did surprise us, however, was the fact that we could largely replicate the *U.S. News* list using just two variables from the magazine: six-year graduation rate and score on the reputation survey. Among the fifty top liberal arts colleges, the fit was almost perfect. Research universities presented a slightly more complex result because the *U.S. News* list commingled public and private institutions. Once a research university's control— either public or private—was taken into account, the result nearly matched that of the liberal arts colleges.

We now had our answer. The *U.S. News* rankings measure not quality—a conceit only *U.S. News* itself still promotes—but *market position.* Once that proposition is understood it becomes perfectly clear why presidents like Rodin and Freeland are attracted to the rankings. Both made improving their institution's market position the focus of their presidencies. At the same time, the fact that the *U.S. News* rankings measure market position and not much else helps explain the growing discomfort of educational reformers in general, and liberal arts college presidents in particular, who want to de-escalate institutional competition by stressing instead the importance of educational values and institutional collaborations.

Customer Satisfaction

U.S. News is not alone in seeking to rank American colleges and universities in order to determine who is best. The University of Illinois, Chicago, maintains a rankings website that contains thumbnail sketches of two dozen separate ranking schemes. In addition to the *U.S. News* rankings, the website lists entries that vary from "Young America's Foundation Top Ten Conservative Colleges" to "New Mobility Disability-Friendly Colleges" to "John Templeton Foundation: Colleges that Encourage Character Development."

Most of these other ranking schemes use methodologies roughly similar to the *U.S. News* collection of statistical variables that are indexed to produce a rank ordering. The most important exceptions to this pattern are the every-other-year rankings of MBA business schools conducted by *BusinessWeek*. Since 1988, *BusinessWeek* has gone in search of what it called the "best B-schools." Instead of compiling a statistical portrait of the schools, however, the magazine chose instead to ask the customer—or, in this case, the two sets of customers most important to business schools: their students and the corporate recruiters who interview and hire them. *BusinessWeek* rankings measure, the magazine proudly tells its readers, nothing less than customer satisfaction.

For its 2006 ranking of B-schools *BusinessWeek* contacted 16,565 recent graduates of the top 100 business schools. In all, 9,298 responded for a more than respectable 56-percent response rate. Only two schools refused to supply the names and addresses of their recent graduates— the Harvard Business School and the University of Pennsylvania's Wharton School. Using public records *BusinessWeek* tracked down and got responses back from 39 percent of the recalcitrant institutions' recent graduates. In the final result, Wharton ranked second and Harvard fourth—the first and third spots went to the University of Chicago and Northwestern's Kellogg School, respectively.

The survey itself was a fifty-item questionnaire that asked about everything from what the graduates thought of the teaching at their schools, to the kinds of career services the school provided, to their initial salary upon graduation with an MBA. *BusinessWeek* went to considerable length to ferret out the possibility that the schools try to game the survey by hiring two CUNY educational psychologists "to ensure that the results were not skewed by any attempts to influence student responses or otherwise affect the outcome of the survey."[5] In the final rankings, a school's score on the student survey received a 45-percent weight in the final rankings.

Also receiving a 45-percent weight was each school's score on the corporate recruiter survey. Recruiters were asked to judge the quality of the students they interviewed for employment in terms of their communication skills, aptitude for teamwork, and analytic skills. Beginning in 2006, *BusinessWeek* began using a weighted average of the recruiter survey that included the current plus the previous two survey administrations in order to provide a more robust and stable total score.

The final 10 percent of a school's score reflected what *BusinessWeek* called "intellectual capital." For this index the magazine, focusing on the school's faculty, noted faculty publications in the field's top twenty publications, from the *Journal of Accounting Research* to the *Harvard Business Review*. *BusinessWeek* also searched the *New York Times*, the *Wall Street Journal*, and its own archives, adding points if a professor's book was reviewed there. The scores were then adjusted for faculty size.

BusinessWeek rankings promise and deliver an ordering of business schools based on the outcomes that matter most to students (salary, career support, engaged teaching) and to the companies that hire them (capacity to communicate, analyze, and be an effective team member). *BusinessWeek* rankings also provide a diagnostic tool that tells the aspiring institution what it has to do to raise in the rankings. The folklore that surrounds the competitive world of B-school rankings abounds in stories of institutions caught short and their subsequent scramble to set things right. My favorite centers on a top-ten business school that suddenly plummeted in the rankings in large part because it had angered its student body. In the midst of the ensuing furor, the school went about the business of recruiting a new dean. One candidate arrived with a detailed analysis of the *BusinessWeek* rankings, which told him, at least, what the school needed to do to right itself.

When he sensed no one was really that interested, he withdrew his candidacy. The school has yet to return to the top ten.

Purposes

Actually the *BusinessWeek* rankings serve both the principal purposes that educational rankings pursue. The rankings provide, as the magazine proclaims, an important measure of "customer satisfaction." In the hands of an adroit dean, the rankings are a guide to quality improvement because they highlight both the successes and the failures that matter most to students and employers. At the same time, the rankings clearly signal market position; those at the top have the same market power among B-schools that the colleges and universities at the top the *U.S. News* rankings of undergraduate institutions have in that domain. And no one seems too worried about the very public nature of the exercise itself. Given the institutions' educational commitment to competition and market forces, one should expect that judgments of quality and market position should be both public and entangled.

For undergraduate education, this commingling of quality improvement and public measurement presents a host of difficulties— just ask the academics and institutional leaders responsible for the National Survey of Student Engagement. The NSSE, as it is fondly known, was the brainchild of Russ Edgerton, who was first the president of the American Association for Higher Education and later the educational director of the Pew Charitable Trust, which provided NSSE's startup funds. His collaborator, Peter Ewell, throughout the last two decades has solidified his position as the researcher who best understands learning outcomes and how they are achieved. Together, Edgerton and Ewell argued that, while it was not really possible to test for learning outcomes, it was possible to test for the conditions that promoted the best learning outcomes—what they came to summarize as the conditions promoting student engagement.

The NSSE itself is a short, four-page survey given to a sampling of college and university juniors and seniors that asks questions about what they typically do both in and out of class, how much they study, how often they write papers, how often they engage in collaborative learning projects, and how many hours per week they work for pay. Toward the end of the instrument the student is asked to evaluate the "quality of your relationships with people at your institution": other students, faculty, and administrative personnel. The student is given a seven-point scale for each group, ranging from "unfriendly, unsup-portive, sense of alienation" to "friendly, supportive, sense of belong-ing" for their fellow students; from "unavailable, unhelpful, unsympathetic" to "available, helpful, sympathetic" for faculty; and from "unhelpful, inconsiderate, rigid" to "helpful, considerate, flexible" for administrative personnel.[6]

The NSSE has been wildly successful, particularly among public institutions and lesser-ranked private colleges and universities. To date, more than 1,200 baccalaureate institutions have administered the NSSE to a sample of their students—and many repeat the administra-tion on an every-other-year or every-third-year cycle. The NSSE has provided these institutions with a clear sense of what is necessary to improve student engagement and, by implication at least, learning out-comes. Faculty members have been put on notice when the NSSE reports they have not been attentive enough. Curriculum committees take note when the NSSE reports that, compared with similar institu-tions, students on the committee's campus do not write enough or do not speak up in class regularly or do not engage in collaborative learn-ing projects on a regular basis.

True, NSSE institutions have been known to festoon their website with NSSE factoids like ranking in the ninetieth percentile on particu-lar survey items. For the most part, the NSSE is advertised as and used for purposes of improvement. From the outset, however, Edgerton, in particular, believed that colleges and universities would grow comfort-able with releasing their NSSE results into the public domain as a kind of natural antidote to the *U.S. News* rankings. Most institutions, how-ever, have demurred, wanting to contemplate their results in private.

More recently the NSSE organization has formed an alliance with *USA Today* in an "Initiative to Focus on Meaningful Indicators of Collegiate Quality." But for the moment, the newspaper will present only the good results, those that highlight what the partners described as "different types of colleges and universities that involve their stu-dents at high levels in effective educational practices."[7]

Critics and observers who want higher education to be more accountable want the NSSE results released—and there's the rub. Will institutions still use the NSSE if the results are both made public and used for the purpose of holding the institution accountable to its accred-itors and, in the case of public institutions, its state's regulatory agen-cies? Won't the temptation be, as Colin Diver has suggested is already the case with the *U.S. News* rankings, to game the system by lessening the probability that unhappy or disengaged students make it into the test's sample? Won't institutions, subtly or not, encourage those students selected to fill out the NSSE to win one for the Gipper by focusing on what is right as opposed to what is wrong with the institution?

Even tougher to gauge would be the reaction of the faculty. Already there is a tendency for the very best or at least the top-rated and most expensive undergraduate institutions not to use the NSSE; they have little to learn and a fair amount to lose. If the past is any guide, faculty will find it in their interest to attack the instrument itself by bringing all their considerable verbal and mathematical firepower to demonstrate that NSSE results are at best inconclusive. What had hitherto been seen as an interesting diagnostic tool, despite some methodological problems, would become in the eyes of many a political tool of uncertain value that would likely be used to bludgeon otherwise right-thinking faculty to adopt a cookie-cutter approach to undergraduate education.

That fate is already befalling another instrument that seeks to measure learning outcomes. The Collegiate Learning Assessment (CLA), originally developed by researchers at the Rand Corporation, later spun off to something called the Council for Aid to Education. The CLA is a Web-based instrument that tests samples of an institution's students in four broad areas: critical thinking, analytic reasoning, written communication, and problem solving. Although the test itself is automated, its grading is not and depends on the ability of the test givers to train a sufficient number of graders of the students' work in response to the prompts the student receives during the time allotted for the test.

Presumptive regulators, in particular, have been much impressed with the CLA. Charles Miller, chair of the Spellings Commission, early on urged his commission to adopt the CLA as exactly the kind of test that would tell the nation which colleges were up to the mark and which were not. From Miller's perspective, the CLA offered precisely the objective measure that would allow everyone—government funders and regulators, accreditors, and potential students and their parents—to at last hold higher education accountable. For higher education the CLA would be analogous to No-Child-Left-Behind tests in primary and secondary education.

The CLA, however, won't work. It is expensive to administer. Its results are difficult to interpret and verify. And it largely tests general education rather than the kind of advanced and technical studies that have been the hallmark of the academic major across American higher education. At least in the pilot administrations made public so far, there has been an uncomfortable correlation between SAT/ACT results and the CLA—hence, the institutions with the most selective admissions practices very likely score highest on the CLA. The Council for Aid to Education counters that the CLA really allows the measurement of value added by using the SAT/ACT results as the benchmark. Here, too, the results have been confusing. Institutions ask, Which is the better measure, the SAT/ACT or the CLA?

Actually a prior technical difficulty renders the CLA less than ideal. While the CLA results are to be used to evaluate an institution and its learning effectiveness, individual students are expected to take the test. Because they have no personal interest in the outcome—their scores, for example, will not be reported to prospective graduate schools or employers—they are not likely to either prepare for the test or necessarily do their very best. Faculty members are quick to point out that they have little intention of being judged by student performances on a test that does not matter to the student. My guess is that, given the choice, faculty members would prefer an old-fashioned beauty contest survey or even the NSSE to the CLA.

More of the Same

Despite the muddle caused by the rankings, two important aspects of the problem are now clearer. First, the *U.S. News* rankings are here to stay, though October now comes in late August with the pre-release of *U.S. News*'s list of "Best Colleges." Autistic savant or not, *U.S. News* will continue to go with the numbers—and the story those numbers tell will remain largely the same.

At the same time, calls for an alternative to the *U.S. News* rankings will increase in both frequency and fervor. Policy wonks and would-be regulators will demand both more transparency and more testing in the name of making higher education more accountable. Advocates for alternative learning paradigms will insist that more robust measures of learning be included in the rankings' calculations. The most coherent and perhaps most successful calls for developing cogent alternatives to the *U.S. News* rankings will come from those like Lloyd Thacker of the Educational Conservancy and Doug Bennett, Earlham College president and chair of the NSSE board, who want to make the conversation about what constitutes a good college or university better reflect the educational values that ought to shape the enterprise in the first place.

There ought to be calls as well to make rankings and institutional evaluations more an exercise in gauging customer satisfaction—more like *BusinessWeek*'s rankings of B-schools. Students actually know better what they want and need than the reformers and critics give them credit for. Ask recent graduates what they thought of the institutions they attended. Ask them if they are happy in the jobs they took following graduation. Ask them how much money they are making and to what extent they are actually using on the job what they learned inside and outside the classroom.

But moving from statistical measures of market positions to customer satisfaction will not be so easy. *BusinessWeek* learned this lesson in 2006 when it sought to match its rankings of MBA programs with a similarly constructed ranking of undergraduate schools and programs of business. *BusinessWeek* wanted to deal with only one hundred or so top undergraduate business programs and actually settled for just sixty-one institutions in its inaugural effort. In all, the magazine got valid e-mail addresses from the colleges and universities themselves for just slightly more than 81,000 current business program students. But only 19,550 students completed the online survey, for a 24-percent response rate. Most analysts think a 35-percent to 45-percent response rate is necessary to draw the kind of conclusions *BusinessWeek* wanted to draw. For its MBA survey the response rate was 56 percent.

By comparison, developing a valid customer satisfaction survey for colleges and universities conferring baccalaureate degrees will prove a gargantuan task involving some 1,800 institutions and a sample of 900,000 potential respondents at 500 students per institution. Best guess cost-estimates run in the neighborhood of $8 to $9 million per administration. It is unlikely that any commercial venture—or even a foundation—would risk that kind of funding, leaving the federal government and its Department of Education as the only likely sponsors. Whether institutions would trust the department not to misuse the data is an open question, particularly given that organization's recent attempts to federalize the accreditation process and its pushing of a record-unit system that would allow it to track individual students.

The payoff, however, if these security and political concerns can be assuaged, would be considerable, particularly if the resulting survey contained some NSSE-like items along with the bread-and-butter satisfaction questions *BusinessWeek* asks of the students in its survey. Initially, I suspect, most consumers will stick with the market position indicator championed by *U.S. News*, though in time consumers too may begin to look at measures that tell them something about the learning environments of the different institutions in which they are interested. The big winners would be the faculty once they got over the notion that the survey's results were just another scorecard or ranking and treated them instead as a set of comparative diagnostic tools. The result just might be a giant step toward creating the culture of evidence the rankings were supposed to engender in the first place.

6 Scandals Waiting to Happen

I was working with a board of trustees filled with corporate executives certain that higher education was in trouble—not their own university, to be sure, but everyone else's. They listened politely as I explained what could—and could not—be included in an effective reform agenda, and then, in no uncertain terms, they told me to stop pussyfooting around. Just like everybody else in the academy, they said, I was afraid to identify higher education's real problems: faculty who can't teach, administrators who don't know how to stop spending other people's money, and students who are more interested in good times than great books. It was midsummer 2002. Enron had imploded the year before. Worldcom had just confessed it had a $3.8 billion accounting problem. Its CEO was about to be fired along with 17,000 of Worldcom's employees. By the standards of corporate malfeasance, I suggested, higher education wasn't doing all that bad—no Enron, no Worldcom, and—and here I paused for effect—no payola outside the normal shenanigans of big-time sports programs.

Turning Up the Heat

I was wrong. What we know now is that the conditions for a really stinky payola-like scandal were just beginning to ripen. The first public inkling, however, would not come for another four years. Then in one of his last official acts as New York's attorney general, Eliot Spitzer let it be known that he had begun an investigation into the relationship between the big lenders providing student loans and the financial aid officers who were in a position to tell continuing as well as incoming students which lenders were on their institutions' preferred lists. Four months and an election later, New York's new attorney general, Andrew Cuomo, used the media, in general, and the *Chronicle of Higher Education*, in particular, to put the squeeze on some of the nation's best known colleges and universities. First, Cuomo announced an expansion of Spitzer's original investigation by requesting information from an additional sixty colleges and universities as part of what the *Chronicle* began calling Cuomo's "expanding . . . investigation into whether student-loan providers encourage campus financial-aid administrators to steer borrowers their way."[1]

Armed with these new data, Cuomo attacked. The problem, he said, was what he called "an unholy alliance" between higher education institutions and lenders. In announcing his intention to sue Education Finance Partners (EFP), one of the bigger providers of student loans, he minced no words in charging EFP with aggressively offering "kickbacks and inducements" in order to have its products placed on the colleges' preferred lender lists. Shortly thereafter, four hundred additional institutions received letters from the attorney general asking about their relationships with lenders in general and in particular what inducements they had accepted to steer their students to a set of preferred lenders. Dallas Martin, president of the National Association of Student Financial Aid Administrators, accused Cuomo of character assassination and demanded an apology. "I know my members," Martin said. "They play by the rules. They are ethical. They don't cut corners. They don't take bribes."[2] As it turns out, Martin, like the rest of us, didn't know what he was talking about.

Cuomo struck back, announcing that thirty-five institutions had accepted his demands to pay restitution to students and accept a new code of conduct. What set the higher education world abuzz, however, was the announcement that Cuomo's probe had gotten personal and in the process snared some pretty important fish. First was Matteo Fontana, a top official at the U.S. Department of Education, responsible for overseeing the federal government's student aid operations. Fontana had held and subsequently sold more than $100,000 worth of stock in Student Loan Xpress after he joined the department in 2002. Fontana was placed on administrative leave and in May submitted his resignation. Next on the firing line were three key student financial aid officers from three of the nation's top universities: David Charlow, whom Columbia quickly fired as its chief student financial aid officer; Lawrence W. Burt, who was fired from his job by the University of Texas, Austin; and Ellen Frishberg, director of financial aid at the Johns Hopkins University, who was first placed on administrative leave and then allowed to resign from Johns Hopkins. Charlow and Burt, like Fontana, had held significant amounts of stock in companies providing students loans. While Frishberg had declined the offer of stock, she had accepted consulting fees as well as tuition assistance from a major provider of student loans.

In June, Margaret Spellings, already on edge because of the failure of her Commission on the Future of Higher Education to spur either more accountability on the part of the nation's postsecondary accrediting agencies or more support from within higher education itself, got roasted by the congressional committee responsible for her department. She had, the members made clear, allowed the student loan scandal to fester on her watch. George Miller, the panel's chair, wanted to know whether the department's "monumental" failure to monitor the student loan industry was "simply laziness"? Or was it "incompetence? Was it a deliberate decision to look the other way while these things happened? Or was it a failing more sinister than that?"[3] About the same time, Cuomo began collecting his pound of flesh. Million-dollar restitution payments were extracted from Columbia, Johns Hopkins, the University of Pennsylvania, New York University, and Citibank.

More of the Same

Not so coincidentally, 2007 was an equally bad year for the quasipublic agencies the states had been setting up to provide students access to private loan funds at reasonable rates. In that year, three of these agencies found themselves the focus of newspaper exposés of their policies and perks.

In Iowa the *Des Moines Register* targeted the Iowa Student Loan Liquidity Corporation that dominated the state's market for student loans. What had begun as a relatively small, quasipublic agency created to purchase student loans made by banks had, by 2007, become a lender to students and an agency with more than four hundred employees and a loan portfolio of more than $3 billion.

When the *Register* gained access to the agency's internal e-mails, the fat was in the fire. The most damning tracked the agency's "continued hypergrowth" and the benefits of "an aggressive, offensive strategy to bring in new loan volume." That aggressive marketing, along with special incentives and favorable arrangements with many of Iowa's colleges and universities, allowed Iowa Student Loan to boast that it had captured 90 percent of the market for student loans. What galled the *Register* and eventually Iowa's governor and state legislature was that en route to that mark, Iowa Student Loan had helped earn the state the dubious distinction of the nation's second-highest debt burden per college graduate in the nation—an average debt of $23,680 per graduate in 2006, compared with a national average that year of $18,918.[4]

The icing on the cake, as far as the legislature was concerned, was the $250,000-plus annual salary paid the agency's executive director, the absence of public access to the agency's books and board meetings, and the fact that each board member received a $1,000-fee for attending each meeting. The *New York Times*, covering the story as a sequel to its extensive coverage of the Cuomo investigation of shady practices in the loan industry, quoted Iowa State Senator Michael Connolly as putting Iowa Student Loan on notice: "If they're going to act like an aggressive profit-making corporation and pay their CEO a quarter of a million dollars a year and pay their board members $1,000 a meeting, then maybe we should cut them loose." Jonathan Glater summed up the *Times*'s take on the issue: "The states are focusing, to a degree, on issues similar to those raised in the national student loan scandal of the spring: lax oversight and, in Iowa, whether incentives to colleges led them to steer students to Iowa Student Loan. Other questions are particular to state-affiliated, nonprofit lenders, like whether they should be held accountable for lavish spending, be subject to greater public scrutiny or retain a right to issue tax-exempt bonds."[5]

Missouri had the same story to tell. A quasi-governmental student loan agency—the Missouri Higher Education Loan Authority or MOHELA—had grown rich and powerful serving a multibillion-dollar market for student loans. MOHELA had also attracted a lot of attention. The governor, among others, allowed the agency to sell off a small portion of its $-billion loan portfolio and use the proceeds to support physical improvements in the state's public colleges and universities. The governor's initiative, independent of its merits, was made politically palatable to both MOHELA and its higher education supporters by a state audit that detailed the perks the authority had provided key personnel along with their salaries, bonuses, extra payments, and severance packages. For an official audit report, the document made for juicy reading. In recent years MOHELA had spent $2.3 million on severance packages for just four top officials, provided individual performance bonuses in 2004 that ranged from $112,500 to $157,500, allowed senior executives to cash in their overtime for more than $200,000, and granted temporary salary increases totaling $82,500 in 2004. The *New York Times* quoted Missouri State Auditor Susan Montee as observing, "They did not act like a state agency at all. . . . They really had the mindset that they were a for-profit business."[6] When the MOHELA board objected to using some of its assets to fund campus facilities, the governor forced the resignations of a majority of the board, including its chairwoman.

The story in Pennsylvania was achingly similar—a rich and powerful quasi-governmental loan agency that saw itself as increasingly independent and largely immune to the kind of public scrutiny to which state agencies and public institutions were routinely subjected. The Pennsylvania Higher Education Assistance Agency (PHEAA), however, had been celebrated for its inventiveness as well as its success at holding simple greed at bay. Not true, it turned out. One of the less well-known aspects of PHEAA operations was the fact that sixteen of the twenty PHEAA board members were appointed by legislative leaders—and not surprisingly, most were either current or former members of the Pennsylvania legislature. Even less well known was just how well these pros treated themselves. In all three states, news reporters were responsible for uncovering what the loan agencies wanted concealed. In Pennsylvania the resultant news reporting was particularly gleeful. Writing in the *Pittsburgh Tribune-Review*, the steel city's second largest daily, Brad Bumsted made clear his allegiances. It began with the headline—"Pigging Out at PHEAA"—followed by a series of body blows: "After trying to conceal the details of trips to posh resorts from 2000 to 2005, a court order this year required PHEAA to lay the cards on the table: $860,000 in resort expenses that included golf, massages, pedicures, fly fishing, fine cigars and cooking classes." What had it cost to try to block these juicy disclosures? "The state's college loan agency had spent $400,000 in legal bills to keep you from knowing what the lawmaker-dominated board had spent going to resorts like Nemacolin Woodlands in Fayette County and The Greenbrier in White Sulphur Springs, W.Va." And then the coup-de-grace: "Now, on top of all that, the board doled out executive bonuses totaling $570,000 for top staff, including a $180,857 bonus for CEO Dick Willey, whose annual base salary is $289,119. He gets nearly a cool half-million dollars overall."[7] Willey would not last out the year, though his pedigree was PHEAA to a tee. Prior to joining PHEAA as CEO he spent twenty years inside the Capitol in Harrisburg as executive director of the Pennsylvania House Majority Appropriations Committee, where he served as principal advisor to the Speaker and majority leaders responsible for developing priorities and strategy. He was also once the executive director of the Senate Minority Appropriations Committee and a senior governmental affairs consultant for the law firm Stevens and Lee.

The clincher had been a state auditor's report revealing that in sum, PHEAA had awarded more than $7.5 million in bonuses to top officials. Willey's last bonus of $185,000 was actually greater than the total salary paid to Pennsylvania's Governor Ed Rendell. The state's auditor general drew the obvious conclusion: the "$6.4 million in bonuses/incentives could have provided 1,702 Pennsylvania students a maximum education grant, which ranged from $3,300 to $4,500 during the audit period. Or, PHEAA could have provided 2,563 borrowers $2,500 apiece in loan forgiveness."[8]

When Is Enough Already Too Much?

The payola scandals involving big players in the student loan market and the exposè of the pay packages and high living of those in charge of a host of not-for-profit state student loan agencies made the big headlines. The continuing story, however, was the steady upward climb of presidential compensation across higher education. The data on compensation come from the Internal Revenue Service (IRS) 990 Form required of almost all nonprofit organizations and nearly every accredited college or university. In addition to reporting its basic revenues and expenses, the organization is required to report for each executive management employee, for each member of the organization's board, and for the organization's five highest paid employees the amount received from the institution in four categories: loans and advances, compensation, contributions to employee benefit plans and deferred compensation plans, and expense account and other allowances. At the end of each tax year, the IRS makes most complete 990 Forms available through a variety of databases.

In the tracking of presidential compensation in higher education, the designated scorekeeper is the *Chronicle of Higher Education*, which draws on both the 990 databases and its own survey of executive compensation. Its analysis is reported each fall in a special supplement. The headline it attaches to each pretty much tells the story.

2007: The Rising Price of Presidents
2006: Paychecks at the Pinnacle
2005: Under Scrutiny

The sub-headline for the 2005 executive compensation supplement—
"The Internal Revenue Service and the U.S. Senate have turned their
attention to college pay and perquisites"—signaled that the *Chronicle*
that year would focus on the sad case of Benjamin Ladner who was
ousted from the presidency of American University in Washington D.C.
after his lavishing spending on entertainment and travel became public.

The major story in the *Chronicle*'s Executive Compensation supplement broadened the target, asking "The Million-Dollar President, Soon
to Be Commonplace?" The answer was a resounding yes! In a single year
the number of presidents at public universities making more than a half-
million dollars a year had nearly doubled, though as before, the pay of
the presidents at the nation's private medallion universities drew most
of the attention. Topping the list was E. Gordon Gee, then still at
Vanderbilt University, whose publicly reported compensation was
$1.2 million. With remarkable understatement, the *Chronicle* observed:

> The number of chief executives in higher education moving into
> the highest ranks of compensation accelerated in the past year.
> While the salaries do not have the eye-popping quotient of those of
> corporate CEO's—whose median compensation was just over
> $6-million among the 350 largest U.S. corporations—the steady
> upward march of higher-education compensation is increasingly
> spreading from private institutions to public colleges and
> universities.[9]

The IRS Form 990 and *Chronicle*'s surveys cover most compensation for
most presidents but not all the high fliers, the members of what the
Chronicle has taken to calling the "millionaires' club." To get the full
picture of the earnings of these presidents requires pouring through the
proxy statements of the corporations on whose boards these presidents
sit. The *Chronicle*'s 2005 Executive Supplement, covering compensation for 2004, provided an intriguing glance into just how entwined private higher education and corporate management were becoming. In
that year, Vanderbilt's Gee, in addition to his million-dollar-plus compensation from the university, received "as much as $275,000 in annual
pay for membership on the boards of Dollar General Corporation,
Gaylord Entertainment Company, Hasbro Inc., Limited Brands Inc., and
Massey Energy Company, plus stock options and shares." Rensselaer
Polytechnic Institute (RPI) President Shirley Ann Jackson's annual compensation from corporate sources included "as much as $525,500 in
annual pay for memberships on the boards of AT&T Corporation,

Federal Express Corporation, Marathon Oil Corporation, Medtronic Inc., Public Service Enterprise Group, and United States Steel Corporation, plus stock options and shares. She also received $60,000 in annual pay for membership on the board of the New York Stock Exchange." The University of Pennsylvania's Judith Rodin received as "much as $318,000 in annual pay for memberships on the boards of Aetna Inc., AMR Corporation, Comcast Corporation, and Electronic Data Systems, plus stock options and shares." William Brody of the Johns Hopkins University received from corporate sources as "much as $96,000 in annual pay for memberships on the boards of Medtronic Inc. and Mercantile Bankshares Corporation, plus stock options and shares. He also served on the board of Aegon USA, the privately held American subsidiary of Aegon NV, a Dutch insurance company."[10]

In California this link between executive pay and corporate governance helped speed the departure of the University of California System's Robert Dynes as well as tarnishing the standing, if not the reputation, of one of the University's rising stars—the University of California, San Diego (UCSD) Chancellor Marye Anne Fox. This particular drama unfolded after the media's discovery that Dyne's office had not fully revealed the pay packages or arrangements used to attract and retain top administrators across the ten-campus system. But what had been originally presented as a bureaucratic slip-up quickly mushroomed into a scandal of California proportions. A state audit of the University's pay practices revealed $334 million in extra compensation to employees, much of which, the *Chronicle of Higher Education* reported, "was improper and not reported to regents or the public."[11]

At this point, though Dynes temporarily kept his job, he effectively lost control of the university he was supposed to manage. He had to confess that he had fully kept track of neither how much extra compensation his campus chancellors were earning nor what was expected of them in exchange. In this case the devil that made him do it, he told Paul Fain of the *Chronicle of Higher Education*, was a competitive environment for talented academic leaders, coupled with the high cost of living in California, for creating a climate of secrecy in which university officials at times tried to "disclose as little as possible" about compensation. He also blamed some mistakes and violations on both an outdated human resources system and bad advice from underlings.[12]

Marye Anne Fox was one of those talented academic leaders that the University had attracted to California to head the San Diego campus with its emphasis on cutting-edge scientific research. Though the term is often overused, Fox could rightly claim to be a world-class chemist, a member of the National Academy of Sciences and the American Philosophical Society, and a fellow of the American Academy of Arts and Sciences. She was also a proven administrator, having served as the vice president for research at the University of Texas–Austin and chancellor of North Carolina State. Bringing her to California was a major feather in Dynes's cap. To attract her, however, UCSD needed an attractive package to supplement her $350,000 annual salary. In a self-congratulatory note, the *San Diego Union-Tribune*, as part of its coverage of Dynes's growing liabilities, reported that the president had been forced to defend the "decision in 2004 to pay UCSD Chancellor Marye Anne Fox $248,000 in previously undisclosed compensation. That payout, with other benefits, brought Fox's compensation for her first year at UCSD close to $700,000, according to data released in response to a public records request by the *San Diego Union-Tribune*."[13]

To more permanently bridge the gap between her market value and her stated salary, Fox was given permission to join eleven corporate and nonprofit boards, four of which paid her a total of $668,231 in cash and stock awards in the most recent fiscal year. That service was not a secret and in fact the previous year had been the subject of another story in the *San Diego Union-Tribune* in which Fox was quoted in effect as saying that she could more than handle the extra hours for such service because she used her vacation time. Nonetheless, she was technically over the limit in the number of boards she served on—somewhere in the policies of the University of California it was discovered that ten board memberships were the maximum allowed—so, in the furor surrounding the system's handling of extra compensation for senior executives, she resigned from the board of Pharmaceutical Product Development, a Wilmington, N.C.-based clinical research company that, as the *Union-Tribune* reported, paid her "$179,800 in cash and stock awards in the past fiscal year." The newspaper further noted: "Fox remains a director at medical device developer Boston Scientific Corp., chemical manufacturer W.R. Grace and Co. and software company Red Hat Inc. She also serves on the boards of six nonprofits and foundations: Burroughs Wellcome Fund in North Carolina; Dreyfus Foundation in New York; Welch Foundation in Texas; United Way of San Diego County; Rady Children's Hospital-San Diego; and the San Diego Regional Economic Development Corp."[14]

Practices, Policies, and Values

None of these peccadilloes—not the payola in the loan industry, not bonuses and junkets of the state loan agencies, not the extra compensation itself or the secrecy in which it was originally awarded by a University of California president who was in over his head—come close to matching the corporate malfeasance of the Enron and Worldcom scandals. What is troubling about them, however, is that the pace of such misadventures seems to be quickening—that and the fact that it is becoming increasingly easy for an investigative reporter or a diligent state auditor or an ambitious state attorney general to smell out those things that seemingly shouldn't pass anyone's smell test in the first place.

There is an obligation to ask, What happened? Indeed, what happened to that presumption that American higher education was special, protected from and at times seemingly oblivious to the pursuit of privileges and perks that has always been a feature of the American landscape? To be sure, there have always been scandals, though more often relegated to the sports pages and those stories that focus on college purchasing agents looking for kickbacks from suppliers. What is particularly troubling about the people caught in the events I have been describing is that they are from the heart of the enterprise and in fact represent some of higher education's biggest success stories. Columbia University touched on the sadness and inexplicableness surrounding the scandal when it observed in its announcement of the firing of its longtime financial aid director and university alum that David Charlow was a "longtime, well-regarded employee [who had] failed to uphold the trust that had been placed in him by the University."[15] Charlow's mistakes included holding $100,000 in stock in a company he put on the Columbia preferred lender list and a multitude of social events hosted and paid for by the lender's president.

Among the commentators who tried to make sense of the fact that the payola scandal had ensnared some heretofore exemplary citizens was Barmak Nassirian, an associate executive director of the American Association of Collegiate Registrars and Admissions Officers (AACRAO)—the professional organization most admissions and financial aid officers belong to. As he looked out across a landscape now cluttered with the wrecks of promising careers, he talked sadly about how many American colleges may have started down a "slippery slope" in the original intention of helping students arrange affordable financial aid packages only to be swamped by the banks' maneuvering. He told the *Chronicle of Higher Education*, "They have created an environment in which otherwise perfectly decent, honorable people can't tell right from wrong. . . . The problem with getting entangled in the seemingly innocent act of robbing Peter to pay Paul is that you find yourself sort of increasingly developing a hearty appetite for robbing Peter."[16]

That slippery slope concerns us here. I did not know David Charlow, but Ellen Frishberg was a student in the University of Pennsylvania's Executive Doctorate Program in Higher Education. Had you asked any of us who taught her in graduate school, we would have told you she was at least one college financial aid official who had her head screwed on straight—bright, energetic, truly tough minded, and, as a student, completely fearless. Indeed, it was well known within the program that Frishberg was someone you could go to if you needed to know something about how the market for student loans worked and whether there were any ethical questions that needed to be addressed. It was, therefore, no surprise that one of the facts that came tumbling out of Cuomo's investigation and a subsequent report by Ted Kennedy's Senate Education Committee was that Frishberg had turned down the opportunity to acquire stock in Student Loan Xpress, a company on whose advisory board she served. "I told them it was not allowed in my position," the *New York Times* reported.[17] David Kasakove, her lawyer, similarly told the *Times*, "She never intended to do anything that would be perceived as harmful to either Johns Hopkins University, its students or their parents and has always acted in good faith."[18]

But Frishberg had accepted $43,000 in consulting fees and $22,000 in tuition reimbursement for Penn's doctoral program in higher education management. In an e-mail she sent to an officer at Education Lending, then Student Loan Xpress's corporate parent, she noted, "I am searching for 1/2 tuition support—know any good scholarship programs? (I already know where to get loans)—or why don't you put me on retainer to Ed Lending?" Robert DeRose, the chief executive of Education Lending, replied, "How much is 1/2 tuition? If we can help you we will."[19]

All the institutions caught up in payola and excess compensation scandals, including American University, had complex and detailed conflict-of-interest policies. All had practices and review procedures to prevent exactly what happened—and yet it happened anyway despite a longstanding tradition within American higher education that membership in or association with an academic institution would not lead to personal emoluments. But, as in the exchange between Frishberg and DeRose, it was all so easy to slip into a comfortable banter that led almost inexorably to an exchange that in fact was as inappropriate as it was informal. She asked; he responded, saying he could help, tell me how much.

What greased the slippery slope, quite literally, was the extraordinary amount of money the burgeoning market for student loans was generating. The three quasipublic, nonprofit, state loan agencies that ran into trouble in 2006–2007 had amassed loan portfolios and other assets of $84 billion (PHEAA), $6 billion (MOHELA), and $3 billion (Iowa Student Loan). To be in the student loan business in the first years of the twenty-first century was an opportunity to garner quick returns and exaggerated profits. Student Loan Xpress, the distributor of so many of the incentives at the heart of the Cuomo probe, was a classic example. The company didn't exist until it was cobbled together by Education Lending Group, itself a new entrant in the student loan sweepstakes. In the beginning, key assets of Student Loan Xpress were three executives with established reputations for finding new ways to market student loans. They were particularly good at relational marketing, which meant they were good at showing potential clients and customers a good time. Student Loan Xpress began life as a marketing arm for Education Lending Group. Then in 2005, both before and after engaging in the activities that became the focus of Cuomo's inquiries, Student Loan Xpress was sold to CIT Group, a Fortune 500 company that specialized in both arranging and providing financing for a full range of businesses. As recently as 2002, Student Loan Xpress had posted a $28.3-million loss. By the time of its sale, however, the company had its own $3-billion loan portfolio and annual profits of about $10 million. CIT Group purchased Student Loan Xpress for $318 million. Such was the industry's growth potential on the eve of Cuomo's investigation.

With so much money flowing through the system and so many executives who were good at making other people feel good about shared opportunities, the student loan imbroglio was a scandal just waiting to happen. But the sheer magnitude of the funds flowing— rather than the fate of those who could not resist temptation—is rightly at the center of this morality tale. Higher education had never seen anything like it—sums of money vested in paper instruments that could be bought and sold, not just once, but over and over again, that ran into the billions of dollars and sometimes into the tens of billions of dollars. By 2007 the federal government was annually guaranteeing $70 billion in subsidized loans to college students. Private lending—the monies lent out to college students who had exhausted their eligibility for a federal loan or were not eligible in the first place—had increased more than tenfold over the last decade to $17 billion annually. All those zeroes created the sugarplums financial aid officials and state loan executives found so hard to resist.

Some may want to argue that such loose change is exactly what Bok, Kirp, and Vedder, along with the anticommodifiers, are so exercised about. I think not. Regardless of whether colleges and universities became vendors in this market, its sheer size and liquidity would have overwhelmed whatever resistance might have been raised within the academy. The growth in presidential salaries reflects the same trends, particularly at those institutions whose boards boast full rosters of corporate managers who have themselves benefited from the financial excesses of the credit and related markets. Put corporate executives on the board, and they will use the same yardstick to measure the performance, perks, and pay that their companies use to gauge their own market value and hence their compensation. Even better, put presidents on corporate boards, and they will become accustomed to compensation conversations that know few bounds. If law or tradition prevents paying the president a salary commensurate with his or her perceived value to the institution, then provide extra opportunities in the form of additional corporate directorships that provide both extra pay and generous stock options.

It's not commercialization per se that is getting higher education into trouble; instead, the vendor culture sees nothing wrong with regularly spreading a little—and sometimes a lot—of good will. Spurred on by the success of the Cuomo investigation, news reporters have begun looking everywhere for further evidence of higher education's lax ethical standards. One such inquiry snared three admissions officials at three of the nation's medallion research universities—Columbia, Penn, and the University of North Carolina, Chapel Hill. Each had joined the advisory board of a Japanese company specializing in helping its clients to win admission into top MBA programs in the United States. When pressed, all three said that they received free trips to Japan for meetings of the advisory board, and two said they received consulting fees as well; the third declined to answer the question. All three insisted, and were backed up by their respected institutions, that they had vetted the relationship with the appropriate campus offices.

The most embarrassed of the three, Judith S. Hodara, a senior admissions official at Penn's Wharton School, allowed that her relationship with the Japanese company was not a singular occurrence; in fact, she had set up her own consulting company, IvyStone Educational Consultants, whose website prominently featured Hodara's position at Wharton. The day all these details came to light, the University of Pennsylvania issued a terse statement to the effect that "Penn does not consider this type of situation to be appropriate, which is why it has been ended." Hodara took down her consulting firm's website, announced she was discontinuing her consulting business, and resigned from the Japanese company whose business was to help its clients to gain admission to places like Wharton.[20]

There is one more example of the pervasiveness of these practices and the media's newfound interest in exposing them. While the *New York Times* normally is restrained in the amount of ink it devotes to covering higher education, it can seldom resist the opportunity to embarrass some of its most avid readers. In July 2007 the *Times* ran a round-up story detailing a host of practices that had recently come to the newspaper's attention. The common thread was the willingness of vendors to provide financial support for a variety of meetings at which they would have the opportunity to rub elbows with key college and university officials. With ill-disguised glee, the report began with an account of a Sustainable Operations Summit at which vendors, for a fee of $18,500, were guaranteed "15 one-on-one sales meetings with officials at the conference." The setting for the conference was as noteworthy as the opportunity to purchase time with the college and hospital officials attending the meetings: "a resort in the high desert north of Albuquerque, with a championship golf course, swimming pools, a spa and views of distant mountain peaks." Next the *Times* reporter found a rival consultant who was properly indignant. "This is a form of trying to buy influence. People are paying for access." As if organizing a tennis match, the *Times* reporter extracted a response from the University of Rochester's Director of Energy Initiatives: "It doesn't bother me. . . . That's part of the world we live in today. I don't think there is a conflict."[21]

The real message of this story is that everybody does it, literally. Hardly a higher education organization exists today that doesn't fund all or part of its annual meetings or special conferences by soliciting contributions from vendors. The National Association of Student Financial Aid Administrators, the professional organization to which most financial aid officials belong, did it until Cuomo forced them at least to prevent lenders from sponsoring the organization's meetings. NACUBO, the National Association of College and University Business Officers, was "offering six levels of sponsorships for its annual convention in New Orleans this month. The most expensive level, called the diamond, costs at least $30,000." The American Council on Education (ACE), higher education's umbrella organization, had an even more ambitious sponsorship program. As the *Times* reported, ACE "using a fund-raising technique worthy of a presidential campaign, created a President's Circle; corporations that pay at least $200,000, according to the council's Web site, get opportunities for meetings with university presidents and chancellors. The money is used to support programs and research, officials said."[22]

Just how touchy the subject of vendor sponsorship had become was reflected in a series of quotes the *Times* reporter extracted from Terry Hartle, ACE's senior vice president and principal architect of the Council's political agenda.

> Because of the controversy about sponsorships in the student lending world, our people were thinking about whether or not it was a good idea to continue to do that. . . . It's obviously something that we moved to correct pretty quickly.
>
> A lot of things that were deemed practical and acceptable in January 2007 are now completely out of bounds.[23]

It was the story's last line—but hardly an end to the controversy.

Into the Wind

Those who go in search of a moral to extract from this mess might begin by considering the following image: a young man confronts a scene of mayhem and carnage, covers his eyes with his hand, and then proclaims loudly, "I can't bear to look," all the while spreading his fingers just wide enough to take in the scene in considerable detail. The challenge now facing American higher education is finding a way to actually examine what has happened and why. Even were the nation's colleges and universities not commercial enterprises constantly in search of increased market share, the vendors' push to expand their own businesses would be just as powerful; there would still be the free trips, the sponsored events, the consulting fees, and the opportunities to serve on boards of directors and advisory boards. The fact that most colleges and universities—including most publicly funded institutions—play much the same game as their vendors makes all the more difficult the task of recognizing behavior that has crossed the line. Such actions help the vendors help the institutions—and vice versa.

The examination I have in mind will need to begin with the frank acknowledgment that higher education is truly a big business involving substantial, even outrageous sums of money that have the ability to spread a fog of complacency over the whole enterprise. It will necessarily be a discussion that focuses on the fundraising that has become such an important aspect of presidential service and the ends to which those funds are put. It ought to be a discussion that reexamines the idea of whole groups of institutions establishing buying cooperatives. Necessarily it will be a discussion about student loans and lenders and about the role such agencies can and should play in the operations of the institutions their businesses indirectly support.

But mostly the discussion needs to be about institutional values. Derek Bok is right. Controlling the commercial impulse to let markets—and only markets—shape the future requires a habit of explicitly and repeatedly talking about purposes, about ends rather than means. And in the end, that discussion will not prove productive unless it is also about that sense of separateness and hence awareness of being special that has historically been a hallmark of academic enterprises. Colleges and universities are supposed to be different, less given to the pursuit of money, more committed to egalitarianism, tougher to win a place in, and hence tougher in enforcing those community norms that define the academy's purposes.

Instead there is a growing presumption that colleges and universities—their faculties, presidents, staffs, and governing boards—play by the same rules as everybody else; they, too, allow a rough kind of situational ethics to define behavior and define conflicts of interests. This presumption gnaws at the academy, making cynics of us all, pitting those who see themselves as the "have-nots" against those they perceive as the beneficiaries of the new commercial order.

Often this gnawing gets quickly personal. In the fall of 2007 I joined the *Chronicle of Higher Education*'s team of commissioned bloggers for a fee that worked out to be fifty cents an hour. Like many first-time bloggers I tried engaging potential readers by weaving personal stories into my postings. One such attempt began with my report of a bicycling trip in the Netherlands that included a long ride into a twenty-mile-per-hour headwind whose constancy, I reported, had loomed ever larger in my imagination. I then continued, "My survival solution was to spend as much energy as I could afford working through what I have come to see as a wondrous puzzle: Why should an enterprise devoted to rationality, clear thinking, and precise exposition spend so much of its time arguing about a set of words that have literally lost their meanings?"[24]

What I was looking for from those who commented on the posting was a discussion of higher education's increasing habit of engaging in discussions of issues whose real import is too often lost in a fog of linguistic ambiguities. What I received instead was a blast that centered on the personal—and I do mean personal—rewards of my Dutch excursion. Did I pay for my vacation, or was it on someone else's tab? Had Bob Zemsky morphed into Morris Zap?

Did I respond? Did I protest that I always pay for my own vacations? Of course not. To do so would have been—well, like spitting into the wind.

7 | The Four Horsemen of Academic Reform

Margaret Spellings stood before us just as she stands before most audiences—smiling, comfortable, and confident, forever displaying her can-do, will-do determination. Though the challenge was large and time was short, just about a year, she expressed no doubts that her assembled commissioners would deliver a "comprehensive national strategy" addressing what the *Chronicle of Higher Education* called "such sweeping issues as access, affordability, accountability, and quality."[1]

Without meaning to, the secretary had stumbled into what I subsequently realized was a linguistic cul-de-sac. Though she was celebrating an enterprise devoted to rationality, clear thinking, and precise exposition, she was asking her Commission to pursue goals that, for all their familiarity, had lost their meaning. Access, accountability, affordability, and quality are the four horsemen of higher education reform—goals that are talked about and ardently affirmed, but that in fact too often lead nowhere.

In the time since the Commission's demise, I have tried to understand what each of Spellings's four horsemen might have once meant and just how seriously we ought to take—or not take—calls to make them the cornerstones of a federal higher education policy. This much is clear. Any reform agenda for higher education will, at some point or another, have to deal with the four horsemen. This volume is no exception, and hence this is as good a place as any to try to clear the confusion that these issues have introduced into the debate over higher education reform. Mostly I seek to make clear that the challenges ahead are not so neatly packaged as these four labels might seem to suggest.

Access

For more than fifty years, unfettered access to a college education has been the first goal of federal, state, and local higher education policy. Those who wanted a college education, who had prepared themselves to earn the degree, and who had exhibited the discipline and stick-to-it-ness necessary to succeed deserved a chance. A person's race or ethnicity or gender, financial circumstances, political and religious beliefs, or physical incapacities could not be allowed to matter. Moreover, the term itself—access—reflected a deeply held belief that unfettered participation in the nation's higher education system required the elimination of a set of very real barriers that had historically limited participation to the advantaged few.

The first barriers to fall were products of racial and religious discrimination; outright legislated segregation in the one case and, in the other, a more subtle but no less discriminating set of quotas and understandings used to limit the educational participation of first Catholics and later Jews. We forget at our peril just how persistent as well as successful these exclusionary practices were. Both African Americans and Catholics, in particular, developed their own institutions in response to exclusion, and they maintain them today as not-so-subtle reminders that no one who has felt the sting of discrimination is ever fully sanguine about their place in a culture in which they remain a minority.

Through the 1950s, the relatively meager supply of colleges and universities represented a second major barrier to full educational access in the United States. In 1950, the nation had only 1,851 baccalaureate institutions, collectively enrolling just 2,659,021 undergraduates. Not surprisingly, the decennial census that year reported that just 6.2 percent of the population had college degrees. Fifty years later, the nation had 4,084 combined baccalaureate institutions and associate-level community colleges; the latter was a fundamentally new kind of institution created in response to the demand for more access to a college education. Collectively these institutions enrolled 14,791,224 students. As of 2007, the census reported that 28.7 percent of the population had earned a baccalaureate degree, and another 25.3 percent reported that they had some college but not yet a bachelor's degree.

The lowering of yet a third set of barriers, mostly psychological and cultural, that had once taught most Americans that "college education is not for me—it's for them" helped fuel this extraordinary expansion. Amidst the hurly-burly of today's admissions arms race, it is important to remember that as late as 1950, Harvard had just 1.3 applicants for each place in Harvard College's freshman class. You simply knew whether you would be welcomed at Harvard or at any of the other institutions that made up the ancient eight. You even knew if you belonged at the local college and state university without being told. In part these barriers were demolished by parents who simply insisted that their children were going to have opportunities that had been denied them. And in part they were demolished by local, principally public school systems that rapidly expanded their college prep tracks in recognition of changing political and economic realities.

The final barriers to be attacked were financial. Through the 1970s, the growth of public systems of higher education and the rapid expansion of community colleges kept the price of a college education mostly within the reach of most middle-class Americans. But prices were rising then as now, particularly at those institutions, both public and private, with selective admissions. At the institutional level private colleges and universities began practicing what would come to be known as need-blind admissions and backing up their offers of admission to students whose families could not pay the full freight of sending a son or daughter to the college of choice by offering financial aid in the form of grants and later loans. On the federal level a Nixon administration not remembered for its social conscience introduced a series of federal programs that gave grants directly to students, allowing them to attend the institution of their choice. From that beginning grew the federal student aid program, with its Pell Grants and Stafford loans, which today dispenses more than $100 billion annually in the name of providing access to a college education to every American regardless of personal financial circumstances.

Do additional barriers remain today? Yes, but they are of a different kind requiring quite different policies and strategies. Developing them necessarily begins with the recognition that the nation has actually won the battle of access. In 2007, the year for which current statistics are now available, two out of every three high school graduates matriculated at an institution offering some form of higher education. Community colleges enrolled 35.9 percent and baccalaureate institutions 64.1 percent of these students.

Those readers who are growing uncomfortable with the direction this argument is taking will want to point out (shout, probably): But those statistics are not the same for all groups! And indeed they are not. Among white high school graduates, about 73 percent enroll in college; for African Americans, the proportion enrolling in college is 56 percent; for Hispanic Americans, it is 58 percent. Inner-city and rural youths are less likely to enroll than the children of suburbanites. Rich kids go to college at a much higher rate than poor kids. But in every case, the percentage of high school graduates matriculating in a college or university, two-year or four-year, has steadily increased over the last two decades. The targeted barriers to access have largely come down.

One other set of numbers troubles those committed to the necessity of providing equal access to opportunity for all Americans. While the percentage of Americans with a college education has increased, the gap between minority and majority experiences has persisted to an alarming degree. Given that a college degree is now the principal portal to middle class status, it is simply not acceptable that one's ethnicity, in particular, remains a tag predicting likely success at reaching that destination. The problem, however, is not one of access—or at least the kind of access that is achieved by the removing of barriers, be they legal, cultural, psychological, or financial. Providing equal educational opportunity—what I have taken to calling "access to success"—requires a different mindset and a willingness to invest public funds in programs other than federal and institutional financial aid.

Affordability

For me, the linguistic quest for an affordable higher education is the most problematic of the four horsemen. This much is clear, however: An American higher education has become ever more expensive. Some would say, with fair justification, that paying for a college education in this country has now become obscenely expensive. But ever higher prices in higher education are nothing new. For more than a half century, the average price, even the average net price, of a year in college has been increasing faster than the underlying rate of inflation, except during the decade of the 1970s when the average prices colleges and universities charged merely kept pace with double-digit inflation.

By the time Spellings appointed her Commission, however, a host of foundations, researchers, and policy wonks had declared that an American higher education had become truly unaffordable—increasingly beyond the reach of Americans of ordinary means regardless of their talents and ambitions. Robert Dickeson of the Lumina Foundation for Education probably said it best in the title to his Lumina Foundation Report—*Collision Course: Rising College Costs Threaten America's Future*. The media have happily amplified the message. In a special report on the increasing indebtedness of young adults, "Thirty and Broke: the Real Price of a College Education Today," *Business Week* observed, "the cost of higher education . . . has increased so dramatically in the past decade and a half—up by 63 percent at public schools and 47 percent at private—that more students have to borrow tens of thousands of dollars to attend, ensuring that many of them are paying off those loans well into their 40s."[2] American higher education was once again on the nation's radarscope—and the escalating tuitions American colleges and universities charge were putting them there.

This issue had taken a remarkably long time to crystallize. Through the 1980s and 1990s, most reporting on the cost of attending an American college or university was occasioned by the College Board's annual announcement that college tuitions had again risen substantially faster than inflation. Then in 2000, *Measuring Up*, the State-by-State National Report Card compiled by the National Center for Public Policy and Higher Education, focused renewed attention on higher education's affordability. Along with Preparation, Benefits, and Completion, Affordability became one of the Report Card's signature criteria. In its first year, *Measuring Up* gave out five As and eleven Bs, while just thirteen states earned a D, and only three states received an F for affordability. Two years later just one state, California, earned an A, four states earned a B, and thirty-three states received a D or an F. By 2004 there were no As, just one B, and two Cs. The remaining forty-seven states received a D or an F. It was a matter of going from sort of okay, to bad, to worse in four years. As *Measuring Up 2004* declared, "The vast majority of states have failed to keep college affordable for most families."[3]

Well, not exactly. When something is unaffordable it means it won't be purchased. Health insurance—and with it access to health care—is now unaffordable for a large and growing number of American families. We know that to be the case because an increasing number of American families do not have health insurance. That seemingly is not the case for American higher education, given that in most years enrollments have continued to rise even as have the prices students are expected to pay.

Market researchers often talk about affordability in terms of the would-be customer's "willingness to pay" for a specific product and that same customer's "ability to pay." Thus far, most American families and most students have shown both an ability and a willingness to pay the prices colleges and universities charge. Indeed, most purchasers of higher education have, over the last decade, been shopping up, consistently choosing higher-priced over lower-priced options. The baccalaureate institutions that are hurting the most for enrollments are, for the most part, those with the lowest tuitions.

Much of the debate about affordability is both linguistically confusing and politically dangerous. Those who declare boldly that the sky is falling—that American higher education is either already or about to become truly unaffordable—make two fundamental mistakes. First, they presume that students and families are still expected to pay for college out of current earnings and savings. The fact is that a college education has long since become something that one purchases over time, most often at attractive interest rates. Savvy middle-class families know that it is smarter to take out a PLUS loan while investing their savings in financial instruments that promise returns that exceed the interest they will pay on loans used to pay for their children's college education. Families that are culturally or ideologically adverse to debt miss out on this modest opportunity at arbitrage to offset some of the high price of a college education. Students with demonstrated need substantial enough to qualify for a Pell Grant are able to secure additional financing at subsidized rates. The average indebtedness of students on graduation from college in 2005 was less than $20,000, or roughly the price of a low-end new car. Students and their families who wanted a more upscale product took on more debt, but again, debt that was in line with their other longer-term purchases.

The second mistake made by those who push the affordability agenda is to apply an absolute standard to the problem. If a college education costs more than, say, X, then by definition it is unaffordable even though students and their families continue to purchase it in ever greater numbers. The better approach is to look at behavior—who is and who isn't purchasing higher educations—and then to ask higher education's potential customers how the cost of a college education is affecting their educational choices.

That is what The Learning Alliance (TLA) did in the fall of 2004 at the behest of the Rendell administration in Pennsylvania. As part of its review of the *A Rising Tide: The Current State of Higher Education in the Commonwealth of Pennsylvania*, TLA commissioned a survey of young adults across the Commonwealth focusing on their attitudes toward higher education in general and its costs in particular. The survey was designed and administered by Berwood Yost, director of the Floyd Institute for Public Policy at Franklin and Marshall College, in collaboration with his colleague, Terry Madonna, the director of the Keystone Poll, the standard benchmark for political polling in Pennsylvania.

Survey findings attest to the confusions that had already become an integral part of the discussion of affordability. Of the sample 86 percent agreed with the statement, "Regardless of the cost, tuition at Pennsylvania's public universities is a worthwhile investment." Just 9 percent disagreed. At the same time, only 63 percent agreed with the statement, "The cost to get an education at one of Pennsylvania's public universities is affordable"; 25 percent disagreed, and 12 percent said they didn't know.

One question on the survey asked whether costs had determined the choice of a college or university. Of the respondents who either had attended or were currently attending an institution of higher education, three-quarters reported that there was not a college or university that they had wanted to attend but did not "because it cost too much." Forty respondents (about 9 percent of the total sample), however, said they had intended to go to college but felt prevented from doing so. As a group they reported that they were prepared for college, had reasonable if not outstanding grades, and were well motivated. The reason these respondents cited most often for not going to college was that they "needed to work." The cost of attendance was a close second. Yost and Madonna summed up their findings:

> The responses of young adults who wanted to attend college (9% of the total sample), but who did not do not suggest that cost is a problem for a large majority of young adults. Cost (33%) was the most frequently mentioned problem among those who planned to attend college but did not; however, they mentioned many other reasons, too. Starting families (23%), having a job that did not require a degree (10%), a lack of motivation (8%), and planning to attend at a later time (5%) were other reasons that interested students never attended college. When these responses are calculated to reflect the total sample, it turns out that fewer than one in twenty (4%) 18–30 year olds in Pennsylvania did not attend a

higher education institution because of concerns about cost, which is nearly the same proportion (3%) who did not attend because they were starting families.[4]

In its formal report to the governor, TLA estimated that up to 8 percent of this population felt their opportunities for a higher education were hindered by higher education's high price tag. Included in this group were students who reported they initially enrolled in a college or university but had to drop out because they could no longer afford the price of attendance. Two characteristics of this excluded population are worth noting. First, the respondents who said that costs were a primary reason for not attending college were more likely to report much higher tuitions for both public community colleges and state universities than those institutions actually charged. Second, they were twice as likely to be African American or Hispanic or to come from the rural part of the state.

Make no mistake—8 percent is a substantial number. Its import, however, lies in telling us that making a higher education more affordable for those who are unable to afford it—as opposed to those who believe the price is too high—requires very targeted investments designed to assist the 8 percent who need immediate help rather than the 92 percent for whom a college education remains affordable.

Increasingly, questions focusing on access and affordability have been joined in a push to increase federal aid, on the one hand, and, on the other, to force colleges and universities to restrain if not actually roll back their price increases of recent years. But would more financial aid really make that much difference?—or, put differently, Is cost the principal barrier to equal access to an American college education? As part of the same study of higher educational enrollments across the Commonwealth of Pennsylvania, TLA assembled the relevant statistical data identifying the community characteristics that promoted college enrollments. The resulting statistical model taught five basic lessons.

First, income matters. To no one's surprise we noted that high school seniors from communities whose families on average have higher incomes are more likely to attend college than students from communities with lower family incomes. To say that income matters, however, is not tantamount to saying that potential students from lower income families were being excluded from attending a college or university in Pennsylvania.

Second, higher levels of unemployment translate into increased college enrollments. When jobs become scarce, young people are more likely to stay in school. Taken together, these two lessons underline the key importance of economic development in stimulating college enrollments, provided that increased economic activity translates directly into increases in family incomes and that those who turn to postsecondary institutions to increase their employment skills reap benefits in the labor market.

The next three lessons changed our understanding of the dynamics of college enrollments. Third, the quality of primary and secondary education, as reflected in the how well eleventh graders in the county did on the Commonwealth's assessment exams, matters a lot. The most powerful measure was how well these students did on the standard reading test; school districts whose eleventh graders performed poorly on this exam sent far fewer students on to college. Should we have been as surprised as we were?—probably not. Students who can't read for comprehension at a ninth-grade level are not going to succeed in college, and they know it. Without improvement in academic preparation and a substantial increase in the number of students who are college-ready, it seems unlikely that there can be substantial increases in college participation rates—or any significant lessening of those barriers that limit postsecondary enrollments.

Fourth, familiarity engenders interest. The more colleges nearby, the more likely students from the same communities will plan to attend college.

Fifth, and finally, the absence of a low-risk higher education portal is in itself a substantial barrier to postsecondary participation. Here the lever most readily available to policymakers is an old one: increasing the spread of community colleges across the Commonwealth will increase college participation rates—though not necessarily college success rates.

There are two interesting footnotes to this discussion of access and affordability, as exemplified by the Commonwealth of Pennsylvania. About 15 percent of Pennsylvania's students attend schools in rural communities. To the extent that they pursue a college education, these youngsters remain at significant disadvantage—in part because they are more likely to attend a poorly performing school, in part because college attendance is not a strong tradition in their communities, and in part because they are less likely to have ready access to the kind of low-risk higher education portals that community colleges provide.

Along with rural Americans, the others in this debate about access and affordability are adults—either those returning to higher education to complete degrees, first-time enrollees, or workers who seek new and more advanced skills. One good thing the Spellings Commission did was to draw attention to the very real needs of this population of learners.

It is worth noting as well that exactly how to make a college education more affordable is among higher education's more intractable problems. Initially those who worried most about a college education's affordability focused on public institutions and the fact that their increasing prices were directly related to per-student reductions in public appropriations by the nation's fifty states. It seems unlikely, however, that the states will dramatically increase their support for higher education. The states have discovered, in good times and bad, that students and their families will pay more for their college education, thus allowing the states to promote other spending priorities, including the lowering of taxes.

More recently, the outrageousness of the tuitions of the nation's most selective institutions has drawn the ire of the media and policy makers. But these critics have no better answer to higher education's fifty-year cost-price spiral than do the college and university presidents whose inaction they so frequently lament. Those who call for greater efficiency sooner or later stumble over the fact that most of the costs they find wasteful—climbing walls are one favorite target—are in fact responses to student and family demands for better service and additional amenities. Those who study the shifting allocation of funds within the academy regularly point out that instructional costs are already a shrinking proportion of the average college or university's budget. Were calls for lower prices to succeed while the costs imposed by regulation and the need to supply ever more amenities increased, the result would be institutions less able to fulfill their educational missions. The alternative, of course, would be to pay the faculty and everyone else in the institution lower salaries, which ironically is the strategy most often employed by underfunded elementary and secondary schools.

Sooner or later the price spiral in higher education will have to be addressed. My guess is that breaking the gridlock on costs will require some kind of dislodging event that leads to a substantial reduction in the going price of an undergraduate degree. What won't reduce costs or lower prices are tough or inflammatory speeches demanding that colleges and universities cut out the frills, make their faculty work harder, and learn from businesses the discipline of outsourcing.

Accountability

Reform's third horseman is the call to make higher education more accountable. Before colleges and universities give away the store, however, someone ought to ask, "Accountable for what?" and "Accountable to whom?"—real questions too often glossed over by higher education's putative reformers. There is instead a presumption on the part of what I have come to call the "accountability police" that colleges and universities are not accountable—paired with a sense that a college education is too expensive and not worth the money, given that college students are not learning enough. Finally there is the assumption that if the public had more data, accrediting agencies more power, and state governments more gumption, the nation's colleges and universities could finally be held accountable.

Here is a stab at making sense of the rhetoric. Being accountable ranks right up there with being nice and responsible. Not being accountable is the same as being selfish, out of control, and irresponsible. Simply raising the subject is enough to put higher education on the defensive and its principal spokesmen on edge.

That higher education is not accountable to anything or anybody outside the academy itself is a charge that won't hold water. What the critics who pursue the accountability agenda really mean is "higher education is not accountable to me" or, occasionally, "to us." They don't like that colleges and universities are accountable to a market that favors selectivity, brand names, national visibility, winning sports teams, and, in the case of the nation's medallion universities, major research portfolios.

Professional programs are accountable to their cognizant accrediting agencies. In the fields of law, medicine, dental medicine, veterinary medicine, business, and engineering, those agencies exercise the real power they know they have. For undergraduate education, however, accreditation remains a hodgepodge of regional agencies that talk tough but in the end don't make enough of a difference. As an inevitable result, the kind of accountability the market exacts becomes ever more important.

Given these circumstances, just two principal avenues remain for making undergraduate education accountable to someone else or something other than the attributes the market currently rewards. One could join with Lloyd Thacker and his Educational Conservancy to create a consumer movement that understands and then seeks to make educational values more of a factor in the college choice process. Such a movement would be akin to the kind of consumer movement that changed the cars Americans bought and, in the process, made *Consumer Reports* a national buying guide.

The other alternative is to construct an accountability process that tests the quality of higher educational products—both courses and degree programs. What I have in mind will appear draconian as well as impractical. Nonetheless, focusing on the testing of products rather than the testing of students helps make clear what accountability ought to mean. Imagine a federal higher education agency modeled after the U.S. Food and Drug Administration (FDA). To ensure safe and effective pharmaceuticals the FDA conducts clinical tests of new drugs before they are released to the market and then insists that their manufacturers continue to test and report on the drug's safety and efficacy. A higher education look-a-like would be expected to do the same thing—test products and monitor their continued efficacy. This proposal differs from other calls for increased accountability by focusing specifically on educational products, insisting that they be rigorously tested, and establishing an external mechanism for post-test monitoring.

Several insights result from playing this imaginary game. To begin with, all testing schemes confront a basic problem: any test proposing to measure learning outcomes requires, as a minimum, that the taker of the test have a direct interest in his or her performance on the test. The test taker needs to believe that the results really matter personally. Few proponents of the testing of students as a means of holding institutions accountable for learning outcomes are prepared to say to those students: You cannot receive your baccalaureate or associate degree unless you achieve a satisfactory score on the national test measuring how much you learned while in college. Absent that kind of incentive, large numbers of students will either avoid or skate through the test simply to get it out of the way.

Suppose, however, some agency like the U.S. Department of Education was actually willing and able to test everyone every year or every other year and make the student's academic standing depend on his or her test scores. There would likely be a very limited number of tests—perhaps even a single battery of integrated tests—developed, and if the results were to actually influence the funds an institution received or the kinds of student it enrolled, all but the most selective and richly endowed institutions would make it their business to teach to the test. Medallion institutions wouldn't have to worry because the students they attract are proven test takers whether they learn anything or not.

At the same time, holding individual institutions accountable for the quality, efficacy, and safety of their educational products will require a substantial bureaucracy. The requisite agency would almost certainly have to be federal, resulting in less institutional autonomy as well as institutional diversity. Inevitably, one size would be expected to fit all regardless of institutional history, mission, religious affiliation, or location. The result would be a visible federalizing of the American system of higher education.

Actually, a full-blown federalized testing regime is not required. Today at least some graduating seniors at nearly every baccalaureate institution are being tested by examinations whose outcomes matter mightily to them. In many institutions a majority of graduating seniors take the GRE, a GRE Subject Test, the LSAT, the MCAT, the GMAT, or a licensure exam in a host of subjects ranging from engineering to nursing to education. Were the Department of Education able to make public the mean, median, 75th percentile, and 25th percentile scores for each exam for each institution, the result would be greater transparency, though not necessarily greater accountability.

Would the adoption of such a system lead to faculty teaching to the test? Not likely, since a wide variety of tests would be in the mix, though no doubt institutions would want to help their students prepare for the tests by offering coaching sessions, perhaps even for-credit classes getting students ready to be judged and evaluated. Wouldn't institutions discourage poorly performing students from taking the tests? Again not likely, because to do so would stand in the way of the students' own goals. Wouldn't the comparisons among institutions be unfair given that only the best students at each institution would be likely to take one or more of the tests leading to further study? While the results would in fact be thus biased, my guess is that the bias would not vary greatly among institutions, making possible valid comparisons among them. Finally, wouldn't the results be highly correlated with the SAT or ACT? Here the answer is yes—making the most meaningful comparisons those among institutions whose students upon entrance have roughly the same SAT or ACT scores.

There is another alternative to a federal testing regime. Most institutions, regardless of mission, religious affiliation, or location, have remarkably similar transcript systems that, for the most part, are in machine-readable formats. In the 1980s Joseph Johnston of the Association of American Colleges (AAC; now the Association of American Colleges and Universities—AAC&U), along with my colleague Susan Shaman and I, conducted a massive transcript study to determine the correctness of the charge that there had been a marked decline in the rigor of undergraduate education across the nation— fewer requirements and less course sequencing, leading to an absence of curricular coherence. That charge had been made in an earlier AAC-sponsored study, *Integrity in the College Curriculum*, which had relied heavily on the testimony of educational reformers. Our task was to see if a statistical analysis could either confirm or refute that study's finding. What we found, more than a quarter of a century ago, dismayed and baffled us. It was true. Undergraduate curricula in almost every kind of college and university were being "destructured," just as the authors of *Integrity in the College Curriculum* had charged. Anything and everything was possible: this realization proved the observation of one faculty member we talked to; he had assumed in each class he taught, regardless of its numbering or presumed place in the curriculum, that almost every student enrolled in the course had little or no prior understanding of his field's basic precepts.

The larger disappointment, however, was the fact that neither *Integrity* nor our analysis led to any noticeable change in what was happening to college curricula. The authors of *Integrity*, particularly Williams College's Frederick Rudolph, were celebrated and quoted. We were congratulated on the cleverness of our statistical routines and on the software we developed to help individual institutions build greater structure back into the undergraduate curriculum. The software went largely unused; academics everywhere were intrigued, but not enough to take on the tough task of forging the necessary consensus to require more work from their undergraduates and each other. The faculty had learned only too well the pleasure of allowing each to do his or her own thing. Reinstituting requirements would have made faculty responsible for what their students took with them into the next set of courses in an ordered and sequenced curriculum.

And that turned out to be the most important lesson of all. Presenting evidence of a problem—no matter how compelling—is not sufficient to change academic practices. Faculty freedom and autonomy trump evidence every time. Those who argue that greater transparency, that is, more evidence as to the academy's problems and failings, will either compel faculty to change or force public entities and accrediting agencies to change always underestimate the inertia in the system. The lamenters will complain that it is cowardly for those outside the academy to give in, having first settled for issuing strongly worded statements filled with angry words. The efficiency pundits will similarly protest, all the while proving relatively powerless to change either practices or customs within the academy.

Quality

The country bumpkin among the four horsemen of reform is quality—a term so bereft of practical meaning today that it is now commonplace to talk about high quality, higher quality, and highest quality as a means of distinguishing among competing claims to excellence.

No one is against quality. Almost everyone is ready to concede that American higher education, whatever its faults and shortcomings, is the envy of the rest of the world and in that sense truly world class, perhaps even in a class by itself. Jonathan Grayer, the former *Newsweek* marketing executive the *Washington Post* picked to run its Kaplan subsidiary, was in many ways the most interesting as well as the most unusual member of the Spellings Commission. Under his leadership Kaplan, Inc. has grown from an $80 million per year test-preparation company to a diverse education corporation with more than $2 billion in revenue in 2007. Kaplan serves more than one million students annually and has more than 27,000 employees in the United States and abroad.

On the Commission, Grayer's role was principally to explain and where necessary defend the interests of the growing for-profit educational sector. But periodically the Harvard graduate (Harvard College, then Harvard Business School) would let loose, challenging the rest of us to think differently. At one point he suggested an alternative way to think about quality. Having been reminded by a recent declaration in the *Economist* that American universities were the best in the world, Grayer said he thought such statements did not apply to the bulk of American higher education but only to its most selective institutions. To reinforce his point, he sketched on a napkin the hypothetical quality curve reproduced in figure 1.

The sketch suggests that American colleges and universities are like the little girl with the curl in the middle of her forehead. When they are good (the right end of Grayer's sketch), they are very, very good—and

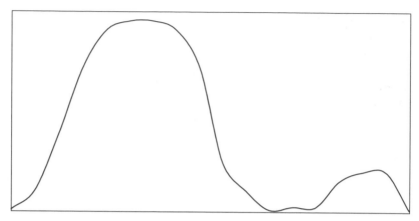

Figure 1. Jonathan Grayer's napkin sketch of a hypothetical quality curve for U.S. higher education.

when they are not, well, they are just sort of mediocre. This observation, among other things, helps explain why the United States ranks in the middle rather than at the top of so many international comparisons focusing on the quality of national systems of higher education.

The comparative scale on which American higher education clearly ranks at the top is expenditures. Grayer's sketch pretty much duplicates the relative expenditures per student of American colleges and universities: In American higher education, those institutions with the highest expenditures per student—those toward the right end of the quality scale—are the same institutions with the most selective admissions and hence the most competitive students. Whether these students rise to the top because they are among the best and brightest to begin with or because the institutions in which they enroll have more resources to invest in their educations is a question worth pondering, particularly if the question before the house is whether money buys quality. Most observers of American higher education would argue that the quality of student inputs remains more important than the quality of the educational process—in part, at least, because the educational processes employed vary so little across the range of baccalaureate institutions.

But there are other equally troubling aspects of the cost-quality dilemma. Richard Vedder's work, both before he joined and as a member of the Spellings Commission, focused on how American colleges and universities spend their monies and on the aspects of American

higher education that make it so expensive without returning a commensurate quality premium for most students pursing a baccalaureate
education. This research made Vedder among the best known and most
widely read of the nation's efficiency pundits. Charles Miller, the chair
of the Commission, regularly points out that American colleges and
universities really don't have a bottom line, and hence productivity
and efficiency gains constantly elude them—though that observation is
probably more true of the highly selective best institutions on the right
of Grayer's graph than of the bulk of the colleges and universities
responsible for educating most undergraduates. Taken together these
arguments suggest that American higher education is at or near a crisis
point in the sense that, as a nation, we are spending more and getting
less from our system of higher education.

Two aspects of that system are of particular importance here.
First, the institutions on the right of Grayer's sketch have almost no
incentive to be either more efficient or more productive. Rather, their
success depends directly on their ability to raise ever more funds—
through more research contracts, through bigger gifts and campaigns,
through larger yields on their endowments and other investments,
and through escalating tuition revenues, which are as often the product
of new programs as of increased prices. Internally realized savings are
rare; in part, they are so difficult to achieve, and, in part, it has proved
so much easier to raise additional revenues than to squeeze current
operations. As a result, the kind of productivity-centered changes that
came to characterize much of American industry and commerce in the
1990s largely skipped over higher education's most elite institutions.

The second aspect of the American system of higher education
worth noting here is that most institutions in the middle of Grayer's
sketch still seek to emulate those institutions to their right despite the
fact that they have substantially less resources and are fundamentally
more dependent on tuition revenues and state appropriations (largely
granted in lieu of tuition). To be sure, these institutions have compelling reasons to be more efficient, but they achieve their savings
largely by squeezing salaries, hiring adjuncts rather than full-time
instructors, and eliminating most perks associated with current
expense budgets. Despite more than two decades of economic pressure
in these institutions, however, their basic production function has not
changed. In terms of the organization of the curriculum and the
specifics of the academic calendar, what transpires in these institutions still duplicates the calendars and curricula of the nation's

best-endowed colleges and universities. The only real differences are the teaching loads of the faculty.

The growth of a for-profit higher education segment further highlights how little traditional higher education has changed. For-profit higher education realized first that the traditional higher education production function was not sacrosanct: that alternative calendars that create savings could be successfully adopted; the institution rather than individual faculty could own the curriculum; it was possible to use a largely contingent workforce whose benefits were vested elsewhere; and some curricula would be far more profitable than others. Moreover, for-profit higher education is teaching the institutions in the middle of the cost-quality curve—those institutions most directly threatened—another lesson; quality pays when it responds directly to student needs. For-profit higher education is winning an increasing share of the market, not by competing on price, but by emphasizing responsiveness, flexibility, and convenience.

Not Much of a Posse

Posses are traditionally portrayed as armed riders summoned by a sheriff to enforce the law. In asking higher education to focus on access, affordability, accountability, and quality, Margaret Spellings was hoping that the result would be more than just reining in the enterprise's wayward ambitions. She wanted, I believed then and I believe now, a recasting of the way American colleges and universities respond to national challenges and opportunities, and she sought a transformation of the nation's colleges and universities that revitalized them, made them more inclusive, more responsive and efficient, more willing to take chances in pursuit of better ways to teach and learn.

Alas, she bet on the wrong horses. In remarkably short order, access, affordability, accountability, and quality have morphed into slogans with which to batter higher education's mythical establishment. Focusing on the four horsemen, however, can provide a starting point by suggesting that two concerns in particular belong at or near the top of a higher education reform agenda. First, we must understand why so many socioeconomically disadvantaged students start but do not complete their college education. As TLA's Pennsylvania study observed, the problem of collegiate success begins well before students enroll in a collegiate institution; short of a dramatic improvement in underperforming middle and secondary schools, no amount of financial aid is likely to close the educational gap between advantaged and disadvantaged youngsters.

Second, the nation will have to cast a much wider net when thinking about how best to control costs and limit price increases. We must fundamentally rethink the use of technology, the amount of time students spend in pursuit of a baccalaureate degree, and the particular mechanisms used to finance a college education. The truly difficult part will entail developing a system-wide strategy that moves forward having first accepted the reality of limited state funding and the fact that the search for sustaining efficiencies will once more prove illusory.

As important as they are, however, inclusiveness and financial stability are but part of a higher education reform agenda worth investing in. Of equal importance are three critical concerns we discuss next: how global markets are changing postsecondary education, the spread of ubiquitous electronic information technologies and their but modest impact on collegiate teaching, and the growing realization that the neurosciences have much to tell college faculty about how learning occurs.

8 | Flat-World Contrarians

Colleges and universities are forever on retreats—presidents convene them, trustees love them, consultants depend on them for their livelihood. Most retreats focus on institutional issues: the preparation for a campaign, the quality of campus life, the strength of the curriculum, or, as is most often the case, simply the need to get better organized. Beginning in the summer of 2005, however, an inordinately large number of such gatherings took a different tack, inspired by the publication of Tom Friedman's *The World Is Flat*. The book, thick though it was, was a natural read for academics: this narrative full of clever stories and individual success stories was current, and above all its message resonated with the academy's sense that the world had indeed changed. Higher education's future lay in going global!

I was certainly among the smitten. For the last three decades, I have spent a substantial portion of each year working and traveling outside the United States. Like many academics, I have in my study a world map full of black and red pins testifying to the fact that professionally I have been busy going places I have never been before. When I read *The Lexus and the Olive Tree*, Friedman's initial volume on the push for globalization, it seemed as if I had spent a lifetime getting ready for the world Friedman was describing. I began using *The Lexus and the Olive Tree* in my classes, noting with a twinge of alarm that universities were largely absent as principal players in the drama

Friedman was describing. In his new world of global connections, universities were like warehouses, full of interesting people who were fun to drop in on and have lunch with. But universities per se were not global players, not part of the growing network of connections that defined the rampant globalism that so fascinated Friedman.

By the time Friedman came to write *The World Is Flat*, he had clearly changed his mind. Universities and the education and research they provided were essential—both as means and as ends in themselves. But by then I was not so sure. Beneath Friedman's obvious skill at storytelling and his inventive cleverisms—I am particularly fond of DOS Capital 2.0 from *The Lexus and the Olive Tree*—lay a remarkably robust definition of globalization. An enterprise or industry could be said to be global if its transactions were transparent, its products widely distributed without reference to national boundaries, and its prices set in fully convertible currencies. In global enterprises both time and space come to mean less and less. In this world without places to hide, cultural sanctuaries, or golden ponds on which to drift in quiet contemplation only the pursuit of high-value commodities matters.

In a global world technology is king. Production cycles become ever shorter. Labor becomes increasingly mobile. Consumers constantly broaden their searches for better products at better prices. Individual enterprises lose their competitiveness unless they become integral parts of an expanding set of networks.

Two decades into the global revolution, this list of attributes can be said to apply to few, if any, of the world's leading universities. Most observers outside the academy would argue, correctly I believe, that universities, in both their operations and their governance, remain opaque, even obtuse, rather than transparent. Few transactions can be said to be instantaneous, while the time necessary to develop new educational programs has probably lengthened rather than shortened. True, there is an international labor market for young scholars, principally postdocs, for Asian and Latin American PhDs trained in Europe and the United States returning to their own countries or continents to begin their careers, and for very senior academics with international reputations. But these transnational patterns of long standing suggest that globalization had little if anything to do with their particular emergence.

Student markets have remained decidedly local. Even less global are the mechanisms by which prices are set for a university education. In most settings and most countries, even in the European Union to a still considerable extent, governmental subsidies to both students and institutions reflecting local conditions and local political considerations determine what students pay and, in some cases still, how much students are paid. While some students shop internationally for better prices as well as better products—Canadian universities continue to seek U.S. students by offering comparable educations and degrees at lower tuitions—most international flows of students reflect the kinds of local economic and political circumstances that have historically resulted in outward migrations.

As a result the academic world has become aggressively more international without in fact becoming much more global. Students travel more; faculty wander more broadly; leaders of these international enterprises find themselves spending more time abroad attending to the interests and soliciting the support of their international alumni. They proudly proclaim their interest in recruiting ever more international students, both for the revenue they bring and the boost such students give to claims that their universities are among the world's most prestigious. Scientific research is—and for more than three decades has been—the principal exception. Colleagues distributed among a half dozen or more countries now routinely compose research teams that have made the Internet a major tool of global collaboration; indeed, the Web owes much of its initial success to the scientists' demand for a ready means of transmitting data and communicating results.

What higher education does internationally is decidedly not global, at least not in Friedman's terms. To understand why, we must consider higher education's current fascination with things international in terms of three broad dichotomies that lie at the heart of what it means to be global.

Customized versus Standardized

Perhaps the most visible result of economic globalism is the standardization of products and hence production. In an era of globalization, a rose is a rose is a rose, and a Toyota is a Toyota is a Toyota, whether it is assembled in the United States or Southeast Asia or Europe from parts manufactured in an even larger array of countries. Products with the same names and the same brand identities look, feel, even smell the same worldwide. What is true of manufacturing is equally true of banking, fast foods, consulting, and retailing. With remarkably little variation, the templates are all the same. This standardization of products is also leading to the standardization of training among multinational companies that understand that their workers, as well as their consumers, belong to a homogenous global community.

Training yes, but not higher education. The services and products universities provide remain singular, unique, and largely customized. Whereas global enterprises readily embrace the notion of interchange, each university remains steadfast in the certainty that it and it alone has both the right and the ability to define what constitutes a successful educational outcome. In the United States a major battle is now brewing over whether governmental agencies can require either the public universities they pay for or the private universities they charter to accept, as valid courses, credits earned in another American college or university. There are also those champions of free trade who believe that educational products can be brought under the regulatory umbrella of the World Trade Organization (WTO), though their cause has attracted little attention and less support among the world's principal universities.

Instead, an international competition for students and faculty in which the competing universities stress their individuality, uniqueness, and nationality is being championed. Whether the student being recruited is from Thailand or China or the Czech Republic, making the sale inevitably requires the recruiting university to demonstrate why its style of university is best and why its particular national setting offers special opportunities not readily available elsewhere. It is a kind of selling in which truly global enterprises almost never engage.

Here versus There

Executives and directors of companies that have gone global often talk about theirs as a journey of three phases. First, their companies were national or regional enterprises in which most of their customers, as well as their workers, were local, along with their production facilities and sales staffs. Then their companies went international, which, for the most part, meant opening sales offices abroad and learning the art of exporting their domestically produced goods and services. Going global was the third stage in which the distinction between here and there was abandoned. Production began to take place everywhere as their hitherto foreign operations and branches became fully integrated subsidiaries of a multinational enterprise. While most of a company's workforce remained tied to a new global set of localities, the leaders of the enterprise began to come from and go anywhere—Chinese executives could be found running European operations, Americans running production plants in Brazil, and Europeans, resident in the United States, leading the company.

For the world's research universities, however, the distinction between *here* and *there* is stronger than ever as the leaders of these institutions struggle to reconcile their interest in being global with their need to preserve the importance and vitality of their *home* campuses. Among these leaders, perhaps no one is more sensitive to this challenge than Johns Hopkins University's President William Brody—a friend of Tom Friedman, an articulate commentator on what globalization is likely to mean to institutions like his, and, at the same time, a stout defender of and investor in the two Baltimore campuses of Hopkins. When you visit Baltimore, Brody's challenge is readily understood. The medical campus is massive, dominating the skyline with a phalanx of buildings that bespeak power and money as well as research and service. The arts and sciences, along with engineering and most of the university's undergraduate programs, are located ten miles across town on an expanded and newly renovated campus that is a jewel of Georgian architecture. With increasing poignancy, Brody asks his colleagues two questions: What has to happen on the Baltimore campuses of Hopkins to make people want to come here from around the world? Or, more prosaically, how does Hopkins rationalize its historical investments in place and expensive physical facilities in an age of globalization?

Brody's question is probably *the* question the leaders of universities everywhere are asking as each confronts the challenge of devising an international strategy that feeds their home campuses, providing them students, revenue, and visibility. Indeed, most programs of international education are designed to do just that. Among lesser institutions, this need to bring the cash home is transparent. Programs and campuses are established abroad to provide credentials fully recognized in the home institution's country of origin. The students pay less than students attending the home campus, costs of instruction are reduced through the use of local faculty, and the operating margins are sent back to the home institution to help defray the cost of operations there, to offset revenue losses occasioned by enrollment shortfalls or declining public appropriations, or both. When students on foreign campuses later transfer to the home campus and choose to enroll for their postgraduate coursework, the economic benefits to the home institution are further enhanced.

Australian higher education has probably been the most forthright in adopting this model. Shortfalls in public appropriations to universities across the system led to an expectation that upward of 10 percent of their operating revenues would come from foreign students and/or foreign operations. As a result, Australian higher education has come to dominate the market for international education across much of Asia.

This model of international exchange is more colonial than global, at least as Friedman has defined the term. The surpluses earned from both foreign operations and the recruitment of foreign students are sent home for support of and investment in the home campus. Unlike the modern multinational corporation, which sees itself as a global network of sales and production facilities in which the center is increasingly less important, the university that competes internationally remains a spoke-and-hub distribution system in which the home campus (the hub) remains at the center of the operations, connecting its international operations not to one another but to itself.

For a while, it seemed as if the world of research would be the globalized exception to this colonial model for broadly distributing educational services. The European Organization for Nuclear Research (CERN) in Switzerland provided the model of how a well-run and commonly financed research center with facilities and services no individual campus could provide trumped the need of the home campuses to control the flow of personnel as well as capital.

Perhaps the best financed example of a nation trying to extend the lessons of CERN to gain first-mover advantage was the decision by Singapore to have its universities team up with major research universities in the United States and Europe. Brody's Johns Hopkins was an early collaborator, working with the National University of Singapore to develop a host of research programs centered in the medical and health sciences. The idea was that principal researchers from Hopkins would relocate to Singapore, bringing their scientific skills, grantsmanship, and research teams with them. In the end, however, the National University of Singapore severed its arrangement with Hopkins principally because the latter's research scientists, though they visited often and often for extended periods of time, were unwilling to transfer their sense of place from Baltimore to Singapore. Despite the attractions of new labs and generous support, in the final analysis "here in Baltimore" proved more important than "there in Singapore."

Real versus Virtual

Not by coincidence, the initial burst of enthusiasm for the globalization of higher education accompanied the dot-com revolution of the 1990s. The lure was the Web with its promise of anytime, anywhere communication and hence learning. Major universities everywhere were caught up in the contagion. In the United States, Columbia University and New York University each launched major distance-learning initiatives using the Web as the delivery vehicle—initiatives in which each institution invested $40 million or more of its own capital.

At the same time, groups of universities banded together to offer cooperative educational programs, creating in the process enterprises that on paper at least had all the characteristics of truly global enterprises: standardized products, degrees and credentials recognized worldwide, and provider networks instead of single-institution branding. An interconnecting technology that was becoming ubiquitous throughout the world made possible all of this activity. The best branded and financed of these networks involved some of the world's very best universities. Often the networks grew out of collaborations of business schools worldwide.

It didn't work. The products didn't catch on. There was open speculation as to the real worth of these Internet programs despite their associations with strong brands. The technology proved both limiting and awkward: the prices were out of line with the real value of the offered products.

In the end, too few would-be students really believed a virtual experience would convey the same benefits as a real one. What students everywhere wanted was face time, contact, and personal exchange. Despite their penchant for consuming standardized products in other domains, when it came to their own education they wanted what most students traditionally have wanted—a personal, at times even intimate, experience.

Perhaps it is too soon to declare the experiment a failure. Although the first movers have largely abandoned their efforts, both interest in and limited capital for a less grandiose set of educational products remains. Most have assumed that the earlier failures were the product of promising too much and delivering too little. My guess, however, is that something more was involved. The first predictors of an emerging global market for higher education assumed that education, like other service industries, was about to be remade by the forces of globalization. To date, they have been proved wrong.

America's Network University

In the meantime, however, it is safe to predict that higher education is a different kind of product—not ready to be standardized, still associated with particular places and specific traditions, and largely immune to the pressures for consolidation and amalgamation that have transformed the global providers of other service products.

Taken together these three dichotomies—customized instead of standardized, here instead of there, and real instead of virtual—provide an interesting approximation of the preconditions that would have to be met for a truly global market for higher education to emerge. First, there would have to be a much more rapid development of and widespread commitment to the standardization of educational products. The goals, standards, and common definitions the European Union is striving mightily to achieve through the Bologna Process would necessarily become worldwide benchmarks. The three-year baccalaureate would become *the* standard degree accepted everywhere along with a full set of professional and advanced degrees. More than that, course content, and probably teaching modalities as well, would be similarly homogenized and made interchangeable, much as manufacturing products today are interchangeable.

Perhaps that process is already underway. In preparation for the next round of WTO/General Agreement on Tariffs and Trade (GATT) talks, Karen Hughes, then of the U.S. State Department, circulated a memo outlining the scope of a March 2007 Berlin meeting that had been called to discuss the definitions of educational services:

> In late 2006, the ISO Technical Management Board (TMB) established a new technical committee (ISO/TC 232 Educational Services) to work on the development of standards in the field of educational services. The proposal to ISO submitted by Germany, noted that there is a need to create a suitable framework for preparing standards in the field of educational services. It is our understanding that the technical committee will consider standards proposals relating to other areas of non-public education that share the common concern of encouraging cooperation in quality assurance, whereby particular emphasis is placed on the

exchange of models and methods and the establishment of common criteria and principles. Core elements are ensuring the quality
and effectiveness of the education or training and improvement of
knowledge transfer whilst also enhancing the transparency and
comparability of the range of educational services provided.[1]

It is possible to read this note as pertaining only to vocational education, though the chair of the U.S. delegation reported that many participants simply assumed that the international definition of educational
services would apply equally to all of postsecondary education.

The American education enterprise that best exemplifies the growing importance of standardized products in a flat world is the University
of Phoenix. In just thirty years, as its website proudly proclaims, the
University of Phoenix has become "the largest private university in
North America, with nearly two hundred convenient locations, as well
as Internet delivery in most countries around the world."[2] It succeeds
because it has developed a standardized set of products that it monitors
closely and changes frequently. At the University of Phoenix the corporation, and decidedly not the faculty, owns the curriculum. Faculty,
along with learning specialists and others, help design the curriculum
by using their experiences in the classroom, real as well as virtual, to
modify and adjust offerings and when necessary to abandon them. But
no member of a Phoenix faculty can say, as those of us who inhabit traditional colleges and universities regularly proclaim, "It's my course."
And what is delivered in any one of Phoenix's nearly two hundred sites
is likely to be delivered in most, if not all, of them.

Along with a commitment to standardized products, for higher
education in the United States to truly go global there would have to be
a fundamental lessening of the importance attached to physical place
and the uniqueness of campus brands across higher education worldwide. Global enterprises are essentially multinational networks of producers and service providers. The kind of cooperative networks that
have been tried in virtual education, linking otherwise competing
providers in a host of countries and/or regions would become a principal, perhaps even a dominant, mode of organizing the provision of
standardized educational services. Campuses would become less
important both as symbols of excellence and as specific places of
research and scholarship. What happened in one part of the network
would become interchangeable with identically designed and delivered programs in other parts of the network.

But that is not the lesson embedded in the development of the modern American campus. In the 1990s I was briefly in charge of the University of Pennsylvania's campus planning effort—charged, with the help of a prominent architectural consultant, to develop a new master plan for the Penn campus. Part of my assignment involved talking and working with a group of the university's most influential trustees who had determined that the university lacked architectural standards as well as vision, having just built a major new building using the wrong color brick. What I learned was that the trustees, particularly those with major corporate responsibilities, wanted the university to use a one-hundred-year standard when building new facilities. In their own corporations, however, these same trustees were opting for remarkably temporary physical facilities—spaces without style or architecture that were seldom built to last and were best leased rather than owned. Though the label globalism was not yet in vogue, corporate America was preparing for a global world in which the physical distinction between here and there was being obliterated as multinational enterprises were preparing to do business everywhere, anytime, all the time.

Here again the University of Phoenix offers the most concrete example of what it means to be an educational provider in a mostly flat world. Phoenix rents almost all of its facilities, as often as not in corporate parks. It has no tie to either space or place—its name is a convenience that the Apollo group, Phoenix's owners, adopted to get its operations chartered in Arizona when it was initially blocked from doing business in California. The lesson the University of Phoenix teaches for those who would do business in a flat world is pretty simple: own the product, not the box.

The third and final necessary condition for making higher education a truly global enterprise is a successful revolution making electronically distributed and asynchronous education (e-learning) readily available worldwide. Despite the promises of the technologists, e-learning has a long way to go. For the most part it remains clunky, linear, too often little more than electronically distributed workbooks. What would be required is a constantly growing catalogue of electronic offerings that had the same impact MRIs have had on the medical profession and video games have had on the entertainment business. It is hard to imagine any process that achieves the first two of my necessary conditions—standardized products and a dramatic lessening of the importance of both space and place—that does not depend directly on the ready availability of a growing catalog of state-of-the-art electronic learning products.

From where I sit, none of these three conditions is likely to be met anytime soon. More important, meeting those conditions would not likely result in universities that are either more interesting or more efficient, or even necessarily more productive. More likely they would become increasingly dull places that were not much fun to visit let alone to work at. To understand why, we need to return to Friedman's conception of a flat world. He has in mind a world in which the network is the thing—not just electronically, though neither he nor I, for that matter, can imagine a flat world in which the technology is not what binds us all together.

Not Exactly

One problem inherent in *The World Is Flat* is the seductive quality of Friedman as storyteller. The reader comes to believe without fully understanding what he or she is committing to. One lesson of the higher education retreats in which *The World Is Flat* has been the principal and often the sole reading is simple: too many participants come away thinking that it is important to understand that what happens here is now directly influenced by what happens there. From this perspective, the big take-away is an understanding that American higher education can no longer pretend it exists in a bubble of its own making. Hence the future of American as well as all higher education lies in adopting an international perspective—sending our students and faculty there, recruiting their students and faculty to come here, adopting wherever possible strategies of collaboration and cooperation.

Well, not exactly. Beneath the anecdotes and clever labels lies a conception of the world that is fundamentally at variance with the presumptions of the modern academy. What makes the world flat, Friedman tells us, is the ability of people to connect directly with the producers of the products they want, the creators of the ideas and opinions they either value or want to explore, and the people they most want to spend time with whether virtually or face to face. A flat world is one without *intermediaries*. Because the connections are direct, there is no need for arbitrators of taste or fashion or facilitators of ideas or conveners of events. In a truly flat world you are on your own, largely unencumbered by institutional arrangement.

Colleges and universities, however, are first and foremost intermediaries. They certify knowledge, award credentials, establish modes of conduct, and, even as they provide opportunity, establish well-worn pathways that constrain choice. People have to choose the colleges and universities with which to associate; at the same time, institutions must choose which students and faculty they wish to admit to their individual communities. While simultaneous as well as serial connections are possible—principally in the form of multiple enrollments and shared appointments—they remain the exception. Universities thrive—some would say exist—because they offer not general but specific connections; they help both students and faculty to organize as well as limit their choices.

In a truly flat world, colleges and universities would have to look and operate much more like the University of Phoenix. There would necessarily be fewer separate institutions. Instead, there would be a limited number of ever-expanding networks in which individual campuses or outlets would become interconnected nodes. Students would collect their course units from a variety of sources—much as modern Girl or Boy Scouts collect merit badges—that would be subsequently tallied and verified by some central authority charged with awarding degrees. In a flat world, education would be more about the commodity than the experience simply because the former and not the latter can be cast in standard format and tested for completeness.

Three Options

Faced with this prospect, traditionally organized colleges and universities would essentially have three choices as they devised their strategies for succeeding in a much altered landscape. First, they could deny the analysis and say in the process that Friedman was wrong. The world's rush to interconnectiveness will not result in a landscape devoid of intermediaries. From this perspective, the push of globalism becomes just another fad, which will fade with time and disappointment.

Second, they could embrace globalism and all of its consequences. Colleges and universities following this track would likely begin an accelerated search for new partners with which to connect. Individual campuses would quickly become outlets offering a standardized set of learning products. As in all franchise operations, location would become increasingly important and transient students increasingly the norm.

Third, colleges and universities could become flat-world contrarians. This option differs from the first in that being a successful contrarian requires both an understanding and, on some level, an embrace of what is being opposed. True contrarians are seldom curmudgeons. Rather than endlessly complaining, a contrarian university and its faculty would have to say and mean something like, "we're the institution that lets you embrace the connectivity a flat world promises. We're your anchor, one of those special places that is in but not wholly part of this world." A flat-world contrarian's future would depend on its ability to give people something to hang on to, a mooring or anchor that would let them lean out without falling off the merry-go-round. Colleges and universities that came to play this role would have to be resourceful, nimble, entrepreneurial, probably rich, and, above all, wise in the ways of connecting with entities that are not similarly moored or anchored.

All three of these scenarios are inherently problematic. The first—operating on the assumption that the world is not becoming flatter—won't work because Friedman is not wrong. The world is becoming an ever more connected enterprise in which intermediaries are playing a diminishing role. Large numbers of people will seek their postsecondary education in fundamentally different ways—from outlets, from the Web, from networks that promise that all educational credits and credentials meeting the network standards are fully transferable. To stand aside valiantly claiming to be above the fray will only mean someone else—probably dominated by for-profit providers like the University of Phoenix and big state systems—will organize the networks, set the standards, and, in the end, garner most of the enrollments.

Embracing a flat educational world, however, has substantial problems as well. To some extent, a system of educational networks consistent with Friedman's notion of a flat world has been foreshadowed by the increasing insistence of state legislatures that students at publicly funded institutions be allowed to transfer credits earned in one public institution to another. Once the credit becomes a fully convertible currency, the conditions for network education have been met, provided the state system embraces all forms of postsecondary education. To date, the system that comes closest to meeting this condition is the State University of New York (SUNY), which combines two- and four-year institutions, technical institutes, and baccalaureate colleges and universities. All that remains is for that system and then others to adopt systemwide graduation requirements, curricular standards, and transferable credits.

Public systems of higher education wishing to become integrated networks offering a full range of educational products (degrees, courses, certificates) have both built-in advantages and disadvantages. They will find it relatively easy to set prices and approve offerings. Big, as opposed to small, state systems will have the further advantage of sufficient demand, distributed locations, economies of scale, and geographic diversity. At the same time in their unionized faculty they are likely to encounter some of the stiffest opposition to making their systems Phoenix-like. Increasingly unionized faculties at public institutions are insisting on substituting full-time for part-time faculty and for preserving the ability of a faculty member to call a course his or her own. But networks, as Phoenix has amply demonstrated, require flexibility and interchangeability as well as willingness on the part of those who teach the curriculum to see themselves as deliverers rather than owners.

Small private institutions are likely to enjoy few, if any, advantages and almost all the disadvantages. Many have remote locations. Most have stubborn traditions of going it alone. Inevitably they will be squeezed between the University of Phoenix network on one side, and on the other, the public systems that have converted themselves into Phoenix-like networks. One way to think of the small college predicament is to remember what is happening to the village hardware store in America. More of the business is flowing to the big box stores—Wal-Mart, Home Depot, and Lowe's, all of which can stock a wider range of products while offering more convenient locations and lower prices. One way to survive as a small, locally owned unit is to band together in a purchasing and merchandising cooperative, as in the True Value network of stores. But the more the old store begins to become a True Value look-alike, the less the store retains the advantage of uniqueness. I have no doubt that the Council of Independent Colleges (CIC), the National Association of Independent Colleges and Universities (NAICU), regional associations like the Appalachian College Association (ACA) and the Great Lakes Colleges Association (GLCA), along with associations of religiously affiliated colleges like the Association of Jesuit Colleges and Universities (AJCU), will, in the face of growing competition from both public and for-profit networks, want to link their members in such a way as to help them compete. In the final analysis, however, such networks will have a tough time matching prices and product ranges offered by the bigger, more completely integrated networks with which they find themselves competing. Only occasionally does a Wal-Mart or Home Depot or Lowe's lose in head-to-head competition to a local True Value hardware store.

The third option—to become a flat-world contrarian—will have the greatest initial appeal; although many will try, only a very few will truly succeed. Some will fail because they confuse being a contrarian with being a "stand-patter." Others, particularly smaller private institutions, will lose out because they lack sufficient heft. Indeed, most institutions will discover that the deck has already been stacked against them. In an increasingly flat world of networks and connections, most institutions will discover that their only viable option lies in becoming an integral part of a successful network, though membership means that they will be substantially less independent and unique than they have been in the past.

Some institutions—my current guess is about sixty American universities in all—will succeed brilliantly in becoming true flat-world contrarians. The winners will be large, rich, and iconic. They will be engines of basic as well as applied research. Their campuses will continue to be important destinations. Their defining characteristic, the one that will most likely separate them from everyone else, will be the adeptness they exhibit at making connections—with both other successful flat-world contrarians and the emerging educational networks and systems that will teach most undergraduates as well as most graduate students pursing professionally oriented master's degrees. Flat-world contrarians will increasingly resemble the tertiary health care centers that both thrive among and depend on their linkages to the physicians' networks that are coming to dominate the practice of medicine in the United States.

Currently the best model of what such an institution might look like is the Massachusetts Institute of Technology (MIT), which has maintained, and indeed increased, its standing and independence, even as it has gone about the business of adroitly building a host of connections across what the leaders of that institution saw as an increasingly flat educational world. MIT's most visible thrust has been its OpenCourseWare Project, which, starting in 2001, began making all MIT course materials available on-line free of charge. It is and was an expensive undertaking made possible by funding from the William and Flora Hewlett Foundation and the Andrew W. Mellon Foundation. Only an institution of MIT's standing could attract the required $6 million per year the Project is currently spending, and only an institution of MIT's visibility could attract the attention that makes the project such a success.

In the spring of 2007 the *New York Times* ran a story that asked all the right questions. Would the faculty support a project that some might have claimed gave away course materials the faculty, and not the institution, owned? Here the answer was a resounding yes; this affirmation suggests just how important changing faculty predilections is to succeeding in an increasingly flat world. And, the *Times* asked, "If M.I.T. gives away this material . . . [will] students still pay the $33,600 tuition to attend?" And the answer? Classes remained filled, and, "if anything, university officials say, the material has served to stoke the interest of potential applicants." The story continued,

> "It is so much bigger than we could have ever imagined," said Shigeru Miyagawa, a professor of linguistics and Japanese, who was on the committee that originally proposed the plan. "The number of visits that we get is beyond belief. We really didn't know who would be using it when we went into this at the very beginning."
>
> The president of M.I.T. at the time, Charles M. Vest, anticipated as much, saying, "there will probably be a lot of uses that will really surprise us and that we can't really predict."[3]

That capacity to respond quickly and effectively to changing as well as unforeseen circumstances is the important lesson here. MIT found the money, harnessed the technological know-how to make the project work, and provided the kind of international brand that made it and its website an international destination. At the same time, the MIT culture allowed the institution, in partnership with its faculty, to change an important parameter governing the intellectual property rights of its professors.

In an increasingly flat educational world, then, MIT occupies one end of a spectrum that is likely to stretch across the educational landscape, ending in the highly standardized, even regimented, networks exemplified by the University of Phoenix. Caught in the middle will be most institutions. Public systems will likely become networks more like the University of Phoenix or will find their markets increasingly usurped by the for-profit networks, both real and virtual. The really disadvantaged institutions will be those that are smaller or private or remotely located and find themselves unable to become flat-world contrarians because they possess neither the brand nor the resources needed to forge an independent path. The successful contrarians, like MIT, will continue to be idiosyncratically independent even as they use their standing in the market to establish new connections.

Perhaps none of this will transpire. Perhaps nations as well as individuals will choose not to be so interconnected; perhaps universities will fear terrorism or product contamination or cultural degradation. Perhaps it will prove possible for colleges and universities to put Humpty Dumpty back together again, all the while changing little if any of their core operations or values. My bet is that such a future is not very likely.

Still, it is interesting to note that in February 2008, the *New York Times* sought to make it official—front page, Sunday edition, above the fold, color picture. American higher education was betting on the global option. To the *Times* it was a veritable "educational gold rush" as American institutions of nearly every stripe joined the parade of universities opening branch campuses around the world.[4] But as I have observed here and elsewhere, not that much was new except the proliferation of outlets in uncertain places. It was all about the money—about American higher education becoming an export commodity.

The story of our fascination with things international is a cautionary tale that teaches two basic lessons. First, international higher education will never supply the funds American higher education requires to either sustain or improve itself. The success of Australian higher education cannot be replicated here. Like every other gold rush, the winners will be few and the losers many—a case of too many institutions chasing after a very limited number of truly profitable international ventures.

Second, market forces will not yield the kind of reforms—better teaching, more engaged students, more affordable as well as accountable institutions—that the lamenters seek. In a flat world all the market forces align with products that are more standardized, more broadly distributed, and more clearly interchangeable. Here as elsewhere, the market favors, not traditionally configured colleges and universities, but those like the University of Phoenix; they alone fully understand that in a flat world networks and convenience matter most.

9 | The Wrong-Way Web

Globalization, Friedman argues, was a product of merging two irresistible forces. First, the unexpectedly rapid liberalization of economic systems resulted in convertible currencies, binding trade agreements, transparent business practices, reduced tariffs, and a mindset that made "country of origin" considerably less important. In a process that resembles nothing so much as the mad dance of the sorcerer's apprentice (recall the early Walt Disney cartoon in which Mickey Mouse plays the hapless apprentice), countries, cities, individuals, even tribes and clans rushed to expand markets, produce standardized products, and embrace business models that stressed just-in-time manufacture and service delivery.

The second irresistible force was the rapid spread of a set of ubiquitous electronic technologies that made the dance possible in the first place. The new world of instantaneous electronic transfers—symbolized by, but not limited to, the World Wide Web—first transformed currency markets and then allowed for the electronic distribution of services. The new electronic technologies made real the promise that time and space could be eclipsed. Like the Scarlet Pimpernel, innovative businesses were suddenly here, there, and everywhere—simultaneously.

The combination of new technologies and economic liberalization promised a new world order; Friedman captured something of this euphoria in the title of his book, *The World Is Flat*. The demand for goods and services would expand, leading to ever bigger markets. Innovations would flourish, leading to an era of new products and services. And everyone could participate; for perhaps the first time in history the playing field would be level. An outmoded system of imperial privileges would give way to a global economy in which innovation would confer first advantage.

As I have already noted, higher education's take on this transformation was often paradoxical. It was good to be global—to be part of a brave new world of connections and expanding markets. For higher education in general and American higher education in particular, however, going global principally meant sending our students *there*, having their students come *here*, all without really changing what we did or how we did it. At the same time, a host of top-line American universities, both singularly and in like-minded collaborations, embraced the Web as a means of delivering high-quality graduate education everywhere simultaneously—almost always with financially disastrous results. Columbia University lost in excess of $40 million on its venture. New York University lost even more. The high-profile collaboration of a dozen of the world's top business schools offering a top-of-the-line business degree online went nowhere. By 2005, when Friedman published *The World Is Flat* as a sequel to *The Lexus and the Olive Tree*, it was apparent to almost everyone that the Web was not going to do for most established colleges and universities what the twin forces propelling the globalization were doing for—and to—the world's economy. What survived were a variety of "dumbed-down" online universities offering courses targeted to adult and working learners, designed for students interested in spot courses, and intended for students in developing countries (though to date that market is still more talked about than actually served electronically).

The failure of an online international market for top-end universities was probably the most visible sign that e-learning was not changing higher education. There were, however, plenty of other, largely domestic omens, starting with the failure of digital ventures to yield the revenues that the advocates of e-learning had promised. The most quoted projections were supplied by Michael Moe in his 2000 Merrill Lynch white paper, *The Knowledge Web*:

- Our estimates for the U.S. online market opportunity for knowledge enterprises will grow from $9.4 billion in 1999 to $53.3 billion in 2003, representing a CAGR (Compound Annual Growth Rate) of 54 percent.

- At an estimated $105 billion, the spending power of college students is huge. Not surprisingly, a growing percentage of their spending is moving online. Currently, students spend $1.5 billion online, an amount which is expected to almost triple to $3.9 billion by 2002.
- We estimate that the U.S. market for online higher education alone will grow from $1.2 billion in 1999 to $7 billion in 2003.[1]

The Big Promise

It was all part of the big promise. E-learning would revolutionize the college classroom and change how faculty taught and students learned. Demand for both degrees and skills courses would literally explode. As in the case of global e-learning, the new technologies would allow domestic higher education to establish whole new markets by reaching out to learners who had failed to complete their higher educations and to those with degrees who needed new skills and wanted to shift vocations. At the same time, colleges and universities, eager to become both more productive and more efficient, would seek and acquire the very electronic processes that were recasting the world of business.

It never happened. For e-learning, the first decade of the twenty-first century has proved to be one of lowered expectations, redefined boundaries, and unexpected twists. The skeptics have had a field day, asking not just once, but over and over again: Why haven't computer-based technologies actually changed higher education? Why haven't colleges and universities achieved the productivity gains that other industries have achieved through the introduction of electronically mediated processes? Why haven't the new technologies in general and the Web in particular spurred colleges and universities to adopt the reforms the policy wonks have argued for so fervently? Why, in fact, has classroom teaching changed so little, if at all?

In fairness, this set of questions, despite the power of repetition, ignores a great deal of real change. Most colleges and universities have adopted the same electronic business practices that have made industries more efficient in their processing of orders and their delivery of products. Potential applicants can shop and apply online. Enrolled students register online, pay their bills online, reserve library books online, receive assignments online, get their grades online, and when the need arises, complain online. Most big universities, along with a growing number of midsized and wealthier smaller institutions, either have in place or are in the process of acquiring ERP (enterprise resource planning) software enabling them to integrate all business and record-keeping functions within a single computer system. Computer-based technologies have revolutionized research in every domain. Library processes and procedures have been rendered unrecognizable by the rapid adoption of computerized search engines and document storage systems. Not least, computerized technologies have forever changed how colleges and universities identify, cultivate, track, and eventually harvest donors, big and small.

That said, however, the larger truth remains; in their basic teaching operations colleges and universities have remained blissfully impervious to the kinds of changes the new technologies have introduced almost everywhere else. Asking why has even become something of an academic specialty initially spurred by two early studies of a revolution yet to happen. The first was Larry Cuban's *Oversold and Underused— Computers in the Classroom*. Published in 2001, Cuban's study focuses on the use of computers in a variety of public school systems located in and around the Silicon Valley. In prose that often reflected the antibusiness bias of the commodifiers then excoriating higher education's embrace of market practices and rationales, Cuban described what the new technologies were expected to bring to K–12 education. By using the language of their corporate sponsors, Cuban quoted Louis Gerstner Jr., then IBM's CEO, "Before we can get the educational revolution rolling, we need to recognize that our public schools are low-tech institutions in a high-tech society. The same changes that have brought cataclysmic change to every facet of business can improve . . . the efficiency and effectiveness of how we run our schools."[2]

The new technologies in themselves, business leaders and allied school reformers argued, would bring about the necessary changes. Schools would, as Gerstner proclaims, become more productive and efficient. Teaching would be transformed into an engaging and active process. Just as important, students would be much better prepared for the jobs the new technologies were creating in the workplace. The challenge was clear—get more computers into the classroom.

Money to buy the computers and wire the schools flowed. The Clinton administration made more than $2 billion available starting in 1996. A special McKinsey and Company study estimated that by 1998–1999 spending on educational technology by K–12 education had grown to $5.5 billion dollars annually, or roughly $120 per student. Over the course of the 1990s, the ratio of students to computer had dropped from eighteen students per computer to just five students per computer. Having detailed the rapid spread of computers in the classroom, often placed there through the energetic lobbying of business interests, Cuban summed up the big promise for K–12 education: "In seeking to achieve three divergent purposes, techno-promoters across the board assumed that increased availability in the classroom would lead to increased use. Increased use, they further assumed, would then lead to efficient teaching and better learning which, in turn, would yield able graduates who can compete in the workplace. These graduates would give American employers that critical edge necessary to stay ahead in the ever-changing global economy."[3]

Cuban was even better at detailing how little difference the schools' substantial investment in hardware and software made in the lives of their students and their teachers. In ten of the eleven preschool/ kindergarten sites he studied in detail, the machines were "used infrequently." This marginal use reflected both an absence of sustained technical support and a real confusion as to whether computer-based activities were really appropriate for this age group. Cuban then argued that this practice taught a straightforward lesson: "these preschools and kindergartens seek primarily to conserve traditional civic, academic, and social values rather than turn children into future Net-workers."[4]

The site studies of secondary schools produced the same results, which Cuban described in terms of four unexpected findings. Less than 10 percent of the teachers who actually used computers in the classroom could be considered serious users. Even in the classrooms of teachers who were either serious or occasional users, their students' use of computers was more often than not "peripheral to their primary instructional tasks." Despite all the talk about how young people were embracing the new technologies, Cuban reported that only 5 percent of the high school students he observed could be said to have had "tech-heavy" experiences, and these occurred mostly in nonacademic subjects or when students served as part of the school's technical support system. Finally, the most devastating as well as unexpected finding of all proclaimed that "less than 5 percent of teachers integrated computer technology into their regular curricular and instructional routines."[5]

Cuban concluded by examining three scenarios that might explain why, even in the Silicon Valley and despite the direct expenditures of substantial sums of money, the new technologies had had so little impact on schools, teachers, or students. First, the "slow revolution" scenario offered the solace that it is too early to judge. Be patient, and in time what has proved ubiquitous elsewhere will prove ubiquitous in education as well. Cuban's second scenario, what he called the "history-and-contexts" explanation, focused on the web of assumptions and social beliefs held by taxpayers, parents, public officials, and teachers, all of which make rapid change difficult and frequently impossible. Not only are the new technologies inadequate, but they are also no match, at least in the short run, for deep-seated beliefs about what constitutes learning and how best to improve educational performance.[6]

Third, Cuban's "textually constrained choice" focused on how alternative strategies for improving school performance—reducing class size, more preschools, better driven curricula—trump the new technologies in competing for the attention of those both within and without K–12 school systems. In a summation that echoed in my own explanations of why e-learning has had so little impact on collegiate learning, Cuban predicted, "Even if every single child had a personal computer at home and in school in the next decade or half-century as a consequence of the slow revolution, I believe that core teaching and learning practices—shaped by internal and external contexts—would remain very familiar to those who would visit mid-twenty-first-century schools."[7]

As Cuban was finishing his study of computer use in K-12 education, Bill Massy and I were starting our Thomson Corporation study of e-learning in postsecondary and corporate education. And, as with Cuban's work, the study's title was both summary and come-on: *Thwarted Innovation, What Happened to e-learning and Why*. Even more than was the case in K–12, the impact of electronically mediated learning on the collegiate level never came close to matching the hype. There was the same big promise: e-learning would revolutionize teaching while simultaneously reaching out to whole new audiences of learners. And, as Michael Moe promised, first adopters would achieve substantial advantages in terms of efficiencies, economies of scale, and market share.

We discovered instead that conditions closely parallel those that Cuban had encountered in K–12 education. Because there was little demand, there was little market for e-learning. There was the same built-in inertia associated with a standard teaching model. Faculty, for the most part, lacked both knowledge about and interest in e-learning. When we asked individual faculty if they were familiar with e-learning, the most frequent answer was, "Yes I use Blackboard, and I am getting really good at PowerPoint."

Our most unexpected finding was that there was also little student interest in e-learning. The students we encountered were often bemused by their professors' experiments with e-learning. As one honor student at the University of Texas, Austin wrote: "The fairy tale of e-learning assumes that classroom technology enhances the learning experience for both the professor and the students. The reality of such educational technology is far from ideal. Often poorly integrated into a course, its use skews the balance of content and technology and lessens dynamic interaction among students and between students and faculty."[8] Students really want to present themselves, to showoff—a phenomenon that was plain to us, though we finished our interviewing before Facebook, MySpace, and YouTube burst on the scene. From distance learning they want principally convenience, not new modes of learning. Most students have no more interest in alternative teaching modalities than the faculty who teach them.

Where's the Demand?

In the years since the publication of *Thwarted Innovation*, the reasons for higher education's tepid embrace of the new technologies has become clearer. For me personally, the "aha" moment occurred at the San Diego meeting of the Spellings Commission in February 2006. Before us were three technology experts: a distinguished dean of engineering, a young computer-science faculty member, and the chief information officer at one of the nation's most technologically adept universities. Each had come to plead for more money to support the development of open-source educational software. More exasperated than usual, I mused during the comment period that technologists needed not more money, but more customers. The genesis of my observation was my finding in *Thwarted Innovation*: there was no demand for e-learning software, particularly on the part of faculty, and hence no market.

It turned out that the good dean was even more exasperated. He was not interested in hearing that customer demand might be required to spur e-learning's development. Looking me in the eye he said, "You don't understand. If we build it they will come." For nearly twenty years, I had used that line from the 1989 film, *Field of Dreams*, to parody the assumption by educational researchers that what intrigues them will interest those whose lives they are trying to change. I called it the "Kevin Costner principle of strategic change" after the star of the film about an Iowa farmer who hears a mysterious voice telling him to turn his cornfield into a baseball diamond. Suddenly it was not parody but fact—the deeply held conviction that the new technologies in themselves would drive educational reform. Faculty would change how they taught because they could not resist the beguiling power of the new technologies.

Sometimes the spread of an innovation does follow the "If we build it" scenario. It's not clear, for example, that there was a huge demand for a new kind of MP3 player prior to Apple's introduction of the iPod. But that device proved beguiling enough to spawn whole new forms of communication, including, but not limited, to podcasts. What became clear to me that afternoon in San Diego, however, was that e-learning was no iPod. This innovation would not drive change; rather, innovation could spread only in response to someone else's demand for change. In short, the technologist needed not more grant money but more customers who were willing and able to invest their own time and funds in a set of innovations that solved *their* problems rather than satisfying the technologist's inquisitiveness.

Much the same point can be made by looking at the adoption of the new technologies in two professions whose principals resemble faculty members in terms of the training and education they receive and the professional independence they enjoy. The practice of law has been fundamentally changed by two computerized search engines: Westlaw.com and LexisNexis. What lawyers do, particularly younger lawyers in large firms, has changed forever. The search engines, along with the efficiencies and cost savings electronic search introduced, merged with other cost savings and cost avoidance strategies that have helped redefine the roles and responsibilities of partners as well as clerks and young associates. Indeed, the need to achieve those savings helped create the demand for the electronic search engines in the first place.

Medicine is a second example of a profession that has been fundamentally changed by the introduction of the new technologies. Here, too, the drive for cost savings helped create the necessary demand, though two other needs proved even more powerful. The first was the demand for less invasive diagnostic procedures. Once, if you were suspected of having Hodgkin's disease, the only way to chart the cancer's spread was to perform a laparotomy, which involved opening up the patient something like a sardine can just to have a look around. I know; I have one of those scars. Today that diagnosis is done through a series of scans.

The scanning technologies answered a second, subsequent demand as well. In an age of increased litigiousness, physicians needed to reduce the risk of being sued for missing a diagnosis. As a result, ironically, many health care economists now believe the scanning and related technologies are being overused. If in doubt, order the test even if the result is substantially elevated costs. It should be pointed out, as well, that once the scanning technologies took hold, a large number of physicians discovered the profitability of owning the equipment and diagnostic centers that were performing the very scans prescribed by the physicians themselves.

There is simply no parallel development in higher education. For the most part, faculty have neither sought out nor felt compelled to adopt new, electronically mediated ways to teach. There is not, as Richard Vedder and his fellow efficiency pundits have lamented, demand to make the delivery of classroom instruction either more efficient or less costly. And on those occasions when lowering costs does become the paramount goal, the most effective strategy is not to invest in the new learning technologies but rather to hire more adjunct faculty.

Had the technologists been more attuned to what higher education needed, they might have focused more of their developmental efforts on a set of instructional challenges that lie at the heart of higher education's current curricular dilemmas. First and foremost is the need to find new ways to teach the STEM disciplines—science, technology, engineering, and math. American education still does a reasonable job at instructing science majors, teaching them what they need to know and how to learn more. The problem, however, is that the rest of the population is becoming ever more scientifically illiterate. My guess is that science faculty today are ready to try just about anything except the dumbing-down of their disciplines. They want students to understand the role scientific principles play in defining problems and organizing the knowledge base. They want nonmajors to understand what it means to solve problems scientifically and the importance of verifying results. No less, they want nonmajors to understand something of how the world works. These faculty need new means of conveying that information.

Instruction in languages other than English for native speakers of American English is a second example of a field that ought to be more than ready to try alternative teaching strategies. Missing here is sufficient demand on the part of those who fund higher education—governments, foundations, parents—to spend more of their funds on the learning of a foreign language.

The Problem with the Web

The absence of sustained demand and a viable link to educational reform only partially explains why higher education's response to the new technologies has proved so modest. The rest of the story involves the nature of the World Wide Web and its limitations as a platform for learning.

The balance of my explanation begins with the observation that the Web itself is not a learning platform. It is rather a utility for connecting people with people and people with things. Think Amazon.com or Netflix.com, or any of the dozens of sites you use to make airline and hotel reservations. MySpace, Facebook, even YouTube are sites that primarily allow you to see other people's postings, and then they encourage you to share your own experiences. Facebook probably says it best when it describes itself as "a social utility that connects you with the people around you."[9]

Blogs distribute ideas. Wikipedia is a collection of definitions and short essays collectively posted. The Web is primarily used to buy and sell things—books, cars, hotel rooms, antiques, clothes, gardening supplies, exotic spices, tools—you name it, and you can in all probability find a vendor who will sell it to you online. The Web also distributes information. A host of sites will help you interpret a variety of symptoms as a means of learning what questions to ask your doctor. If you are buying a car, a half dozen sites—some charging a fee, some free—will provide you with benchmark prices for both the car you are buying and the one you are selling. These are the Web's best uses—distributing information and processing orders.

The Web's primary function as a distribution system helps explain why Blackboard and other course management systems are the most widely used e-learning technologies across higher education. Course management systems give students what they want most—their assignments, their course packs, and their grades. The same point can be made by focusing on *Virtual U*—the intricate and detailed learning game of how a university operates developed by Bill Massy with the support of the Sloan Foundation. You can download *Virtual U* on the Web—its takes less than three minutes—but you cannot play *Virtual U* on the Web; the permutations of possible combinations are simply beyond the largely linear interactions (again, think making airline reservations or buying a book) that dominate Web applications.

Alas, the great majority of learning routines that students can access through and use on the Web (that is, online) are in reality not much more than automated workbooks where multiple-choice exercises let students call up discreet learning modules and questions in a largely preset order. And when a Web-based or online server is chosen to process the user's responses, the designer of that e-learning program confronts a host of obstacles. If the program is to be widely accessible, it will necessarily have to work for students with low-end connectivity. It must accommodate the limited set of display conventions available for standard Web applications, and even then the designer cannot be sure which conventions a particular Internet service provider (ISP) makes available. Not surprisingly, the most reliable designs are the most simple.

One should not be surprised with these limitations. The Web began primarily as a network for distributing messages and data among a limited number of research scientists in the physical sciences. To run their complex, often collaborative experiments, they needed to be able to communicate quickly. For the most part, their experiments produced large data sets that needed to be processed by individual members of the team working in different locations. Thus, from the get-go, the Web was conceived primarily as a distribution device for exchanging messages and distributing data. E-commerce websites like Amazon.com, Netflix, and the shopping networks extended the capacity of the early Web to increase the number of messages sent and the kinds of data distributed. In higher education, Blackboard and the course management systems played the same role.

In general, mainstream e-commerce websites have shied away from the kind of real-time programming and simulation that e-learning's advocates promised. The routines themselves are expensive to develop, their actual presentation on different platforms hard to control, and the returns difficult to translate into revenue streams. If the product was complex, like a movie in a DVD format, better to have a short preview, a catchy review, and a simple read-and-click order form for sending the movie in the mail. Just over the horizon is online distribution of the movie itself, although, even in that innovation, the Web acts as a distributor of goods and services.

What Will It Take?

Understanding the obstacles e-learning has encountered—relatively little demand, a fascination with technology that too often trumps an interest in education, and an attempt to make the Web something it really isn't—provides a platform for understanding what it will take to make the new technologies central to the reform and transformation of education systems in general and the nation's higher education system in particular.

To make e-learning ubiquitous will require faculty who seek new ways to solve old riddles and technologists who understand that their business is using technology to help people solve their own problems. When I challenged the three technologists appearing before the Spellings Commission, I had in mind a relationship between teachers and technologists in which the former defined the problems the latter tackled rather than the latter enticing the former with the wonders of what the new technologies can do. Even then I suggested two problems with which the technologists might start: how to use the multiple dimensions of e-learning to recast foreign language instruction, and how to use the power of e-learning to make more college graduates scientifically literate.

But I also need to be clear. The technologists have not been ignoring faculty-driven discussions of how best to change teaching or faculty-generated lists of the problems the professoriate needs to take on collectively. Quite the contrary, however, the faculty members who do most of the teaching have generated precious little discussion of either topic. In this regard, those regulars at Association of American Colleges and Universities (AAC&U) workshops and meetings are now, as they have been in the past, a decided minority. Some reformers hope that confrontations with the new technologies and technologically adept students would help jump-start the necessary conversations. I wish this were the case, but it isn't. Given present trends, at least, e-learning is not likely to help trigger the transformation of higher education.

Put another way, e-learning's blossoming will require a fundamental shift in the culture of teaching. As long as most faculty are satisfied with the current tools of the trade, experimentation and some successes will continue, but a real revolution is unlikely. Students will have to demand more, and faculty will have to respond to that demand by first understanding that the power of e-learning lies in its ability to teach by design rather than by instinct; there will have to be a commitment to course design as opposed to course assembly. For e-learning to reach its full potential, faculty will first have to recognize the technology as a means of solving problems that traditional pedagogies too often ignore.

Two technological shifts will also be necessary: a dominant design and a focus on learning objects. One standard rule of innovation is that a new technology takes off only after a dominant design has been widely accepted. Course management systems have proliferated and thrived because they have achieved a dominant design—that is, they fundamentally look the same and perform the same tasks. For e-learning to become a dominant innovation, a dominant design, particularly for the learning objects that are e-learning's building blocks, must emerge. It is a matter of making them not just easier to create—although that too is important—but also more interchangeable and more easily linked with one another. In this context, it helps to think of a railroad marshalling yard in which the cars are the learning objects being assembled behind locomotives that are the user-interface drivers of an efficient e-learning system. The marshalling yard only works if the cars all have the same gauge and common couplers.

Finally, for e-learning to truly take off, colleges and universities must invest in what the trade calls "sticky" learning platforms—websites, probably, to which students and faculty return again and again. Amazon.com works because customers return again and again, in part because Amazon.com actually "learns" to recognize the customer's particular interests and needs. Course management systems must develop a similar kind of "stickiness" by becoming real learning platforms like Amazon.com. I have long been struck by the fact that a course management system like Blackboard stores great volumes of personal data—grades, course selections, often writing assignments and answers to problem sets, career goals and aspirations, and in some cases, course evaluations. On a commercial website, these data would be constantly monitored and "mined" for insights and preferences using CRM (customer relationship management) software. This set of algorithms mines data to reveal the kinds of books a customer likes or the movies the customer wants to rent or the products the customer is likely to select from a catalog.

In an academic setting, such data mining could help students better understand their own learning styles while assisting faculty in developing teaching strategies that better match how their students learn. Faculty could begin using the data from course evaluation systems to better craft their syllabi and stop using writing assignments and problem sets that thwarted rather than encouraged learning. Again, for course management systems to evolve as I have suggested will require faculty and students interested in using data to change the environment for collegiate teaching.

Why e-learning and the
New Technologies Matter

Despite the travails of the past several years, e-learning has retained a core of true believers who argue, still forcefully, even persuasively, that a revolution is at hand—that the computer will do for learning today what printing did for scholarship in the fifteenth century. The story of e-learning is still unfolding; no one really knows what tomorrow will bring. This much, however, is clear: the underlying information technologies on which e-learning depends are themselves too ubiquitous, and the people committed to developing learning platforms too smart, for universities and their faculties not to take seriously the prospect that major changes will flow from their efforts.

The problem is that American colleges and universities cannot afford to wait. If I am inclined to make fun of those technologists who believe in a field of dreams, I am nonetheless persuaded that the kind of transformation higher education requires will ultimately depend on the wholesale adoption of the alternate ways of doing business their technologies now promise. I also understand that ultimately innovators need their field of dreams, if only because those dreams stir their imaginations and stoke their curiosity. I also understand that I have stumbled into a rhetorical cul-de-sac. If, as I have argued, most collegiate faculty, either singularly or collectively, will resist defining tasks they need accomplished in terms the technologists can understand and respond to—and if those same faculty will ignore technological innovations that do not respond to their sense of what needs to be improved and why—then nothing will happen. Somehow, somewhere higher education will have to find a way out of this cul-de-sac, will have to define means as well as ends in such a way that the transforming power of the new technologies will become central to defining higher education's future.

A Critical Experiment

From the impact the new technologies have had on other, similarly constituted enterprises, we know that the process will be more dislodging than peaceful. Nearly everything changes—how decisions are made, how decisions are defined, and the organizational structures that are charged with the defining and making of those decisions. Just how dramatic those changes are likely to be is reflected in a transforming experiment now underway at the University of Minnesota's new Rochester campus (UMR). Responding to increased demand for undergraduate places in general and the prospect of developing collaborative programs with two Rochester icons, the Mayo Clinic and a historic IBM lab and manufacturing facility, the new campus was officially chartered in 2006. By the fall of 2007, a new chancellor, Steven Lehmkuhle, had been recruited from the University of Missouri system.

Taking advantage of the fact that he was truly beginning with a blank slate, Lehmkuhle set about creating an institution that would take full advantage of the new learning technologies; in the process he developed a roster of learning programs that defined the twenty-first century in both their focus and their organization. A program for full-time undergraduates leading to a Bachelor of Science in the Health Sciences took full advantage of UMR's association with the Mayo Clinic. The goal of the program was specific: to educate and train students fully prepared to pursue a health-profession career in the workplace immediately following graduation or enroll in a graduate program leading to an advanced degree or gain admission to a leading medical or dental school.

To drive the design process he recruited Claudia Neuhauser from the University of Minnesota's Twin Cities campus to be the project's principal architect. A mathematician by training, Neuhauser was both a Howard Hughes Medical Institute Professor and Distinguished McKnight University Professor in the department of Ecology, Evolution and Behavior on the University of Minnesota's Twin Cities campus.

From the outset, Neuhauser wanted a Bachelor of Science in the Health Sciences degree that would be delivered differently because it would be organized differently. The basic instructional unit would be a module; many of these modules would be delivered in technologically smart classrooms; others would be delivered as self-paced e-learning experiences. Students would be able to test out of modules while receiving full credit for what they knew or were learning on their own. Modules could be grouped or taken separately. Each module would include assessment tools that enabled the instructor to monitor the effectiveness of the learning strategies the module used and would allow students to monitor their own progress through the curriculum.

Even more dramatic in the sense of being different as well as unexpected was the program's staffing structure. Rather than having a school or department assume responsibility for the program, Neuhauser, with Lehmkuhle's support, created a Center for Learning Innovation (CLI) with the mission "to advance learner-centered, technology-enhanced, competency-based, assessment-driven, and community integrated education." Lehmkuhle named Neuhauser the center's first director and subsequently the campus's first vice chancellor. The core faculty and staff of the CLI, at least initially, were to be four research scholars, whom Neuhauser formally labeled "Design Faculty." She sought a team of fully vetted academics—either tenured or on the University's tenure track—who were subject experts in their disciplines and committed to working in an interdisciplinary environment. Taking their cue from Ernest Boyer's scholarship of learning, core faculty were to be equally engaged in research on learning and research focusing on the frontiers of their scientific disciplines. Their job descriptions stressed their responsibility for developing a "learning architecture and design" that included learning objectives, learning objects, module definition, quality assessment, and learning space design.

Supporting the Design Faculty would be a cohort of "Student-Based Faculty," younger scholars with a primary interest in teaching and, like the Design Faculty, a commitment to a curriculum that was technology enhanced. Much of the student mentoring and advising was to be the responsibility of the Student-Based Faculty, who would also be front-line instructors delivering the program's technology-enhanced learning modules. The staffing table was rounded out with the appointment of a set of postdocs, apprentices really, ready and willing to work with both the Design Faculty and Student-Based Faculty. With Lehmkuhle's support Neuhauser sought an instructional team that was staffed and organized much like the teams that had come to dominate interdisciplinary research in sciences. Neuhauser was the PI, the Design Faculty were the senior as well as creative members of the team, the Student-Based Faculty were the workhorses, and the postdocs were the utility infielders. What the CLI did not look like—though it served the same organizational purposes—was a traditionally organized academic department. Working with a blank sheet of paper, Neuhauser and Lehmkule went about the task of creating a fundamentally new structure.

The CLI's relationship to the new technologies was similarly at variance with the dominant experience in American higher education. The program used the Web, but was not Web based; that is to say, it was not online. In designing when and how to use technology, Neuhauser and her colleagues first asked, "What do our students need to know and know how to do?" Then they asked, "What kinds of learning objects are available to help us meet our goals?" Also different about the curriculum that UMR was developing was its underlying assumption of technology enhancement. Nobody needed to be convinced. Those responsible for the Bachelor of Science in the Health Sciences program, students as well as faculty, knew from the outset that they were engaged in e-learning and not some kind of curricular hybrid that expected the new technologies to supplement, rather than replace, traditional modes of instruction.

The first question to ask of the UMR experiment—and it is important to remember that it remains just that, an experiment—is, "Could the program's learning goals and commitment to technology-enhanced instruction have been satisfied using a traditional departmental organization and a curriculum based on courses worth three credits or more?" Neither Lehmkuhle nor Neuhauser thought so, and I agree. Here then is the true cul-de-sac of my tale. Technology-based work is a different kind of work. It needs to be sculpted as well as organized differently. To fully mix my metaphors, it is never a matter of pouring old wine into new bottles. Everything needs to change, and, once those changes are allowed, the payoff in terms of improved efficiency and effectiveness just might be dramatic.

Can we imagine an American higher education that embraces that kind of transforming change? Or will the push of the new technologies ultimately result in a host of new, totally different institutions that at first compete with and then ultimately supplant traditionally configured institutions?

10 Were Learning to Matter

Despite the energy Steve Lehmkuhle and Claudia Neuhauser invested in their alternate organizational structure for the University of Minnesota, Rochester (UMR), their ultimate goal had more to do with learning than with either structure or technology. Their announced purpose was to develop an academic environment in which students learned more because they learned better. Indeed, what is probably the most radical and hence important aspect of the UMR experiment is its embrace of the revolution neuroscientists and others have fomented in their search for a better understanding of how students learn and hence how they might be better served.

For the moment, however, it is also a revolution, like the revolution in learning technologies, that is longer on promise than on actual adherents. Let me put that differently: it is a revolution that too few in higher education pay sufficient attention to and hence have little appreciation for in terms of exactly what the neuroscientists, in particular, have achieved. On the Spellings Commission, only Jim Duderstadt seemed fully conversant with what, over the last decade, had been learned about how people learn. And though he brought the subject up often enough, he was never able to spark a sustained conversation that might have led the Commission to explore either alternate teaching methods or alternative curricular structures.

There is a larger truth here as well. For as far back as most modern professors can remember, discussions of learning have been the nearly exclusive domain of organizations like the American Association for Higher Education (AAHE) and the American Association of Colleges and Universities (AAC&U), and of think tanks like the Carnegie Foundation for the Advancement of Teaching, over which Lee Schulman presided until recently. Outside these rarified atmospheres, talking about learning has largely been dismissed as a misplaced interest in pedagogy.

The absence of a sustained conversation within the academy about the quality and nature of learning helps explain why so many outside of higher education have been taken with Derek Bok's *Our Underachieving Colleges*. Written four years after *Universities in the Marketplace*, in this volume Bok wanted to provide a candid assessment of undergraduate education today focusing on what students did and did not learn and why. As in my recounting of Bok's discussion of commercialization and its consequences in chapter 4, it is important that I let Bok speak for himself.

Written in the same measured style of his earlier works on higher education, *Our Underachieving Colleges* is a volume with a carefully parsed title—underachieving rather than underperforming—that presents an impressive culling of the evidence telling us what today's undergraduates too often do not learn. The result is a catalog of public as well as educational failures.

> Many seniors graduate without being able to write well enough to satisfy their employers. Many cannot reason clearly or perform competently in analyzing complex, non-technical problems, even though faculties rank critical thinking as the primary goal of a college education. Few undergraduates receiving a degree are able to speak or read a foreign language. Most have never taken a course in quantitative reasoning or acquired the knowledge needed to be a reasonably informed citizen in a democracy. And those are only some of the problems.[1]

Given other, more scandalous and best-selling lamentations on the state of undergraduate education in the United States, Bok himself is quick to point out that his critique is different, more restrained, more about good citizenship and what an undergraduate ought to be prepared to do as opposed to be able to recite. He is all but dismissive of Alan Bloom's *The Closing of the American Mind* while outright rejecting Charles Sykes's *Profscam* and Dinesh D'Sousa's *Illiberal Education*. In *Universities in the Marketplace* Bok positioned his argument between the hard left of the anti-commodifiers and, on the right, the efficiency pundits. In *Our Underachieving Colleges* he positions his argument between the hard right for whom the declining quality of an undergraduate education is evidence of a liberal conspiracy and the jeremiads of lamenters who see in the same declines an absence of will and moral virtue largely without political overtones.

In other important ways, as well, *Our Underachieving Colleges* extends Bok's critique of commercialism in higher education. Recall in that volume the issue was not commercialism per se, but the absence of a set of values capable of monitoring and, when necessary, regulating commercialism's excesses. This same absence of an agreed-upon set of values, this time defining the purposes of an undergraduate education, is putting the nation's colleges and universities at risk. With remarkable adroitness, Bok laments that the American professoriate has left unexamined those value propositions that ought to determine how, what, and why undergraduates learn.

What the faculty have been willing to talk about—sometimes even endlessly—is the organization and structure of the curriculum. How much depth is needed? How much breadth? How much attention should be paid to general education? To what extent should student preferences and choices determine what is required as opposed to merely recommended? It is what faculty love to do—develop plans and strategies that somehow become ends in themselves.

For there to be a revolution in learning, however, the faculty's attention needs to be turned elsewhere. Here Bok gets it right—any process intended to improve collegiate learning must begin with a faculty discussion of purposes that is frank, purposeful, and sustaining. Bok suggested that such a discussion ought not to focus on a "single overriding aim" or take the "narrow view" that limits "the purposes of college to the realm of intellectual development. . . . Instead, colleges should pursue a variety of purposes, including a carefully circumscribed effort to foster generally accepted values and behaviors, such as honesty and racial tolerance."[2] The specific educational purposes Bok advocates include an ability to communicate, a capacity for both critical thinking and moral reasoning, a commitment to citizenship, an understanding of diversity, a similar understanding of the obligations as well as the opportunities present in a global society, and, not least, a practical preparation for work.

Two aspects of Bok's list of preferred purposes deserve special note. First, traditionalists who believe an undergraduate education is first and foremost an introduction to the disciplines, and principally Arts and Science disciplines to boot, will be aghast; for them, Bok's commitment to civic purposes and out-and-out vocational education betrays the academy's true purposes. Bok would, I suppose, grin and let the debate begin.

Second, most of Bok's list of preferred purposes can be said to produce measurable outcomes. While he concedes that "some forms of learning are . . . hard or even impossible to measure, . . . many other important competencies do lend themselves to rough but useable assessments."[3] It is more than possible to test if graduating seniors can communicate and perform quantitative analysis, to learn after they graduate if they have become active and informed citizens, if they are conversant with the complexities of diversity and the demands of a global society, and if they are prepared for work, both in their own eyes and those of their would-be employers. Bok has argued forcefully that there cannot be a standardized, one-size-fits-all set of tests as Charles Miller of the Spellings Commission has proposed; rather, Bok recommends producing measurable outcomes in support of stated purposes, within the realm of not only the possible but also the desirable. To repeat, what is required is a consensus on what ought to be measured—and that means a consensus on purposes.

Once purposes are agreed on, the next big challenge facing those who would make learning matter is getting the professoriate to focus on teaching means and methods—in short, a commitment to take pedagogy out of the closet and make it a subject of academic discourse. Bok himself is too long a university professor and too cagey a winner in the rough and tumble of academic politics not to know that in pushing the importance of pedagogy, he was coming dangerously close to touching a third rail. Why have curricular reviews over the last five decades produced such negligible change and even less improvement? The answer lies in a faculty's "habit of spending almost the entire time discussing which courses should be offered or required while devoting little or no attention to the methods of teaching to be used. This approach is convenient for faculties. It allows them to argue over what every educated person ought to know while avoiding the touchier question of how to teach one's courses, a topic most professors would prefer to keep to themselves, beyond the collective scrutiny of their colleagues."[4]

Bok's interest in pedagogy is unabashed, in no small measure because he knows what has to happen: a sustained commitment to active learning. Remember Bok was a distinguished professor of law and dean of the Harvard Law School before he was the president of Harvard. In *Our Underperforming Colleges* he is the quintessential law professor arguing the importance of dialogue—in modern dress, engaged teaching—as opposed to enshrined lectures and slick presentations. What he wants in the classroom is good old-fashioned talk. It doesn't have to be Socratic in form, but the time spent in class ought to *engage* the learner in the complete sense of that term.

Right Diagnosis—Absent Prescription

Despite the fact that Bok specifically rejects the idea of systematic testing of what college students have learned, his critique of American higher education as a learning enterprise was quickly endorsed by the enterprise's principal lamenters. Here was an authoritative voice—elegant and restrained—saying the same things that critics like Charles Miller, John Merrow, and Richard Hersh were making the cornerstone of their calls for the sustained reform of American higher education. Given this embrace of Bok's critique—an embrace he neither asked for nor probably enjoys—it is important to ask, Is Bok right? Does he know what is wrong? And, more important, does he know how to fix it? My answer is "not exactly," and therein lies the difficulty.

Bok is right to focus on values and purposes. He is also right in his focus on the faculty adopting Pogo's notion that "we have met the enemy, and he is us."

He is right about what students don't learn and can't do. He is right about the faculty's interest in the structure and organization of the curriculum and their downright refusal to make their teaching a collective subject for discussion or improvement. He is right about the need for an explicit discussion resulting in at least a loose consensus on the fundamental purposes of an undergraduate education. And he is right to approach the subject gingerly, recognizing that yet another complaint on the inadequacies of the academy will only result in thicker walls and more calloused minds.

The problem with Bok's argument is that it really doesn't go anywhere. He tells us what is wrong. He tells us what has to happen before there is any noticeable improvement. But he is largely silent on the question of means as opposed to ends. No doubt he will want to argue the contrary and suggest, as most reformers do, that in an enterprise that prizes evidence, clearly, judiciously, and in fact gingerly documenting what is wrong and why with American undergraduate education ought to produce the necessary changes. I also suspect he is not too optimistic on this score; knowing that in offering his critique, he joins a long list of distinguished and some not so distinguished commentators on the condition of undergraduate education in the United States.

Put another way, *Our Underachieving Colleges* makes two fundamental contributions to our understanding of the problem and indirectly forecasts how a useful path forward might look. Bok's first contribution is the more obvious. Because he is who he is, he has made the water safe for others of us who would take up the challenge of reforming undergraduate education. If Derek Bok can write elegantly about the failures of the academy, so too can the rest of us, provided of course that, like Bok, we eschew the voice of the prophet and resist the temptation to add yet another harangue to the funeral pyres we are constructing in our minds.

Bok's second, albeit indirect, contribution to the reform of undergraduate education lies in the limits of his argument (I suppose it is a backhanded compliment, though I don't mean it as such): If we understand why Bok's approach won't result in substantial change, then by subtraction we can learn what needs to be done and why. We must begin with an understanding of how the limits of Bok's argument reflect his own predilections. He is right to be exasperated by the faculty's habit of talking about the structure of the curriculum rather than about either purposes or pedagogics. But he leaves unexamined the larger issues embedded in today's undergraduate curriculum—whether courses and course units ought to provide the basic building blocks of an academic calendar that still focuses on the nine months stretching from mid-September to mid-June. To be fair, the faculty who frustrate Bok are even less willing to consider alternate curricular structures whose adoption would force a wholesale reconsideration of purposes and pedagogies.

If we mean to take up Bok's challenge to remake undergraduate education, then we must be prepared to go further than the master— much further. Though some will want to dismiss what I have in mind as too ludicrous for consideration, I am proposing a reconsideration of all the key elements of an undergraduate education—purposes, pedagogies, structural building blocks, and the role and advantages of electronically mediated instruction. Bok, I think, will settle for more conscientious faculty—scholars who, when faced with the evidence of underachieving colleges and universities, will change their ways. I am just not that optimistic. Reform requires both an internal demand for change within the faculty and a set of dislodging events that together will propel faculties along the path to learning reform.

Bok's diagnoses and prescriptions are further limited by the scholarly literature he draws upon to help document that undergraduate education in the United States is no longer good enough. A significant portion of that literature is based on studies conducted at Harvard, most often by Richard Light of the Kennedy School and Dean Whitla who was responsible for some of the most interesting institutional research coming out of Harvard during Bok's presidency. The more conceptual literature Bok draws upon comes from the three scholars whose work has dominated the study of student development on the collegiate level. Over the last twenty-five years, Ernest Pascarella and Patrick Ternsini's three volumes on how colleges affect students provided much of the conceptual literature for the embrace, first by the AAHE and subsequently by the AACU, of active learning as their reform movement's principal pedagogical thrust. For Bok, active learning's precepts confirmed what the faculty of professional schools had known all along:

> In their view, passive lecturing and drill can help students memorize rules and concepts and apply them to a limited range of problems similar to those covered in class, but they do little to equip undergraduates to apply their knowledge to new problems. Merely inviting students to ask questions or allowing them to carry on a formless discussion among themselves is not much better. Instead, instructors need to create a process of active learning by posing problems, challenging student answers, and encouraging members of the class to apply the information and concepts in assigned readings to a variety of new situations.[5]

The third of this triumvirate of scholars Bok drew upon, though admittedly less directly, was George Kuh, now best known as the founding director of the National Survey of Student Engagement (NSSE). Kuh, like Bok, stresses the importance of faculty responsibility; it is not enough that conscientious, successful teachers take responsibility for what their students learn and how they learn it. Kuh argues that successful teachers also know that student engagement—the penultimate benefit of active, motivated learning that occurs in settings in which faculty and students are partners in learning—is the key to better learning outcomes, the principal quality NSSE is designed to document.

The student development literature that focuses on active learning and the student's personal development is a good literature, though, to paraphrase Cole Porter, it's not the best literature if one is truly interested in fomenting a learning revolution. Pascarella, Ternsini, and Kuh are careful scholars, given to neither overstatement nor hyperbole. They, along with Light, Witla, Peter Ewell, and a host of others, have made important contributions to our understanding of the environments in which students learn best. If, however, one's goal is to establish new settings and new modalities in which student learning and undergraduate education can thrive, then it is the wrong, or at least an incomplete, literature.

An Alternative Literature

What would I have had Bok read instead of or in addition to the student development literature? I would have had him follow Jim Duderstadt's dictum and capture what the neurosciences are discovering about how people learn. On the Spellings Commission, Duderstadt began to sound like a broken record, constantly reminding us that if we are serious about improving student learning, we need to know and then take advantage of a revolution every bit as dramatic and wide ranging as the revolution in electronic technologies. Duderstadt, while a former president, provost, and dean of engineering at the University of Michigan, is a nuclear engineer rather than a neuroscientist. But playing both a leadership and a gadfly role for two decades in the National Academies of Science and their affiliated organizations has made him a prodigious consumer of a wide variety of disciplines, including, it turns out, what neuroscientists have been discovering about the brain's capacity for evolving complex learning strategies.

The place to begin, Duderstadt said when I finally decided to take him seriously, was a National Academy Press 1999 edited volume, *How People Learn: Brain, Mind, Experience, and School* by John D. Bransford, Ann L. Brown, and Rodney R. Cocking on behalf of the Committee on Developments in the Science of Learning of the Commission on Behavioral and Social Sciences and Education of National Research Council. In part, the volume provides a summary of the current research on cognition, learning, development, culture, and the brain that forms the basis for the new learning sciences discipline; and in part, *How People Learn* is a loosely organized prescription for how to apply that research on behalf of improved student learning.

From my perspective, *How People Learn* teaches three basic lessons. First, not only do individual people learn differently, but they also learn different disciplines differently. Second, the meaning of learning itself has changed over the course of the last century. Where once learning meant being literate and numerate, today the generally agreed purpose of education is "to train people to think and read critically, to express themselves clearly and persuasively, to solve complex problems in science and mathematics." These "aspects of high literacy are required of almost everyone in order to successfully negotiate the complexities of contemporary life."[6] Third, from the work of the neuroscientists comes the insight that learning physically changes the brain. In sum, learning is about making connections. Understanding how such connections are made—physiologically as well as metaphorically—becomes a necessary first step in the design of effective learning processes.

The problem remains that, outside the learning disciplines themselves, few faculty know much about what the cognitive scientists and neuroscientists have wrought. Theirs is a technical literature that is largely opaque to all but the previously initiated. But that circumstance is changing. For me personally, the best entry point proved to be a relatively thin but nonetheless remarkable volume by James Zull—*The Art of Changing the Brain, Enriching the Practice of Teaching by Exploring the Biology of Learning*. Zull is a Case Western Reserve University professor of biochemistry and biology who made himself an expert on collegiate teaching strategies. Beyond thirty years of experience introducing premed majors to the mysteries of the biological world, Zull offers three attributes that make his volume a particularly fitting introduction to what the neurosciences have to tell teachers about how to redesign their craft. He has been there and done that. He has an uncanny ability to sort through the neuroscience literature in such a way that what is important is highlighted and explained and the rest left for further pursuit. Third, and perhaps most important, he is a superb storyteller who knows teaching and teachers. Zull's stories never let the reader forget that his purpose is to connect what we now know about how the brain learns and develops with the real problems collegiate teachers encounter every day.

As in the case of my explication of Bok's critique of undergraduate education, I want to let Zull speak for himself. Not only what he says but also how he makes his key points are of particular interest here. I have no doubt—as I suspect Zull has no doubt—that many details he

WERE LEARNING TO MATTER

reports as today's understanding of how the brain learns and develops will undergo substantial revision in the decade ahead. I am also aware that those who are operating on the frontiers of the knowledge explosion that is now consuming the learning sciences see Zull as a popularizer rather than contributor to that revolution. So be it. Zull's volume is important, not for its details but for its capacity to connect with the reality of college teaching today. In doing so, *The Art of Changing the Brain* teaches how the products of the learning sciences—were they actually to become part of a collegiate teacher's toolkit—can provide pathways for not just changing but also in fact fundamentally recasting how American colleges and universities provide an undergraduate education.

The place to begin is with the literalness of Zull's title. Taking his cue from the growing capacity of the neurosciences and their imaging technologies to document how the brain changes physically as it learns, Zull's goal becomes an understanding of the physical properties of learning sufficient to persuade teachers they can be much more proactive in creating the conditions that spur their students' learning. He quite literally means "*creating conditions that lead to change in a learner's brain*. We can't get inside and rewire a brain, but we can arrange things so that it gets rewired. If "we"—and here that we includes all who teach—"are skilled, we can set up conditions that favor this rewiring, and we can create an environment that nurtures it."[7]

To do so, we must understand conceptually the physical processes by which the brain—and hence we—learn. Zull was introduced to the physical nature of learning and its importance to teaching by David Kolb, his colleague at Case Western Reserve University. Among concepts Kolb taught him was the notion that the learning cycle actually mirrors how the brain works: "Kolb began by talking about people I had heard of, but never read before, people like Dewey, Piaget, and Lewin. Combining their ideas about development and learning, he described a new 'learning cycle.' He said deep learning, learning for real comprehension, comes through a sequence of experience, reflection, abstraction, and active testing. These four cycle 'round and round' as we learn."[8] Here it helps to remember that Zull is first and foremost a biologist; therefore, he naturally interpreted Kolb's analysis in biological terms.

> In biology, the way things work depends on their structure—their physical structure. . . . Any function found in any living organism must depend on some structure of some part of that organism. . . .

If the function we are interested in is learning, we should look for the structure that produces it, and the place we should look is in the brain. . . . What I knew about the brain told me that the learning cycle should work, and it told me why. For the first time I saw a structure design for human learning, for understanding, and comprehension.[9]

The Brain Itself

The centrality as well as the physical nature of the learning cycle is Zull's first lesson. His second is that the brain is changed—and remember he means physically changed—by experience. In short, we learn experientially. Neither Zull nor the neuroscience he draws upon is the first to make this argument, but each makes it in a fundamentally different way. Neuroscientists start by focusing on the importance of prior knowledge—that is, the facts and understandings physically stored in the brain's neuronal networks. Zull describes the process: "When we speak of prior knowledge, we are speaking of something physical. It builds as brains physically change, and it is held in place by physical connections. We could say that prior knowledge is a thing!" Hence, the "single most important factor in learning is the existing networks of neurons in the learner's brain. Ascertain what they are and teach accordingly."[10]

In practical terms teachers have to make a substantial effort to know what their students already know—even if, or particularly if, what they know is wrong. Until conditions are created that encourage the student to change what he already knows, he will continue to draw on that information (or misinformation) regardless of how often he is told he is wrong or how authoritative the teacher is in telling him what is right.

Here the key is what Zull (and of course others) calls active as opposed to passive learning. It is the importance of the discovery of— as opposed to the acquisition of already processed—understandings and facts. It is more about self-storage than recall. Bok, in his praise of active learning, makes basically the same points, though he bases his confidence in the superiority of active learning on his and his law school colleagues' use of challenge and dialogue as a principal means of making sure that their students own what they have learned. In Zull's hand, the parallel praise of active learning is based elsewhere:

Any learning that involves some sense of progress and control by the learner might be expected to engage the basal structures.

This would be learning that is pleasurable. On the other hand, learning that involves recall of associations would be more connected with the back part of the cerebral cortex, the receiving part of the brain. . . . Active learning that involves choice and actions for the learner is pleasurable and effective for developing concepts and applications. This type of learning gives an understanding of the big picture and the relationships in a topic.[11]

I quote one more passage from Zull on the importance of active learning. I want to give an example of how he uses what the neurosciences and their capacity to literally watch our brains at work tell us about how and why we should be thinking differently about teaching and learning.

A recent brain imaging study bears out . . . [my descriptions of] the brain and different types of learning. Poldrack and his colleagues found that activation of the basal structures occurred when the learner was engaged in postulating answers and getting feedback on them, an active learning setting. But when the learner was simply asked to memorized associations, the basal structures were less active and the back areas of the cortex near the memory systems were more active.[12]

Zull's discussion of learning styles—now a staple of those who argue that in learning, as in life, there are different strokes for different folks—uses what he has learned from the neurosciences in much the same way. Yes, different people have different learning styles, but an understanding of how and where the brain learns makes clear that different learning styles are a function of how particular students approach the learning cycle. One byproduct of this understanding is a realization that there are in fact a relatively limited number of permutations and hence describing a particular student's learning style can be a relatively straightforward exercise.

The learning cycle gives us an interesting way to think about differences between learners. . . . The cycle is based on two polarities: concrete-abstract and reflective-active. Most people lean toward one side or the other of these polarities. Some enjoy the abstract more than the concrete, and vice versa. Some are more active and others more reflective. If we put this in brain terms, we would say that some people prefer using their sensory brain, some prefer using their integrative back cortex, some prefer using their integrative front cortex, and some prefer using their motor brain. A particular student may like new experience, but find that the quiet of reflection makes him nervous. Another student may be happy reflecting and generating ideas but shy away from actually testing them. Different parts of the cycle seem comfortable to different people. These preferences come from our feelings.[13]

From my perspective, this discussion of learning style makes better sense—it's less mysterious, less idiosyncratic, and holds out the promise that in time individuals will be able to map how they learn.

The Art of Changing the Brain is a dozen chapters chock full of similar insights, but that is only half the story. Zull, in addition to providing a portal into what the neurosciences have to tell us about learning, spends nearly equal time translating those insights into practical lessons for both teachers and learners. Some of his lessons will be readily familiar to those already interested in pedagogy; even then, making how the brain works the basis for their importance makes them more relevant to today's discussions of how the academy ought to recast undergraduate education. Other of Zull's lessons are more unexpected, more directly connected to what the neuroscientists and others have learned about how the brain learns; these lessons are thus fresher and somehow more compelling.

Midway through his volume, Zull pauses to provide ten learning axioms that all who teach would do well to live by.

1. Watch for inherent networks (natural talents) and encourage their practice.
2. Repeat, repeat, repeat!
3. Arrange for "firing together." Associated things should happen together.
4. Focus on sensory input that is "errorless."
5. Don't stress mistakes. Don't reinforce neuronal networks that aren't useful.
6. Try to understand existing networks and build on them. Nothing is new.
7. Misconnected networks are more often just incomplete. Try to add to them.
8. Be careful about resurrecting old networks; error dies hard.
9. Construct metaphors and insist that your students build their own metaphors.
10. Use analogies and similes, too.[14]

Later come additional practical lessons starting with constructing learning sequences that encourage students to use different parts of their brain. Make sure, for example, that some problems involve calculation, while others involve estimation. Why? Because "brain studies show that when we make calculations of exact answers to math problems, we use different parts of the brain than when we try to estimate possible answers."[15] It's just as important not to overload the student's working memory. "A classic error of college teachers is to keep shoving information in one end of working memory, not realizing that they are shoving other data out the other end. . . . Recent research suggests that the more things we have in working memory, the harder it is for us to focus on what is most important."[16]

One of Zull's most engaging lessons centers on the importance of stories—an insight those of us trained as historians have long understood. Zull, however, again puts the case differently. "Stories engage all parts of the brain. They come from our experiences, our memories, our ideas, our actions, and our feelings. They allow us to package events and knowledge in complex neuronal nets, any part of which can trigger all the others."[17] Ever the artful storyteller himself, Zull provides both summation and homily as the conclusion to *The Art of Changing the Brain*: "Our exploration of the biology of learning has reminded us of many things we already knew but has also given us a deeper respect for the learner and the learning process. Repeatedly we have been reminded that it is our physical body and its interactions with the physical world that produce learning, and that reality leaves us with faith that we will eventually understand this mysterious vocation and avocation of teaching."[18]

Institutional and Other Constraints

As his homily suggests, James Zull is, in many ways, remarkably old fashioned. He is a teacher writing to teachers about teaching. It is what happens in the classroom and those spaces where teachers counsel and coach their students that matters. His concern is pedagogy writ large—and decidedly not the structure of the curriculum or the organization of the academic calendar. His task is to give teachers, as individuals, a new set of tools primarily derived from the neurosciences' understanding of how the brain learns; and though what he has in mind is truly breathtaking, he remains content to change teaching one teacher at a time.

The principal lesson embedded in the intermittent pace of higher education reform, however, is that changing one teacher at a time is a strategy that won't work. Too few teachers actually take up the challenge, and, even when they do, they have difficulty sustaining their commitment to do things differently. Inevitably a tendency to regress to a mean brooks only modest change in how the academy discharges its educational responsibilities. Change of the kind that Zull envisions requires, at a minimum, an institutional platform and, to be fully sustainable, ultimately a system platform that somehow changes all or most parts of the enterprise simultaneously.

For nearly a century now, there has been no successful simultaneous systemwide effort to change the environment in which undergraduate students learn, though both the lamenters and their organizations would have it otherwise. Nor have all that many institutions taken up the challenge of changing how faculty teach and hence how their students learn. More often than not, such efforts have been centered in smaller, less prestigious institutions whose efforts, even when successful, have only small ripple effects.

Among major research universities, the most persistent and in many ways the most successful reform institution has been Carnegie Mellon University in Pittsburgh. Spurred on by Richard Cyert, who served nearly two decades as the university's president, Carnegie Mellon embraced technology as well as contrarianism as a means of distinguishing itself from other, better resourced (some would say better located) research universities. Carnegie Mellon has also made conversations about teaching and learning university-wide endeavors. The most immediate results for our purposes here are two sets of principles developed by the Eberly Center for Teaching Excellence and its director Susan Ambrose, who also serves as Carnegie Mellon's associate provost for education. Drafted in the spirit of Nobel Laureate Herbert Simon, who for more than fifty years was an active and bracing member of the Carnegie Mellon faculty, the center's two sets of principles—one focusing on learning, the other on teaching—drew on much of the same literature on which Zull based his stories. As a more formal supplement to Zull, the Carnegie Mellon principles provide a convenient summation of what the learning sciences would have collegiate teachers know and observe.

LEARNING PRINCIPLES

1. Prior knowledge can help or hinder learning.
2. Motivation generates, directs, and sustains learning behavior.
3. The way students organize knowledge determines how they use it.

4. Meaningful engagement is necessary for deeper learning.
5. Mastery involves developing component skills and knowledge, synthesizing, and applying them appropriately.
6. Goal-directed practice and targeted feedback are critical to learning.
7. Students must learn to monitor, evaluate, and adjust their approaches to learning to become self-directed learners.
8. Students develop holistically, and their learning is affected by the social and emotional aspects of the classroom climate.[19]

TEACHING PRINCIPLES

1. Effective teaching involves acquiring relevant knowledge about students and using that knowledge to inform our course design and classroom teaching.
2. Effective teaching involves aligning the three major components of instruction: learning objectives, assessments, and instructional activities.
3. Effective teaching involves articulating explicit expectations regarding learning objectives and policies.
4. Effective teaching involves prioritizing the knowledge and skills we choose to focus on.
5. Effective teaching involves recognizing and overcoming our expert blind spots.
6. Effective teaching involves adopting appropriate teaching roles to support our learning goals.
7. Effective teaching involves progressively refining our courses based on reflection and feedback.[20]

Two lenses are important for understanding the Eberly Center's pronouncements. First, its same link to the learning sciences motivates Zull. Eberly is above all else a theory-based teaching center that expects its staff and ultimately the faculty it serves to know about and take full advantage of what has been learned about cognition, about how the brain learns, and about how students and teachers can use that knowledge to improve their capacities for learning. Second, the Center has an interest in and commitment to electronically mediated learning. Through its partnership with Carnegie Mellon's Office of Technology for Education—led by the university's chief information officer, Joel Smith—the Eberly Center spearheads Carnegie Mellon's growing commitment to the use of electronic technology in the delivery of all forms of instruction.

In 2007, the Eberly Center celebrated its twenty-fifth anniversary, a remarkable longevity for an enterprise that on many campuses is viewed as a temporary accommodation of those who would remake how faculty teach and students learn. Still, the professionals who staff the center face the same daunting task as Zull; their charge is providing support to faculty who want to explore how they might teach differently. The institutional ethos says pedagogy is important, and the Eberly Center is a bona fide Carnegie Mellon-funded and verified agency for helping faculty teach better. But there is no mandate; no set of institutional templates or even guidelines make individual faculty members seek out the kind of support the teaching center provides. On their website, the staff of the center are very clear about what they are expected to provide:

- Individual consultations with faculty and graduate students.
- Resources for faculty, including sample syllabi, model grading rubrics, informational booklets and web-based documents.
- Workshops and seminars for faculty, graduate students, and department heads.
- Collaboration with faculty on educational projects.
- Institutional research that impacts educational practice and policy.

And to prevent anyone from suggesting otherwise, the center makes clear that its "consultations are . . . strictly confidential, documented for faculty and graduate student purposes alone, [and] completely. We do not seek out faculty or graduate students, but we are happy to meet with anyone who contacts us."[21]

They succeed because they are skilled, because their work is rooted within the revolution sparked by the learning sciences (principally researchers working on cognitive science and neuroscience problems), and because Carnegie Mellon faculty are more likely to want to explore how better to teach—that is, the Eberly Center and its partner the Office of Technology for Education enjoy the benefit of a faculty demand as well as a demanding faculty. Still, the center operates in a constrained environment. It is principally reactive and responsive to problems, initiatives, even opportunities, but it operates mostly at the margin. It has no overall design responsibilities—no mandate to assist in the implementation of a top-down strategy of educational change.

At UMR, those constraints do not exist, or rather they exist only as long-established expectations of what a solid undergraduate education should comprise. The campus' principal leaders, Steve Lehmkuhle and

Claudia Neuhauser, were remarkably free to design the kind of learning environment they thought best captured the spirit as well as the innovations promised by the learning sciences. What makes their experiment radical is not its incorporation of computer-based learning technologies—though in fact much of the campus' instruction will be delivered using electronically mediated modalities—but rather its curricular structure and its organization. In Rochester, the three-unit course that meets three times a week is gone. In its place are what Neuhauser labels *modules*—learning sequences of varying lengths, each with its own set of learning objectives and its own strategies for assessing a student's progress on an ongoing basis. Gone too is credit for seat time; in fact, it is not necessary to attend the sessions for any particular module as long as the student can successfully complete the tasks the module is designed to teach.

Just as the faculty at UMR are organized differently, so too is the content that their students are expected to master. The campus's first degree program is a Bachelor of Science in the Health Sciences, which is expected to prepare some students to enter medical school and graduate or PhD programs in the biological sciences and other students to transition into technical programs preparing them to more immediately become health care professionals. Students will be required to take a range of modules in four clusters: quantitative studies, which includes but is not limited to the content traditionally taught in introductory calculus and statistics courses; a physical science cluster, including physics, chemistry, and instrumentation; a life/health sciences cluster, which includes a long list of specialized modules ranging from general biology to biochemistry to anatomy and physiology; and finally a liberal education cluster, which fulfills the university's general education requirement but which in fact is a set of modules that links the insights of the humanities and social sciences to the practical concerns being developed in the curriculum's core science modules. Both Lehmkule and Neuhauser are quick to point out that UMR's clusters are in fact integrated; the clusters compel the students to consider just how much physics today impacts chemistry, how quantitative skills often provide the tools for integration, and how even the liberal arts, when considered in a context of integration, provide tools and conceptual insights as important to scientific inquiry as the theorems and theories of the sciences themselves.

In addition to the content-specific modules, the curriculum disperses the program's students into an impressive range of integrative labs melding concepts and practical experiences, learning communities, internships, capstone projects, electives, and, where applicable, specialized training sequences for students seeking to earn a particular health care certificate. Many of these additional learning environments are being supplied by the campus's local partners, principally the Mayo Clinic.

Much instruction in the modules, as well as the partners' supplemental activities, will be problem based. Assessment will be ongoing, purposely designed to tell both learners how they are doing and the faculty which modules and supplemental activities are working, which need adjustment, and which need to be either abandoned or redesigned.

In a special seminar convened early in the planning for the Bachelor of Science in the Health Sciences, Neuhauser defined the proposed curriculum in terms of the Center for Learning Innovation's vision and mission.

Vision
The Center for Learning Innovation will promote a learner-centered, competency-based learning environment in which ongoing assessment will guide and monitor student learning and will be the basis for data-driven research on learning. It will lead the development of an integrated curriculum for a baccalaureate degree in the health sciences and will serve as a laboratory for learning.

Mission
The mission of the Center is to advance learner-centered, technology-enhanced, competency-based, assessment-driven, and community-integrated education.[22]

Neuhauser's dream is possible because she can recruit the faculty she wants, engage a host of consultants, including Carnegie Mellon's Joel Smith, to help select and design the computer-based learning objects the program requires, and be confident that what she has in mind will be judged by the learning outcomes the program achieves.

A Title Explained

My point is simple. Whether the UMR experiment is successful, it demonstrates what is required: a general lessening of institutional as well as individual constraints and a willingness on the part of faculty to make outcomes the test of the efficacy of the curricula they develop. Were that to happen, the resulting learning environments

would be radically different than classroom environments undergraduates encounter today. Zull could not ask for more; as a matter of fact,
neither could Derek Bok, though he would probably be puzzled if not
outright bothered by the emphasis on computer-mediated learning.

However, the probability that such a transformation will take place
remains at best remote—in part because of the system's inertia, in part
because of the cost inherent in recasting undergraduate education, but
mostly because learning doesn't really matter, not at least as it should.
Hence the subjunctive voice enshrined in the title of this chapter—
Were Learning to Matter.

It is clear, for example, that learning does not matter in the marketplace. I have been tracking the market for undergraduate education for
nearly three decades and have yet to find any evidence that the quality
of learning an institution provides determines it success in the marketplace. Instead, the market favors selectivity, brand names, national visibility, winning sports teams, and, in the case of the nation's medallion
universities, major research portfolios. There simply is no example—
save perhaps Brown University in the 1950s—of an institution that
improved its competitiveness by demonstrating that its students
learned differently. And even the Brown example is a little wistful
because that university demonstrated only that its faculty trusted Brown
students by not loading them down with requirements as they pursued
their baccalaureate degrees.

Hence the appeal of Lloyd Thacker's Educational Conservancy and
its attempt to create a consumer movement that understands and
makes educational values more of a factor in the college choice
process. A successful collegiate consumer movement would be akin to
the consumer movement that changed how Americans buy their automobiles and, in the process, made *Consumer Reports* a national buying
guide. One conclusion, then, is that only if and when educational values become a viable market currency will learning likely matter.

James Zull makes something of the same point, but from a different
perspective—that of a long-time faculty member who has often been
confounded by an environment that talked about learning but placed
its bets elsewhere. As was often the case, Zull used a pair of stories to
express his frustration. In the first he tells of attending a Lilly-sponsored
conference on teaching and learning that included a session on
improving teaching in large classes. Zull was all ears given the number
of large biology classes filled with Case Western's army of premed students that he taught. As it turned out, however, the sessions focused on

something else—on how to avoid making record-keeping mistakes when the class numbered 1,000 students or more. I'll let Zull pick up the story from here.

> Finally, my frustration got the best of me, and I blurted out my question. . . . What is your experience with improving learning in large classes? . . . [The presenter] looked blank for a moment and then replied, "Well this session isn't really about learning; it is more about teaching."
>
> That startled me, but I persisted, "But how can you separate teaching from learning?"
>
> In all sincerity, she replied, "You can teach well, do all the right things, without any learning. Learning is up to the student. If I am teaching right, I am doing my part!"[23]

Without meaning to, I suspect, the presenter in Zull's story illustrates Bok's point that conscientiousness, whether on the part of the instructor or the student, is never going to be enough.

Zull's second story has a more personal, harder edge to it. After thirty-five years in the classroom, he had finally come to understand that, in that space, the drama is about the learner and not the teacher or the subject. He was, he confessed, not alone is coming very late to this fundamental understanding. "Recently one of my more honest colleagues blurted out, . . . 'It is all fine to talk about different students and how we can help them to learn. . . . But the fact is that I hardly ever think of that. I mostly worry that I might make a mistake, or that I might give out wrong information. I don't worry about learning.' "[24]

Steve Lehmkuhle and Claudia Neuhauser understood the moral of Zull's tale long before they read his book. The UMR experiment enshrines each of these lessons. They begin with the presumption that learning has to matter—but just to make sure there is sufficient market demand for the new kind of collegiate education they are promoting, they have made a Bachelor of Science in the Health Sciences their first degree precisely because of the growing demand for graduates and specialists in this field. Beyond that, they have made certain that inertia will play as small a role as possible in the design of their learning-centered curriculum—no departments, no standard templates, and a flexible academic calendar along with a commitment to using what we know about how the brain learns to design effective electronically mediated learning modalities. Lehmkuhle and Neuhauser could do all this, they will tell you, precisely because they began with a nearly blank slate.

The underlying questions thus become, How does one engage the rest of higher education, where the slate is anything but blank? How does one forge an effective antidote to Zull's suspicion that faculty dwell on teaching because they neither understand nor want to take responsibility for their students' learning? Or, to pose the question from Bok's perspective, How do you lead a faculty to focus on the doing as opposed to the scheduling and structuring? Personally, I doubt that either more data or more persuasive advocates are going to matter much. What higher education requires is something that breaks the logjam—a kind of dislodging event (or set of events) that forces American higher education in general and its faculty in particular to break that lifelong habit of focusing on discipline and curricular rules and compels them instead to focus on the matter of learning.

11 | Building Blocks

The Wharton School's Greg Shea has an uncanny ability to get experienced—and sometimes not-so-experienced—executives to understand the perils of misdirected management. In the 1990s he was a mainstay in an executive leadership program for senior higher education leaders and managers offered by the Wharton School and Penn's Institute for Research on Higher Education. With ill-disguised envy, I suspect, I would sit in the back of Shea's classroom and watch him take what should have been a skeptical class of presidents, provosts, deans, and vice presidents and march them through routines whose intent was to "re-wire" how they went about the business of making decisions and allocating resources.

One thing these students remembered most about the experience was confronting what Shea called the "necessity of the don't-do list." Shea's point was simple. Too often, inexperienced managers construct endless lists of things that need to be done, though many eventually prove to be only tangential concerns. This problem could be solved, he would get each group to understand, if managers would spend as much time deciding what not to do as they spend deciding what to do. It was a lesson he meant literally; he drove home the point by having the students construct don't-do lists to accompany their to-do lists. For the students—who remember were, in real life, senior college and university leaders—deciding what not to do and why became an essential first step in the building of a focused strategic plan.

Extending Shea's Dictum

Although offered as a lesson in the practical management of an enterprise, Shea's dictum can be applied equally to the task of specifying a reform agenda for higher education. Too often, calls for change begin with a nearly exhaustive list of the problems and challenges facing the enterprise, followed by an even longer list of the steps that need to be taken in response to those ills so carefully catalogued. The report of the Spellings Commission is as good an example as any of what happens when no problem or challenge is considered too small or too tangential to be included in the list of things that must be done. The result is an agenda that overwhelms precisely because it has failed to discriminate.

I am now ready—no doubt more than one reader will say, It's about time!—to specify the issues and challenges I think American higher education needs to address during the next decade. But remembering what Greg Shea taught me, I need to begin with a don't-do list. All the items on this list are, in one sense or another, important. Two have been included because, for the moment at least, no practical solution is at hand and to pretend otherwise would be to waste time and energy. One represents a kind of third rail that trying to change becomes not just quixotic but outright dangerous. The last item, for all its importance to the nation, belongs on a different to-do list, one more focused on higher education's research as opposed to its educational mission. Here, then, is my don't-do list.

Don't Try to Reform the
NCAA's Big Money Sports

In the realm of higher education reform, intercollegiate athletics is the one that got away—permanently. Derek Bok is right when he laments that it's already too late to reverse the tide of athletic commercialism. The sums are too large, the constituencies too powerful, the absence of agreed-upon purposes all too readily apparent.

Is reform necessary?—yes. Is it possible—no, just ask the Knight Commission on Intercollegiate Athletics. Ten years after their initial report, the distinguished panel that composed the commission was painfully blunt in assessing the Commission's lack of success.

> The bad news is hard to miss. The truth is manifested regularly in a cascade of scandalous acts that, against a backdrop of institutional complicity and capitulation, threaten the health of

American higher education. The good name of the nation's academic enterprise is even more threatened today than it was when the Knight Commission published its first report a decade ago. Despite progress in some areas, new problems have arisen, and the condition of big-time college sports has deteriorated.[1]

Big-time football and basketball will not likely change any time soon—witness current discussions as to whether athletes in these money sports deserve to be paid given the substantial funds the sponsoring universities derive from their athletic prowess. The best higher education can hope for is that eventually universities will cut loose their programs in football and basketball, making the university a sponsor rather than an owner of the enterprise.

Don't Tackle Tenure

For much the same reason, though the issues are fundamentally different, higher education's reform agenda should not tackle the issue of tenure. The circumstances of academic tenure have changed and will likely continue to change, perhaps even dramatically. Among university and college staff members who are fully academically qualified—which usually means an individual with an earned doctorate or a corresponding terminal degree—the proportion either with tenure or serving a tenure probationary period has been declining steadily over the last three decades. In many large research universities, the proportion of academically qualified faculty not on the tenure track now exceeds the proportion of academically qualified faculty who are eligible for tenure.

So what is tenure's future? The easy answer is that there will be more of the same—a decrease in the proportion of academically trained personnel who either enjoy or are eligible for tenure, adjustments to the tenure clock to accommodate the growing prevalence of two-career academic families, and continued fussing about how to keep older faculty, in particular, productive and accountable. Nothing on the horizon suggests these trends will either abate or be reversed.

Here the wild card is the fact that too many of the academy's critics, internal as well as external, cannot leave the question of tenure. To the populists among them, tenure is synonymous with elitism and privilege. To the efficiency pundits, tenure is a way of ensuring that a faculty member never has to work too hard. To others, tenure is the stone wall against which every attempt at curricular reform ultimately crashes.

A second wild card capable of altering tenure's future is the possibility of a public outcry on the part of those who have never liked tenure. Why, they will ask, should the academy be exempt from the discipline of the labor market? Were there to be a perfect storm—a perception of out-of-control costs, a sense of students not being served, and a steady stream of arrogant pronouncements by faculty spokesmen to the effect that the academy is different and hence exempt from public scrutiny—the result could be a state in which the legislature abolishes tenure in a fit of spite. However undesirable or, from the academy's point of view, irrational such a political coup de grace would be, it is not beyond the realm of possibility. Could there be a successful battle to do away with or limit the privileges of tenure? The answer is probably yes, but it would be a Pyrrhic victory followed by a decade or more of campus turmoil. Higher education would not be transformed, but stalled, consumed by an angry battle that would employ symbols, not actual change.

There is a second reason for not tackling the question of tenure now. The spread of for-profit higher education and its very different ways of employing instructional staff suggest that the labor market itself could be an agent of change. Here the model is the University of Phoenix, a business that has proved remarkably resilient despite the disdain of traditional academics. It is important to remember that the University of Phoenix has academic employees rather than faculty. Those who teach for the University of Phoenix or one of its principal competitors or imitators are not independent contractors, let alone tenure-eligible faculty. They do not own their own courses. They are not the final arbitrators of either what or how they teach. The academic staffs of the University of Phoenix and similar institutions are contingent workers in both the best and most restrictive sense of that term. They are well rewarded but only as long as what they have to offer in terms of both teaching content and style is valued in the marketplace. The University of Phoenix is not interested in supporting either subjects or individuals whose efforts do not tap an ongoing revenue stream.

Few doubt that this labor model will continue to spread—first through the growth of for-profit entities and eventually by spreading to nonprofit institutions, particularly those serving adult and part-time student markets. Already most of these institutions—principally community colleges, less selective liberal arts colleges, and state comprehensive universities—employ large numbers of adjunct faculty, many of whom work simultaneously for more than one institution. Today they are the academy's gypsies—poorly paid, ordinarily without benefits, often without offices, and almost always without standing in the institutions they serve. The University of Phoenix treats its contingent workforce much better. Were a University of Phoenix-like contingent-labor model to spread, the working conditions for the professionals who serve these markets might actually improve in the sense they would likely be treated as contingent professionals rather than academic gypsies. But that improvement would depend on the institutions that employ them, like the University of Phoenix, abandoning the distinction between "regular" and "adjunct" faculty; instead, the institutions would treat everyone as a part of a contingent academic labor force.

Don't Try to Reform Accreditation

The more external the critic, the more likely he or she will turn to accreditation as a means of reforming individual colleges and universities. To the uninitiated, the accrediting agencies, particularly those responsible for accrediting institutions offering the baccalaureate degree, have (or should have) the power to change both how and what institutions teach. The reason accreditation has not been an agent of enforceable reform, these critics argue, is that there is an all-too-cozy relationship between the accreditors and the institutions they accredit. In support of their argument, they often point out how often the officials of the accrediting agencies and the experts they place on their accreditation teams are drawn from the ranks of established colleges and universities.

Right question, wrong answer. Accreditation has not been an agent of enforceable reform because the accreditation industry is itself a hopeless mess: six different regional accrediting agencies are responsible for undergraduate and graduate education plus two dozen separate, more professional accrediting agencies each jealously protecting its own turf and prerogatives. Although the regional accrediting agencies share insights and occasionally personnel, there is both no common methodology and an irritating tendency to abruptly change how they monitor both themselves and the institutions for which they are responsible.

To make accreditation an agent of national reform would require a major, probably exhaustive campaign to make the accrediting agencies much more like one agency in their ability to gauge the quality of education an institution provides. Testing regimes would have to be agreed upon, as would common definitions of the educational outcomes that accredited institutions are expected to supply—in short, an agreed-upon set of national standards.

To make such an accrediting system work on a national scale, there would have to be a fundamentally different methodology. The United Kingdom and Australia have both experimented with what they call "quality audits." The Australian Universities Quality Agency (AUQA) defines a quality audit as a "systematic and independent examination to determine whether activities and related results comply with planned arrangements and whether these arrangements are implemented effectively and are suitable to achieve objectives."[2] Though the language suggests something like a financial audit, even in this national agency independently charted by the Australian federal government, the quality process involves very little statistical data testifying to the learning outcomes achieved by the audited institutions. Were there in fact data that could be audited, the result would be more like what the reformers have in mind when they link testing and accreditation.

Perhaps the largest problem is that almost no one outside and very few inside the academy either care about or are familiar with how institutions are accredited. Parents and students simply assume the institutions in which they are interested are accredited because they are. Most accrediting reports are not made public, but then again, it is doubtful that higher education's consumers would know how to interpret what are almost always highly nuanced and somewhat opaque essays. The exceptions to this rule are the agencies that accredit professional programs. Not to be accredited by the Association to Advance Collegiate Schools of Business (AACSB), for example, is to be at a significant disadvantage in the market for an MBA education. AACSB sets high standards, mostly reflecting the resources an institution invests in its MBA program. Once accredited, however, and despite a regular review cycle, there is not much mystery surrounding a particular program's accreditation reaffirmation.

Tackling these issues would be a Herculean task promising at best uncertain results. One painful lesson Margaret Spellings learned when she tried to transform the regional accrediting bodies into federal enforcement agencies was just how unpopular that idea was. While the hue and cry was less than what would have been a parallel plan to make the NCAA a federal enforcement agency, the effort taught the same lesson. Some opportunities were lost long ago.

Leave Investments in Research
Infrastructure to Others

One of the most important but worst-named federal reports of the past twenty years was *Rising Above the Gathering Storm: Energizing and Employing America for a Brighter Economic Future*, completed by the National Academy of Sciences' Committee on Science, Engineering, and Public Policy. The report begins with an embrace of Friedman's *The World Is Flat*, moves to a discussion of other models of crisis identification, and concludes:

> Our crisis is not the result of a one-dimensional change; it is more than a simple increase in water temperature. And we have no single awakening event, such as Sputnik. The United States is instead facing problems that are developing slowly but surely, each like a tile in a mosaic. None by itself seems sufficient to provoke action. But the collection of problems reveals a disturbing picture—a recurring pattern of abundant short-term thinking and insufficient long-term investment. Our collective reaction thus far seems to presuppose that the citizens of the United States and their children are entitled to a better quality of life than others, and that all Americans need do is circle the wagons to defend that entitlement. Such a presupposition does not reflect reality and neither recognizes the dangers nor seizes the opportunities of current circumstances. Furthermore, it won't work.[3]

Rising Above the Gathering Storm is comprehensive and, like too many such efforts, has a little bit of something for everyone, but its central thrust is nonetheless true to its central intent. The federal government, in particular, must substantially increase its investment in basic research in the physical sciences, mathematics, and engineering.

The report also talks about the need to make sustained investments in the teaching of the STEM disciplines. Any higher education agenda needs to address that particular need, but one focusing on the general transformation of the enterprise need not—indeed, should not—invest any of its fire power in promoting support of an agenda for basic research. While many who champion this cause will be academics located at the nation's best and richest institutions, their advocacy is necessarily focused on research and not on the general condition of higher education institutions across the United States. No doubt increased expenditures on basic science research will trickle down to the rest of higher education, if only because America's top research universities train the bulk of college and university faculty. But let me note—maybe even shout—that transforming American higher education and revitalizing the nation's capacity for basic research in the physical and related sciences are separate agendas and should remain so.

Building the To-Do List

Most campaigns to transform American higher education have, in the end, proved inclusive to the point of becoming porous. Having launched their critiques, most reformers keep adding details and inevitably new, often tangential issues to an already overcrowded agenda. Moreover, the reformers tend not to waste too much time specifying exactly what has to be changed. At the outset declaring that some issues are "off the table" helps, but that strategy does not guarantee sufficient discipline and focus. Some of us engage in the sticky business of recommending how others ought to transform what they do, and these suggestions should consider philosopher Georges Bernanos's warning: the worst, most corrupting lies are problems poorly stated.

I have now reached the point at which I need to specify the issues, challenges, and problems that belong on that agenda. I will do so with as much specificity and precision as I can muster. In chapter 12 I will tackle the question of strategy—that is, how exactly one ought to go about engendering dramatic changes in an enterprise that has changed for the most part so slowly that the resulting alterations appear largely inconsequential; then I will sketch the agenda I promised so many pages ago.

Learning

It's not something the academy is comfortable talking about and certainly not something it is acting upon—but learning really does belong at the top of any higher education agenda for a variety of reasons. In the first place, learning is the academy's core business, and it has been for a long time, indeed, for something like a thousand years. I have quoted elsewhere, and gladly do so again here, Stanley Chodorow's observation that higher education's business proposition then as now was about access to knowledge and expertise.

> Where there were flocks of students, there was money to be made in teaching. Teaching masters soon came to Paris to take advantage of the opportunity that Peter Abelard and a few others had created. By the middle of the twelfth century, there were dozens of

teachers and thousands of students, and, by the 1180s, it appears, the teaching masters there had formed the guild—the universitas—that would be the seed of the modern university.[4]

The same idea is contained in the title to Martin Meyerson's essays on the history of the University of Pennsylvania, *Gladly Learn and Gladly Teach.*

It's what we do! For all the importance attached to research and service, most faculty spend most of their time teaching or preparing to teach or learning new things to teach to their students. What this teaching intends is learning, on the part of students as well as faculty. But there is a growing suspicion—and in some quarters an already angry conviction—that all is not well with the learning enterprise. Some worry that students today are not learning enough or not learning the right things or not proving capable of applying learning's lessons to new problems and tasks. Underlying these doubts is the worry that today's faculty—that is, us—do not know how to teach or teach so badly that it is inevitable our students learn so little. Derek Bok tapped into this largely undigested glob of worries, suspicions, and doubts in *Our Underachieving Colleges.*

When discussions of learning do take place, they most often focus on just a pair of issues. First, has the form of what is to be learned and hence taught changed? Those who argue that is exactly what has happened point out that successful learning today is less about the static acquisition of knowledge and more about the dynamic mastering of the skills needed to acquire and use knowledge. Where once the successful college student could be thought of in encyclopedic terms—all the facts, formulas, and theories neatly organized for quick and reliable retrieval—a segment of the academy today argues that the successful college student is much more a clever librarian—that is, someone who knows how to ask the right questions and to recognize good answers. This reformulation of knowledge, they say, is the practical recognition that no one has sufficient time or gray matter to master a knowledge base that is growing exponentially every decade or so.

Discussions of the changing nature of knowledge often morph into what a successful learning outcome would be if detailed content were actually becoming less important than a well-executed learning process. The former is static; the latter is dynamic in the sense that learning processes change as the learner seeks new knowledge and tackles new problems.

My guess is that most faculty at most institutions would not know, if asked, what exactly is expected of them when critiques and pundits push the importance of critical thinking, analytic reasoning, and problem solving. Doesn't the traditional physics course with its lectures, labs, and discussion sections, along with its focus on mastering the three laws of thermodynamics, teach critical thinking, analytic reasoning, and, above all, problem solving focused on what physics itself is all about? Doesn't calculus or history or English or sociology or economics do just that—teach the basics of a specific discipline? Isn't that what's really important—not some kind of pop sociology or physics for poets or English literature for accountants?

This line of reasoning (or strategy of counterattack) leads almost inevitably to a second problem nascent in discussions of collegiate learning. How is anybody to know exactly what the student is either learning or actually preparing to do? Those who champion older, more content-centered and fact-specific definitions of learning have a simple answer—test the student, often and rigorously. Recognize that the testing regime is itself a learning process; students learn what they don't know and proceed, if sufficiently prepared and motivated, to learn it so that they can do better on the next test.

Experts in the process of learning just shake their heads. They talk about the silliness of rote learning and how this static definition of learning leads inexorably to teachers teaching to the test. Many of them doubt whether the tests themselves can ever prove to be productive learning experiences. For example, coaching that includes mastering test-taking strategies can greatly improve a student's score on the SAT/ACT and the more general sections of the GRE; however, it is not at all clear whether those improved scores also signal any improved capacity to learn—either the static knowledge advocated by the traditionalists or the learning processes (for example, creative thinking) championed by their opposite numbers.

Were discussions of this sort—even arguments between the sides—ever to become a dominant feature of the modern academy, both sides would quickly discover that they too have wandered into a linguistic cul-de-sac in as much as both would want to cite evidence that their concepts and methods of teaching and learning produce superior results. And there's the rub—there is simply not nearly enough (I am almost tempted to write *no*) data telling us how or what today's college students are learning. It is hard to understand, but it is nonetheless the case: the discussion of learning outcomes so popular today have proceeded without any agreed-upon means of either defining or testing for a learning outcome. Some would argue the absence of testable learning outcomes manifests the academy's reluctance to face the fact that today's students are not learning enough of what they ought to be learning (whatever that happens to be). The absence of adequately defined testable learning outcomes reflects the fact that getting a good answer to the question has to date not proved very important. The United States continues to invest vast sums of money in an enterprise whose most tangible outcomes are only tangentially related to learning. Were this country—or any country—to decide it was important to rethink those investments, I think the academy would suddenly get very good at evaluating which teaching and learning modalities were the best. The question then becomes how best to create those conditions.

If Duderstadt and Zull, along with the good folks at Carnegie Mellon and the University of Minnesota, Rochester and the growing army of neuroscientists in the process of revolutionizing our understanding of how the brain physically learns prove to be right, then the debate about learning I have just outlined will be swept away. Chicken Little learned a long time ago just how foolish it is to predict the end of one world or the beginning of another. Underlying those predictions too often are false signs, badly interpreted omens, and underestimates of the staying power of the status quo. But every once in a while education's prophets prove prescient. Is this one of those times? I don't know, but in contemplating how to recast collegiate learning, it seems prudent to keep in mind that we may all be learning differently in the decades ahead.

Attainment

The numbers tell the story. For the first time in history, the 2000 decennial census reported that most Americans twenty-five years or older had at least some college education. A quarter of the population had earned a baccalaureate degree, and nearly one in ten Americans twenty-five years or older had an advanced degree. In the decade following the 1990 decennial census, the United States had increased its stock of college-educated residents by more than 12 million baccalaureate degree holders—the vast majority of whom had proceeded directly from high school to college.

And yet, despite this substantial growth in the number of college-educated Americans, the United States had actually slipped—some would say slipped badly—in those international comparisons that have become the metrics of globalization. *Measuring Up 2006* framed much of its critique of American higher education that year by focusing on how current and future economic competitors of the United States had caught up and then surpassed the United States in terms of educational attainment. For older adults aged thirty-five to sixty-four, the United States still placed second among the twenty-four developed countries ranked by the Organisation of Economic Co-operation and Development (OECD) using 2003 data. Canada ranked first, with 41 percent of its population having an associate degree (or equivalent) or higher. In the United States, 39 percent of older adults reported having an associate degree or higher. By 2003, however, the United States had slipped to seventh place among developed countries in terms of the proportion of young people aged twenty-five to thirty-four with a college degree—just 39 percent. In Canada and Japan, more than half (53 and 52 percent, respectively) of that age group reported having earned at least a two-year college degree. Ahead of the United States were Korea, Finland, Norway, Sweden, and Belgium.

The most devastating number in *Measuring Up 2006* documented the productivity of the higher education system in terms of completed degrees per 100 students enrolled. Here the United States ranked sixteenth with a productivity index that was 40 percent below that of Japan. Unless one is prepared to argue that the American system of higher education is principally designed to provide spot skill courses to working adults, the ratio reported by the OECD indicates just how rapidly the American system of higher education is slipping behind the higher education systems of its principal economic competitors—at least in terms of its ability to have those who start pursuing a college degree finish the course.

College completion rates have come to play an increasing role in judging the efficiency of both individual institutions and the American system of higher education writ large. The fact that so many start and then do not finish a degree, either a two- or a four-year degree, is taken as a measure of the system's inefficiency and hence its capacity to waste resources: the student's time, energy, and money; the institution's manpower; and the funding agencies' direct and indirect appropriations. Efficiency pundits write and talk eloquently about the dropout problem and the toll it takes on institutional budgets and state subsidies. From these lamentations it is easy to draw the conclusion that if fewer students dropped out, or better yet, had those students most likely to drop out never started, then the overall cost of the system would be substantially reduced—though how that reduction would be translated into leaner institutional budgets is never made clear.

The flip side of high-attrition and hence low-attainment rates is remediation. Traditionally remediation has been narrowly defined as noncredit, pre-collegiate courses principally in math and composition. Most institutions use a combination of high school grades in specified courses plus a student's SAT or ACT score to determine whether that student is exempt from taking the placement exams that, upon entrance, determine which students need to be tested in either math, composition, or both. The actual number of students requiring remediation is a function of how high the institution sets the bar—either in terms of who is exempt from taking the placement exams or what constitutes a passing grade for those exams.

Remediation and developmental education programs are often described as the pathway by which students without the full panoply of required academic skills can gain access to a baccalaureate degree. For nearly all community colleges, remediation and developmental education form a core responsibility. Based on the Learning Alliance's Pennsylvania study and Dave Veazey's study of the alignment between high school curricula and the California State University requirements, my best estimate is that between 50 and 70 percent of entering community college students require some remediation—as much as four courses over their first two semesters, although the average is more likely between two and three courses in their first year. In the California State University system, the proportion of first-time enrollees requiring remediation ranges upward from one-third to one-half of each entering cohort. Middle-market institutions also regularly teach a limited set of remedial courses in composition and pre-collegiate math. Perhaps as many as one in six first-year students in these middle-market institutions enroll in one or two remedial courses in their first semester. Medallion and name-brand institutions, however, have little interest in offering remediation and only then in conjunction with programs designed to support students admitted under special circumstances. Many do not even test their freshmen, using instead SAT or ACT scores and As or Bs in high school math and English courses to establish basic proficiency.

What gives the discussion of attrition and remediation its edge is not the sense of wasted resources, though they are substantial, but the fact that who succeeds in college—that is, who attains a college degree—remains too much a function of the ethnicity and socioeconomic status of the student. Here, again, the numbers tell the unhappy story.

Among white students who enrolled in a four-year private college and university in 2000, two-thirds had earned a baccalaureate degree six years later. Among Hispanic students enrolling for the first time in 2000 in a private college or university, 59 percent had earned a baccalaureate degree six years later. The comparable number for black non-Hispanic students in private colleges and universities was 45.9 percent six years after initial matriculation. In comparative terms, the non-completion rate for black non-Hispanic students in these institutions was 60 percent higher than that of their white counterparts.

There was a comparable gap for students attending a public four-year college or university. Among white students entering in 2000, 57.1 percent graduated in six years; 48 percent of Hispanic students graduated in six years; and 40.8 percent of black non-Hispanic students graduated in six years. Students attending public, two-year institutions were dramatically less likely to achieve an associate degree or its equivalent—and here, too, the student's ethnicity was a major predictor of attainment. One-fourth of the white students in these institutions had earned an associate degree three years after enrolling, but only 17.9 percent of Hispanic students and 15.2 percent of black non-Hispanic students had similarly earned their associate degree in the same length of time.

Many of the strongest advocates for underrepresented and disadvantaged populations see in these numbers proof positive that affirmative action, whatever its political risks, is necessary to produce equal access to educational opportunity. From their perspective, too many people of color have been denied meaningful educational access. It is hard to argue that American higher education is in fact colorblind—the numbers tell a fundamentally different story. Affirmative action, however, even when it is accompanied by student support services, has not solved the problem despite the historical persuasiveness of its rationale. More recently, affirmative action has become a political minefield. Only among the nation's most prestigious and selective institutions, where the losses are beginning to exceed the wins, does the push for affirmative action have significant traction. Given that the hallmark of a medallion college or university—in addition to its high price tag—is a six-year graduation rate of 85 percent or more, these institutions are also aggressive recruiters in search of students of color who will succeed academically once on campus.

Those who believe educational attainment is principally a function of economic status use these same numbers to bolster their case for increased student aid in general and more money for Pell Grants in particular. A college education's ever-increasing sticker price in itself actually discourages young people with limited means from thinking that a college degree is for them. The method of payment compounds the problem. For young people of limited means, borrowed money is not an investment but a harrowing burden to be avoided at all costs. As student debts rise, the inevitable result is a more immediate search for additional employment that first saps educational energies and then ultimately leads to dropping out of college altogether. The answer: put more public money in the pipeline, and the result will be more graduates.

This argument, for me at least, no longer holds water. I really do believe that the number of young Americans who are being shut out of higher education because the price is too high or the loans too great is, as the Learning Alliance's Pennsylvania study documented, about 8 percent of the population of college high school graduates. Though that number is troublesome, it is dwarfed by the number of those not prepared for college. Because of the ready availability of student aid funds, many of these young people start college only to find themselves overwhelmed by what is being demanded of them academically. The growing number of students in remedial programs is but one measure of the problem's magnitude.

To put the matter more directly, even bluntly, the higher education attainment gap is in fact a preparation gap. For the next decade or more, the battle to make a college education equally attainable must necessarily be waged in the nation's middle and secondary schools. The fact that those schools have become more ethnically and economically segregated over the last decade makes the struggle that much more difficult as well as important. To make this argument is not to say that race and wealth don't matter in twenty-first century America; rather, they matter most where basic skills are acquired as well as the appetite and motivation for further learning.

Focusing on preparation rather than access per se helps explain why neither federal nor state programs of student aid have closed the attainment gap. More money for student financial aid is not required, but heftier appropriations designed to improve middle and secondary schools are necessary, along with more uniform access to the kinds of low-risk educational alternatives represented by community colleges.

Advocates for the nation's underrepresented populations do not like this conclusion, in part because it seems to let the nation's colleges and universities off the hook. Hardly. Higher education bears significant responsibility for the state of America's middle and secondary schools. Higher education sets the standards, trains the teachers, and determines how K-12 education aligns with postsecondary education. Given that perspective, improving access and attainment is everyone's responsibility. Charlie Reed, chancellor of the California State University (CSU), knows that and has committed his twenty-three campuses to building, sustaining, and mutually reinforcing partnerships with their feeder high schools. The goal is to cut in half the proportion of first-time freshmen entering CSU who fail one or more placement exams while at the same time increasing the number of high school students who are prepared to succeed in higher education.

Money

No one should take my argument that improving the rates at which disadvantaged Americans attain a higher education depends more on increasing the supply of college-ready high school graduates than it does on increasing the supply of federal or state student financial aid to mean that money doesn't matter—or that money matters less—in higher education. In truth, a money crisis now most threatens the continued success of the American system of higher education.

Higher education lobbyists, along with the organizations that employ them, are fierce in their advocacy of more money for higher education—more money for student aid, more money for research, more money for capital projects, more money for operations—or simply more money. They point out, quite rightly, that the public subsidy of higher education on a per-student basis has been declining; some would add precipitously. Here the problem is one of setting the standard. Should the norm be the 1950s, when fewer than one in ten Americans achieved a college degree? Or should the norm be the 1980s following the great expansion of public systems of higher education and the introduction of state scholarship programs to support students attending private as well as public colleges and universities? Or should the norm be the late 1990s after most state legislatures had figured out that public treasuries did not have the resources—nor, given the growing anti-tax mood of the voting public, would ever again have sufficient resources—to provide a fully subsidized college education to all or even most of its citizens? Europe and a host of developed Asian countries are grappling now with this issue; there are not sufficient funds to pay for the massification of higher education. Ultimately students and their families have to pay an ever-increasing share of the cost of their higher education.

Had I been writing in the first years of this millennium, I would no doubt have argued that, through trial and error, American colleges and universities, along with the public officials responsible for federal and state higher education policy, had evolved a financial system that, while appearing awkward and at times counterintuitive, nonetheless provided a stable financial environment for the nation's colleges and universities. The basic principle was one of shared responsibility. Everybody paid something—everybody was entitled to some help if they could not afford the market prices colleges and universities had begun charging. State government provided direct appropriations to their public systems of higher education. Local governments, often-times in partnership with their state governments, provided base funding for community colleges and, in some states, postsecondary technical colleges. The federal government provided the necessary capital, grants plus loans, that ensured a smoothly functioning market for high-er education. At the same time, the federal government underwrote most costs associated with high-end science principally by funding and managing a competitive market for sponsored research. Most col-leges and universities—but increasingly not all providers of postsec-ondary education—remained eleemosynary institutions entitled to a host of benefits as tax-exempt institutions. Their real property was exempt from local and state taxes, as were the revenues they earned by providing educational and research services and the returns they earned on their endowments. Gifts to colleges and universities similarly provided tax benefits to donors.

Students paid their share of their college costs in a variety of ways. Many worked, both on and off campus. Most borrowed, most often at advantageous rates underwritten by public guarantees and subsidies. No one was expected to borrow more than the earning premium a par-ticular degree was expected to provide. Parents were similarly expected to borrow to help underwrite the cost of their children's college educa-tions. Some, but certainly not all, of the capital underwriting these loans was provided by the federal government, again at advantageous rates. Whether this mixed pattern of self-help, public subsidies, sav-ings, and family and student debt was fair or equitable is the subject of contentious argument. This much, however, is clear: the set of financial arrangements and responsibilities that evolved over the last several decades helped make possible an extraordinary expansion of the market for higher education. I repeat two earlier observations: The market for post-secondary education in the United States more than quadrupled between 1950 and 2000; at the same time, regardless of the price or cost, American families, when choosing a college, consistently shopped up, that is, chose the more costly options available to them.

That was then, and this is now. The arrangements that once appeared settled have suddenly been called into question by a string of unexpected events and miscalculations that have left everyone a lot less certain of how to finance the nation's higher education system. First, the underlying assumption that a college education was in fact a good economic investment came under inadvertent attack. Students and their families had assumed that tuition was more than worth the loans they had taken out to meet the costs of a college education. In late 2007, Harvard University's new president, Drew Faust, announced a major change in the price of a Harvard undergraduate education. Starting with the class matriculating in the fall of 2008, students from families with incomes of less than $180,000 would pay a maximum of 10 percent of that income annually to attend Harvard. It was breathtaking—suddenly "ability to pay" and not the market would determine the price of a Harvard education for middle-class families. For families with greater incomes, the old rules would apply.

The announcement created havoc in the market. No institution save Harvard and a dozen other medallion colleges and universities had the endowment to match Harvard's largesse. Cynics, and I was certainly among them, began asking what Harvard was really up to. It had no shortage of students, no evidence that its outsized price was discouraging middle-class students from either applying or attending. Rather, Harvard had other problems—political problems occasioned by the sheer size of its endowment, $35 billion in 2007, and the fact that its success in the market was annually yielding double-digit increases in value. What exactly was the endowment's purpose? Was it to offset educational and scholarly costs? Guarantee the university's educational quality for an indefinite future? Or had the Harvard endowment morphed into a tax-free hedge fund whose principal purpose was to make money with money?

Suddenly, colleges and universities of every stripe were being asked about the Harvard initiative. Would they give similar price breaks to middle-class families? Couldn't they use their endowment returns to provide more scholarship aid to needy students—never mind that almost no one had an endowment that came close to matching Harvard's. That year's meeting of the Council of Independent Colleges (CIC) devoted a special session to the Harvard initiative, though none of the institutions in attendance, almost exclusively small liberal arts colleges, competed head-to-head either with Harvard or its medallion counterparts for students. All the key issues were raised. Hadn't Harvard's initiative made it difficult, maybe even impossible, to ask middle-class families to take out loans to fund their children's college educations? Wouldn't the Harvard initiative spark a more virulent private-public battle for students in which small, often nonselective private institutions would be squeezed out, caught between the entitlements being offered by the rich institutions and the public subsidies enjoyed by public universities? Jack Maguire, among the nation's best-known admissions and financial aid consultants, joined in the discussion by predicting that the Harvard initiative could well lead medallion institutions to raise their tuitions and ratchet up the price competition in a way that could "snowball out of control." Then the result would be an intensifying competition for top faculty members or, as Maguire neatly put it, "Each of us is likely to see the best faculty migrating to the billion-dollar club."[5]

The second dislodging event that winter was the continued ripening of the payola scandal involving loan companies and collegiate financial aid officers, more institutions and more questionable practices. It was becoming embarrassingly clear just how much loose money was involved in higher education's various financing schemes. A loan game about big money was clearly out of control. Congress quickly moved to reduce the subsidies being paid to banks and other loan originators participating in the federal government's student aid programs. The banks reacted by threatening to abandon the student loan market in favor of more profitable pursuits.

The third event in this tale of woe was the collapse of a housing market too dependent on the continued availability of sub-prime loans. Overnight, or so it seemed, a family's net worth was in freefall. The equity vested in the family's home would no longer be sufficient to support borrowing for a child's college education. Actually, the sub-prime crisis had a much more immediate and potentially disastrous effect on a higher educational financial system that was beginning to look a lot like a house of cards. Everyone began wondering if the banks would still be in the educational loan business, given the new rules limiting subsidies and the general contraction of credit markets. Some major lenders did announce their intention to withdraw from the market; others suggested they would become a lot more choosy about whom they lent money to and indicated that henceforth they would be more attuned to the risk associated with lending to community college students and those attending four-year institutions with low graduation rates. At the same time, a spreading recession dampened the prospect of more money from state appropriations along with the prospect that the states hardest hit by the recession were likely to further reduce their support for higher education.

Like most crises—and kidney stones—this too will pass eventually. As I write in the fall of 2008, the student loan market has stabilized, most big student lenders have continued to make loans available, and the federal government has assumed the role of a lender of last resort. But for one brief, tantalizing moment everything seemed in doubt—the supply of credit, the capacity of families to borrow, the ability of institutions to set prices in response to shifting market conditions. It was a crisis that curtailing higher education's wasteful practices, whatever they might be, would not have solved, just as it was a crisis that was not about affordability—though had higher education and its governmental sponsors not responded successfully, a college education could have ended up a whole lot more expensive for a whole lot of middle-class families.

The crisis revealed an extraordinary vulnerability—to the machinations of a market leader like Harvard, to the sheer size of the student loan business and the nefarious schemes that amount of loose change attracted, and to a credit market that was suddenly in trouble. That vulnerability will continue unless and until higher education collectively reorders its economic practices and policies. Governments will have to rethink the role of endowments and the tax-free advantages enjoyed by not-for-profit higher education—and in the process decide how for-profit higher education ought to mesh with an enterprise that sees itself promoting not just individual advantage but also the public good. Institutions, both individually and collectively, will have to rethink how they set prices and whether in fact alternate ways of doing business will allow a substantial reduction in the prices they charge. And families will once more have to explore whether savings can play a bigger role in the financing of a college education—provided there is an adequate supply of investment vehicles promising both safety and growth.

Not Four Horsemen but
a Trio of Tough Issues

One irony underlying the three issues I have placed on higher education's to-do list is that in defining them better—less as slogans and more as problems in search of solutions—I have made clear just how much needs to be done and done quickly. The learning revolution is upon us; higher education needs to understand its import in terms of what can be done now and what will require colleges and universities in general and their faculties in particular to change how they do business. Higher education will have to rethink what it means to be a learning enterprise, including the role the new electronic technologies and insights from the neurosciences have to play in recasting what happens in the classroom, laboratory, and library. The gap between advantaged and disadvantaged students is large and getting larger. College and universities will be required to do more to remediate past learning deficiencies. The larger challenge for higher education will be to learn to do more to help students in middle and high schools become college-ready learners. Finally, higher education's current financial system does look like a house of cards—too dependent on tax breaks that are likely to be called into question, too dependent on credit markets that can suddenly contract, too unsure of the rationale by which it sets prices and offers discounts, and at the same time unable to imagine alternate production functions that could in fact yield substantial price rollbacks.

Learning, attainment, money—a trio of truly tough issues.

12 | Changing Strategies

The history of American higher education is well supplied with reform movements that have gone nowhere. Despite fervent calls for change most often issued by a commission with an impressive masthead, nothing much happens—or worse, the only visible result is a lot of hurt feelings and a further hunkering down by the college and university leaders on whom successful change ultimately depends. Higher education traditionalists will want to argue that is as it should be: higher education does not need reforming, it's doing just fine as it is, thank you. Cynics and skeptics, lamenters and critics will once again shake their heads, having been reminded anew just how hard it is to change a Teflon-coated enterprise. The public, however, will hardly notice, having decided long ago that the nation's colleges and universities, for all their importance, are beyond their understanding.

That fizzled reform efforts are old should surprise no one, nor should the realization that the history of higher education reform is a story that involves a lot of proclaiming and very little action. My own take on this aspect of the enterprise boils down to three basic lessons.

- *Don't vilify.* Broad-scale attacks that are long on strong language and short on realistic prescriptions can only isolate those within the academy who promote reform.

- *Don't play games*. Don't ask a lot of busy as well as important people to participate in a process that is mostly charade. Most national commissions are staff operations in which the chair and a handful of consultants do all the work.
- *Start with a viable strategy for change*. Within most reform movements there is too often a rush to judgment—an eagerness to tell the world what is wrong and to just as quickly specify how those wrongs can be righted, principally by someone else. No one ever seems to talk about the process of change itself or the need to develop long-term strategies that bring people and organizations together to develop common definitions and shared solutions.

A Process Rather than a Commission

Perhaps the underlying as well as the most important message is that reform, while possible, is very difficult. The task facing would-be reformers is daunting. They have to know what they want and what they are doing. They have to be genuine friends of the academy, agents of change whose proposals are widely accepted as improving the academy, as warding off a calamity that the academy perceives as a clear and present danger, or as responding to changes in the academy's external environment. At the same time, the proposed changes cannot be list-like; rather, they have to grow out of a process that is both central to and centered in the academy. Finally, sustained change has to involve the academy's principal funders and regulators, although these agencies cannot mandate their own prescriptions for change.

Currently the best example of a successful effort to change higher education is Europe's Bologna Process—an effort that began in 1998 when the ministers of education from Germany, France, Italy, and the United Kingdom issued the Sorbonne Declaration signaling their goal of achieving greater integration across European higher education. A year later, twenty-six European ministers of education followed up with a second, more inclusive communiqué spelling out their collective goal of increasing "the international competitiveness of the European system of higher education." Given that "the vitality and efficiency of any civilisation can be measured by the appeal that its culture has for other countries," the signatories to this *Bologna Communiqué* proclaimed, "We need to ensure that the European higher education system acquires a world-wide degree of attraction equal to our extraordinary cultural and scientific traditions."[1] The challenge these reformers tackled was a higher education environment that was too fragmented and too dependent on local customs to allow European universities to become major players in the emerging world-wide market for higher education. Two specific problems concerned those who gathered in Bologna in the spring of 1999. First, they wanted to ensure the comparability and transferability of university degrees across Europe; and second, they wanted company as each of their countries began experimenting with the increased tuition and fees that were becoming necessary to supplement, perhaps in the future supplant, governmental appropriations.

The ministers of education put in place a process of extended consultation and cooperation that would ultimately propel their national systems of higher education along a path of greater integration and cooperation. Everybody had a role; everybody was consulted, although the ministers of education in biennial meetings kept the process on track. Meeting by meeting, year by year, communiqué by communiqué, European higher education's principal constituencies defined and then oversaw the implementation of protocols and agreements that, for European universities, made a commonly defined, three-year baccalaureate degree the standard European undergraduate degree. This process has gone a long way toward creating commonality and interchangeability among and between Europe's competing systems of higher education. What began slowly, almost haltingly, perhaps even accidentally, is now being celebrated as a remarkable achievement in multinational cooperation and reform.

In the spring of 2008 the European Higher Education Area, now grown to forty-six members, began planning for a new round of university reforms to be implimented by 2020. The process itself is now overseen by a representative body commonly referred to as BFUG, for Bologna Follow-up Group. BFUG includes representatives of all the participating countries, key higher education organizations like the European Association of Universities, major student groups, international organizations like UNESCO, the International Association of Universities, the Council of Europe, and the European Union, which has assumed the role as the principal facilitator of the Bologna Process. For each meeting, which occur regularly and often, one or more nations, through its ministry of education, has principal responsibility for planning and logistics and, most important, for organizing the agenda, inviting the participants, and ensuring a rich variety of papers and presentations. The first meetings belong to the policy wonks;

the last say belongs to the ministers of education; and in between, the universities, the students, and the international as well as European organizations that are part of the process will help shape the initiatives to become the hallmarks of the second round of the Bologna Process.

What does American higher education and its would-be reformers have to learn from their European counterparts? At least three characteristics of the European process are worth noting in answer to that question.

- The change process was conceived of as a multiyear, decade-long undertaking. No need to hurry. No need to try to fix everything in a single year of frantic activity.
- It was a process explicitly linking six sets of key actors: ministers of education, university leaders, student leaders, leaders of international organizations, European Union bureaucrats, and policy wonks. The latter analysts help define the issues and shape the agenda. The European Union bureaucracy helps staff the meetings and ensures that schedules are kept and deliverables delivered. University leaders serve as much needed brakes by insisting that the policy wonks proposals have institutional traction. Student leaders, when not overly strident about the fee issue, keep the process honest. The ministers of education are the final authority by providing the necessary political muscle to implement reforms.
- Finally, the process proved both disciplined and focused. A limited number of goals were set with clear benchmarks leading to verifiable implementations.

It certainly makes for an interesting parlor game to speculate about whether a similar process, as opposed to a national commission, might be the better path to the reforming of higher education in the United States. Imagine, for the moment, that the president of the United States, having made energizing American higher education an election promise, asks his secretary of education to organize, not a national commission, but a multiyear, probably a multiterm, process focusing on the future of higher education in the United States. Such a process might look something like the following.

Phase 1. The secretary begins the process with a thoughtful paper focusing on the three higher education issues that concern her the most: the persistent gap between majority and minority students in their attainment of a baccalaureate degree, the need to develop stable funding principles for higher education, and the capacity of American colleges and universities to develop new learning strategies reflecting the insights of the neurosciences and the growing sophistication of electronically mediated instruction.

At the same time she announces her don't-do list—don't get lost trying to reform intercollegiate sports; put off attempts to make the accreditation process more effective; similarly do not waste time focusing on academic tenure; and leave to the president's task force on science and technology the question of the nation's investment in basic research.

During this initial year she quietly meets with a wide variety of college and university leaders, the leaders of higher education's national associations, and a wide range of policy wonks. By midyear she begins to form working groups charged with suggesting strategies for tackling her three principal concerns. By June 2010 she has received a good number of interesting papers that she begins to circulate among higher education's principal constituencies.

Phase 2. This phase of the process is kicked off with a higher education summit presided over by the president and attended by all fifty state governors along with key senators and congressmen. In carefully prepared sessions the president, his secretary of education, and her staff, supported by the key participants of *Phase 1*, succeed in winning a bipartisan political commitment to explore the strategies the secretary has identified as promising. At the conclusion of the summit, the fifty governors pledge to designate their states' chief educational officers as the public officials charged with making sure every state is fully engaged in the planning necessary to implement the principles the governors have just endorsed. This planning to plan and then planning to implement activity consumes the balance of the next two years, with the chief educational officers meeting together at least twice.

Phase 3. With the outlines of an agreed-upon pathway to change in hand, the process takes on a life of its own. Key staff members from The Education Commission of the States are asked both to provide administrative support and to help facilitate the next steps of the process. The elected officials participating in the process work out a way to establish a broadly representative steering committee. This two-year planning period, which spans a presidential election, is increasingly devoted to working out the details necessary to implement the proposed change strategies. Meetings—both large and small, public as well as quasi-private—continue to be held with the explicit purpose of sustaining the consensus to move forward even in the face of a growing opposition from a variety of special interest groups who have known all along their power resides in the old ways of doing business.

During this period there is a pause to absorb the results of the 2012 national elections. Regardless of which party wins, there has been sufficient bipartisan involvement to make it difficult to derail the effort. No doubt another four-year cycle of meetings, consultations, presidential convenings, and public discussion will follow. Patience will become an important strategy in itself.

Could it happen this way? Could the process be truly bipartisan? Could the fifty states actually work together and with the U.S. Congress in first developing and then implementing strategies to promote purposeful change? Perhaps not, but it is certainly worth thinking about.

Lessons for the Reform Minded

Many lessons can be drawn from these experiences.

- Strong rhetoric changes nothing—not even a strongly worded indictment based on what the reformers believe is overwhelming evidence. It is simply not possible to shame the academy into changing.
- Demand for reform must be internal. Faculty do not necessarily have to want to reform, but they do have to see in the proposed reform a means to a desirable end that is important to them. Absent that demand nothing much will happen. The reformer must create conditions that make faculty respond in their own interest—and, to repeat, no amount of rhetoric is likely to create those conditions.
- Public agencies can help engineer change, but their levers for doing so are quite specific and in that sense often limited. Money—the more the better—helps but cannot in itself secure the changes the reformers want. An unwillingness to invest new funds in the enterprise, however, almost guarantees that change will not be forthcoming given higher education's longstanding practice of hunkering down when appropriations are cut and other revenues dry up. Like outside reformers, state agencies cannot prescribe change (unless they are prepared for a long, exhausting battle); what state agencies must do to change higher education is create

the conditions and circumstances that make change possible, even likely.

- It is best to focus on truly systemic change—that is, to promote conditions and circumstances that make most if not all institutions rethink first their assumptions and then their operations—or more precisely, their production functions. The nature of the academy sucks the air out of piecemeal reforms. People lose interest; old ways win out; new problems arise; and not least, the reform itself begins to appear less than perfect.

Still, many within American higher education will be uncomfortable with the idea of a federally organized process. Some, arguing the cure is worse than the disease, then will wonder whether American higher education really needs to be reformed or changed after all. Others, particularly the leaders of the nation's private colleges and universities, will argue that the market, for all its imperfections, is a better gauge of what works and doesn't work in higher education.

The problem, as Richard Vedder and others including Charles Miller have pointed out, is that in the American higher education market the classic rules of supply and demand at best imperfectly hold sway. To put the matter most simply, in a market so awash with federal funds in the form of direct grants and guaranteed and subsidized loans to students and parents and direct purchase of research services competitive pressures are not sufficient to change the system writ large. Perhaps, were there a genuine consumers' movement (like the one Lloyd Thacker champions) the nation's colleges and universities would in time change both what and how they teach. But that, at best, that is a twenty-year proposition with no guarantee that what consumers may want is what the nation, in the end, requires of its colleges and universities.

Making the Earth Shake

Since the publication of *Remaking the American University* in 2005, I have returned frequently to this question of how one might promote—as in assist, facilitate, spur—change across higher education. The imaginary scenario of a Bologna-like reform process was one result of my musing. A second was an extended conversation with Bill Massy during which I found myself arguing that the nation's colleges and universities are not going to be forced to change by outsiders, even outside-insiders like Massy himself. While agreeing that the only ones who understand, who really know where the bodies are buried, are inside the academy, he presented me with the following query. "Suppose," he said, "somebody outside the academy felt it was imperative that higher education change direction. Further suppose that the person I have in mind is what you have called an 'outside-insider,' somebody who has spent all or part of his or her life working for a public agency responsible for higher education policy—someone like Pat Callan; or again, somebody like me, a former professor and senior administrator at Stanford who is now a full-time higher education consultant and researcher; or somebody like John Merrow or even Charles Miller of the Spellings Commission. What are we to do? Just stand idly by even though we know that American colleges and universities are not all they are supposed to be, that is, they could both do more and do it better?"

My initial response was to quip, "Better to spend your time on a feasible project like ending global warming or reducing the world's dependence on fossil fuels." But his question got me thinking: why did reform-minded outsiders or even outside-insiders like himself so consistently fail to launch self-sustaining reform efforts? In constructing an answer that even Bill found plausible, perhaps even persuasive, I began to spell out what it might take to launch a successful reform effort.

I started with the assumption that American higher education writ large will not be changed one institution at a time. Individual institutions can and do change, and very occasionally they transform themselves. But their successes tend to pale with time as the inertia in the system draws almost all institutions back to a mean that brooks only minor changes. Appointing yet another national commission will work no better than before. Traditionally such bodies have been expected to produce a catalog of problems and a matching list of solutions—and there's the rub. National commissions, by their very nature and charters, are temporary bodies without the power to either implement or monitor the changes they have recommended. Their reports become elongated to-do lists full of separable actions to be performed by somebody else. This process at best produces a rationale for change, but not a strategy sufficient to overcome institutional inertia and, in the case of American higher education, the public's traditional disengagement.

Instead, we require a process whose ultimate goal is divining a set of circumstances that quite literally will change most, if not all, of higher education simultaneously. Because a catalog of problems and solutions won't yield the desired change, required, instead, is a kind of *dislodging event* of sufficient force that the academy writ large begins to consider changes that no one institution on its own will likely pursue. The challenge facing reformers is to first imagine a set of changing circumstances—that is, one or more dislodging events—that creates sufficient momentum that change becomes possible, and eventually inevitable.

To understand how a dislodging event might promote reform, you need to embrace the notion the American higher education system is, in fact, a system in which the various parts, despite their unique missions and organizational arrangements, are linked to one another so that what happens *here* is almost always translated into something happening *there*. It helps to think in terms of a hydraulic system, or even a Rube Goldberg contraption, in which pressure on one point or valve is transferred, though often imperfectly, through the whole system. If one wants to change or redesign such a system, all of the parts and various combinations must be considered simultaneously.

In the case of American higher education, what makes the system both complex and at times inscrutable is the fact that it has evolved over the last half century from the interplay of three quite separate forces: a segmented and hierarchical student market along with a largely homogenous market for faculty; an accreditation process that imposes a common set of definitions on nearly all institutions despite their very real differences; and a plethora of federal student financial aid programs that apply a wide array of rules and regulations to all institutions, again regardless of their different circumstances.

Over the last three years I have taken to asking friends, colleagues, students, even potential adversaries, Can you imagine a dislodging event of sufficient magnitude that it breaks the gridlock that now holds attempts to reform higher education hostage? Can you construct a dislodging scenario to which faculty, in particular, will respond in such a way that higher education is changed for better or worse?

My questions have produced three pretty good answers. Although none may prove feasible, or even desirable, collectively they make the idea of a dislodging event seem at least plausible.

A first dislodging event strikes at the federal level. The new Congress could metaphorically "nuke" the current system of federal student financial aid. Having agreed at the outset that the alternative system would receive the same level of federal funding as does the current catalogue of federal programs, Congress, the administration, and the nation's principal higher education organizations would turn the experts loose to craft a system that funds participation, invests in motivation, and rewards institutions that use federal aid funds effectively. Such a system would involve better incentives for family savings, get students (perhaps as early as sixth grade) actively engaged in planning and saving for college, and link what happens in middle and secondary schools more directly to what happens in colleges and universities. In the process, Congress and the administration would have to make better sense of how the nation's capital markets supply the loan funds necessary to make the system work.

Such changes would reverberate across the system. Institutions would have to rethink how they set their prices, use their own funds to offer tuition and other discounts, and more generally fund their operations. Almost certainly we would need to address the question of whether students should receive federal assistance while enrolled in remedial courses. Moreover, we would need to consider the question of whether enrollment in those courses should lessen a student's eligibility for a full four years of support for courses receiving college credits.

There could be lots of wrinkles in the new system specifically designed to increase both participation and attainment. My favorite concept was first suggested to me by Jonathan Grayer, who proposed giving every sixth grader in the nation a $10,000 529 Plan—that is, a federally guaranteed qualified tuition plan whose value would grow as the federally monitored stock accounts increased in value over time.

Actually, Grayer's notion of creating federally funded and guaranteed 529 Plans can be seen as a dislodging event in its own right; the impact of this policy initiative would cascade across higher education and address a whole variety of issues and challenges. To begin, the existence of the account becomes a powerful motivating tool because the funds can only be spent on postsecondary education. Colleges and universities, particularly those in urban environments where high school graduates during the next decade will likely be in short supply, would have both opportunity and rationale for working early with the prefunded middle and secondary school students in their neighborhood. As a result, institutions might be committed to growing and not just recruiting their future students; then faculties might also be more committed to understanding how their would-be students learn as well as determining what they know. Finally, faculty at these institutions might come to realize that, to teach the kinds of students they like to teach, they must take a more direct role in creating the educational contexts in which young students thrive academically.

Federally funded 529 Plans could even help spark a broad-based e-consumer movement in which students and their families learn to ask early and often the really tough questions about the nature and quality of the higher education they are purchasing. Such a system would fundamentally reorder relationships between and among students as consumers, institutions as providers, and banks and other financial entities as suppliers of capital. Faculty would have to accommodate more purposeful consumers who just might turn out to be more informed about what they need to learn. The administrative side of the house would have to rethink how prices are set, what services are provided, and what kinds of information would have to be routinely made available to prospective purchasers.

A second dislodging event targets its greatest impact on those institutions, both public and private, with substantial endowments: at least $200 million for institutions of fewer than 5,000 students and $800 million for institutions with more than 5,000 students. In this scenario, the system that provides federal student aid is not recast; instead, recasting centers on the web of tax and related regulations that define the benefits not-for-profit colleges and universities enjoy. The impetus for change in this domain is the growing realization that institutions with substantial endowments have become like hedge funds; they both use their accumulated capital to make money through the shrewd buying and selling of capital assets. It is not that hard to imagine Congress passing and the president signing legislation requiring college and university endowments to pay the same taxes on the monies they earn from their investments that other, similarly constituted hedge funds are required to pay. A relatively simple rule could differentiate the strictly commercial from the educational: all dividends, interest, rents, and realized capital gains would be taxed at current rates; however, the money owed the Internal Revenue Service would be reduced by the amount of cash the institution withdrew from its endowment to fund educational and research programs. In years when the monies spent exceeded the growth in the value of the endowment, a credit would be awarded to offset future taxes. This proposal would have little effect on institutions with smaller endowments. However, the megabillion-dollar endowments that frequently earn returns in excess of 15 percent and occasionally 20 percent annually would have to choose between substantially increasing their expenditures on education and research and paying substantial federal taxes.

Changing the tax rules on endowments is an example of a dislodging event that would, at best, have mixed consequences. Institutions with large endowments that substantially increased their spending on research and education would flourish, and their students would benefit; the rest of higher education, however, would find itself increasingly disadvantaged in the competition for students and staff. One result could be a drastic consolidation of the industry. Or perhaps state governments would step into the breach, providing more funding to their comprehensive institutions in particular as they sought to keep them more competitive. If a substantial number of institutions chose to pay taxes instead of increasing their research and education spending, then the unintended consequences of their decision just might be a renewed scrutiny of the academy as a source of tax revenue for cash-strapped states and localities. The resulting fracas, at a minimum, would draw state legislatures and perhaps some segment of the public into an examination of just when a college or university is an eleemosynary institution and when it is not. A productive discussion of these issues just might address questions of purpose as well as the economists' and accountants' concerns with how best to organize a charitable enterprise.

My third dislodging event might promote the broadest change in American higher education. What would happen if a Bologna-like process of reform concluded that the standard undergraduate degree in the United States, as in Europe, should be a three-year baccalaureate? Remember the process I described above included all the interested parties: the state agencies responsible for public systems of higher education, the Education Commission of the states as a facilitating organization, Congress, and higher education's key organizations. What might convince such a polyglot group to adopt and then push for such a radical change?

Actually, a host of reasons affirms the sensibility of such a reform. With more and more Americans pursuing advanced degrees, it makes sense to look for ways to shorten the undergraduate portion of their postsecondary educations. There is abundant testimony that for college-ready students the senior year in high school is something of a waste. More of that year's curriculum could be devoted to acquiring advanced college-ready skills in a foreign language, composition, and mathematics, in particular, so that students are ready for more advanced work in their first year of college. Though the community colleges will see themselves as threatened, a nationally adopted three-year baccalaureate degree could well prove a boon to them by clearly identifying and funding them as the places where students go to complete their precollegiate education. Community colleges could continue to provide the first year of collegiate instruction for students of limited means as well as for students seeking a low-risk higher education portal. Finally, provided the four-year curriculum was actually pared to three years, an undergraduate education would see an immediate 25-percent reduction in cost.

In many ways, the second-order effects of a shift to a three-year baccalaureate curriculum make the proposal attractive and establish its bona fides as a truly dislodging event. Suddenly all the questions about teaching and learning would be on the table as faculty everywhere wrestled with questions of how to teach what. To judge whether their now-compacted educational programs were achieving the same learning outcomes as their four-year degree programs had promised, faculties everywhere would find themselves in need of the performance measures they had hitherto eschewed. Technology would likely become a handmaiden of change rather than an educational add-on, while the balance between general and specialized education would have to be restruck.

There would be further second-order consequences as well. Most observers agree that higher education is due for some pruning; too many perilous institutions barely hang on largely by paying lower salaries, hiring an ever-increasing number of adjuncts, and putting off much needed investments in physical plant and technology. Already the pace of mergers and acquisitions has quickened and would likely become something like a stampede as these smaller, less successful institutions became part of larger conglomerations. Others will simply close. In states strapped for cash, the conversion to a three-year baccalaureate degree would likely speed the conversion of their state systems of higher education into networks in which each of the previously independent institutions became an interchangeable node on an educational network that would look remarkably like a not-for-profit University of Phoenix.

These examples of dislodging events are offered as just that—examples. I am recommending a fundamental change in how both those inside and those outside of higher education conceive of the process by which higher education changes what it is about. I am decidedly interested in neither a long list of problems and shortcomings nor the specific solutions particular segments of the population or

political process or even the academy are likely to promote as reme-
dies. Let me repeat my earlier observation. None of us knows what
tomorrow will bring. At best we can organize an ongoing process that
includes all the key players. The meetings that are convened, the com-
muniqués that are issued, the joint working groups that are appointed
all need to focus first on the conditions that will promote change in
higher education. A very explicit and yet open-ended discussion of
how change takes place and a willingness to let a duly constituted
reform process evolve its own agenda are required. To succeed, that
process will need public affirmation, bureaucratic support, and, above
all, time and money. The most anyone can do to steer what happens
next is to suggest a limited number of issues to be discussed when
launching the reform process. I have suggested three—learning, attainment, and money.

Here then is a summary of the argument that has brought me to this
point. To transform American higher education, what is required, in
addition to time and energy, is a process that has the imprimatur of a
full cast of cooperating actors—the president of the United States, the
secretary of education, members of key senate and congressional committees and their principal staff, the governors and key educational
officials from all fifty states, the leaders of organized higher education
including faculty and staff unions, a goodly number of venerated college and university presidents, a wide variety of policy wonks and
their organizations, and, not least, an inquiring as well as curious
media. Getting all these actors to work together requires a process that
is explorative as well as disciplined and focused. The effort must be
conceived as an investment in the academy, rather than a critique or
audit of past or present foibles. The effort must also focus on change
strategies rather than on a list of either problems or solutions. Those
who participate in this process must be allowed to work toward a different set of means and, in some cases, even an altered set of ends,
rather than assured at the beginning that we know tomorrow's needs.
To overcome the gridlock that, for most of the last half century, has
held reform captive, it will be necessary to create conditions that foster
change—even change for change's sake—such that those within the
academy will own the resulting alterations. The transforming of
American higher education requires a process that, despite itself,
comes to consider the impossible. Proceeding along that path requires,
as well, a willingness to consider the kind of dislodging events that can
result in simultaneous change across higher education.

Seeing Straight through a Muddle

Just over two decades ago, the Pew Higher Education Roundtable—a panel of national experts and practitioners who liked to describe themselves "as working stiffs rather than pooh-bahs"—published its first *Policy Perspectives*. That issue's essay was bravely titled, "Seeing Straight through a Muddle," though a close reading of the text would belie its self-proclaimed confidence. The Roundtable set as the focus of its efforts just three issues—cost, quality teaching, and sorting, and then proclaimed: "The agenda for higher education we have laid out is not an easy one: control costs, pay greater attention to quality teaching and learning, ask colleges and universities to play major roles in reforming American schools and reaching out to the educationally and economically disadvantaged."[2]

It's more than a little unnerving that the reform issues I have placed at the top of higher education's agenda are remarkably close to the three issues *Policy Perspectives* gave top priority in 1988. Still, there have been some important changes. Cost containment as an issue has morphed into a more nuanced focus on how the market is reshaping higher education. Quality of teaching has been similarly transformed into a focus on learning, on what the neurosciences have to teach the academy about how the brain learns, and on the potential for electronically mediated learning to reorganize the collegiate learning processes. The issue of sorting, however, has hardly changed at all: it is still about attainment; it still focuses on improving the ability of American middle and secondary schools to produce college-ready graduates; and it is still about differential attainment rates that too easily correlate with ethnicity and economic status.

It is, however, not so much a matter of whether the glass is half empty or half full, but rather a matter of stalled progress and the sense of not knowing how or where to change higher education for the better. I want to close with something of a coda—the kind of preamble I have come to believe any successful reform effort is likely to require. I would remind those interested in reform that the nation's colleges are among the most American of institutions. Their history is America's history, from the founding of the first settlements in Massachusetts and Virginia, through the westward expansion of the nineteenth century, to the emergence of today's network linking public systems of higher education, private colleges and universities, and specialized postsecondary training institutions. It is a history replete with the milestones of public affirmation and public purpose: the Morrill Act of 1862, which made land-grant universities an integral part of the American landscape; the publication in 1945 of Vannevar Bush's *Science: The Endless Frontier*, which helped make the modern research university a uniquely American invention; the GI Bill following the Second World War, which first made access to higher education a national priority; and, in the 1960s and 1970s, the launching and rapid growth of community colleges to the point that they now enroll more than one-third of all students in higher education in the United States.

The emergence of a truly American system of higher and postsecondary education–at once diverse, stable, and successful–is one of this nation's great achievements. For nearly a century now, access to higher education has been a principal—some would say *the* principal—means to personal and societal advancement. Much of America's inventiveness has been centered in institutions of higher education, as has the nation's commitment to a democracy that only an educated and informed citizenry makes possible. It is not surprising that American institutions of higher education have become a magnet for attracting people of talent and ambition from throughout the world.

That world has now changed, becoming tougher, more competitive, less forgiving of wasted resources and squandered opportunities. In tomorrow's world a nation's wealth will derive from its capacity to educate, attract, and retain citizens who are to able to work smarter and learn faster—making educational achievement ever more important for both individuals and society writ large.

Thus, I pose the question that I have now spent more than two hundred pages trying to cogently answer: Will the American system of higher and postsecondary education provide the same competitive advantage in the future as it has in the past? My guess is that most, but probably not all, of the nation's colleges and universities will likely survive, and the very best no doubt will thrive. But to fully answer the challenge contained in my question will require a renewed sense of mission and a commitment to focused and purposeful change. I have come to understand the extent to which American higher education has become a mature enterprise—too often risk averse, more than occasionally complacent, and inherently expensive. This enterprise has yet to address the fundamental issues of how academic programs and institutions must be transformed to serve the changing educational needs of a knowledge economy; it has yet to successfully confront the impact of globalization, rapidly evolving technologies, an increasingly

diverse and aging population, and an evolving marketplace characterized by new needs and new paradigms.

Here I am reminded of Derek Bok's plea that what is most amiss in
American higher education today is a reluctance to talk about purposes—
to which I would add, values and strategies for change. American
higher education will certainly survive, probably in a form that is not
that much different than today. But will it be all that it can be? My
answer: not without a sustained reform process that is open ended,
purposeful, and faculty centered.

Notes

CHAPTER 1. PRELUDE TO REFORM

1. Kelly Field, "Education-Department Panel Will Develop a 'National Strategy' for Colleges," Chronicle of Higher Education, September 30, 2005, A29.
2. Derek Bok, "A Test Colleges Don't Need," Washington Post, March 6, 2006, B07.
3. Peter McPherson and David Schulenburger, *Improving Student Learning in Higher Education through Better Accountability and Assessment*, a discussion paper for the National Association of State Universities and Land Grant Colleges, http://www.scribd.com/doc/1232572/-description-tags-mcpherson.
4. Doug Lederman, "Coalescing around Concepts," Inside Higher Education, April 7, 2006.
5. Ibid.
6. Secretary of Education's Commission on the Future of Higher Education, Draft Report, June 12, 2006.
7. Karen W. Arenson, "Panel's Draft Report Calls for an Overhaul of Higher Education Nationwide," *New York Times,* June 27, 2006; Kelly Field, "Draft Report from Federal Panel on Higher Education Takes Aim at Academe," *Chronicle of Higher Education,* June 27, 2006; Justin Pope, "Commission Draft Report Calls for Shake-up in Higher Education," Associated Press, June 27, 2006.
8. Ralph K. M. Haurwitz, "Chairman Defends Panel's Call for Reforms in Higher Education," *Austin American-Statesman,* June 30, 2006.
9. Secretary of Education's Commission on the Future of Higher Education, *A Test of Leadership: Charting the Future of U.S. Higher Education,* September 2006, http://www.ed.gov/about/bdscomm/list/hiedfuture/reports/final-report.pdf.
10. Kelly Field, "Secretary's Proposals Reassure Some Education Leaders, Disappoint Others," *Chronicle of Higher Education,* September 27, 2006.

11. Kelly Field, "Spellings Lays Out 'Action Plan' for Colleges," *Chronicle of Higher Education*, October 6, 2006, A1.

12. Doug Lederman, "The Sounds of Conciliation," *Inside Higher Education*, September 27, 2006.

13. Sam Dillon, "Secretary Vows to Improve Results of Higher Education," *New York Times,* September 27, 2006.

14. Secretary of Education's Commission on the Future of Higher Education, *A Test of Leadership: Charting the Future of U.S. Higher Education*, September 2006, http://www.ed.gov/about/bdscomm/list/hiedfuture/reports/final-report.pdf.

15. Paul Basken, "Colleges Emerge the Clear Winner in the Battle Over Accreditation," *Chronicle of Higher Education*, February 1, 2008.

CHAPTER 2. THE WINE OF OUR DISCONTENT

1. Richard H. Hersh and John Merrow, eds., *Declining by Degrees: Higher Education at Risk* (New York: Palgrave Macmillan, 2005), 2, 9.

2. Ibid., 17, 13.

3. Ibid., 27.

4. Ibid., 40, 39.

5. Ibid., 78.

6. Ibid., 90.

7. Ibid., 76, 69.

8. Ibid., 69.

9. National Center for Public Policy and Higher Education, *Measuring Up 2000: The State-by-State Report Card for Higher Education* (San Jose, Calif.: Author, 2000), 12–13.

10. Ibid., 9–10.

11. National Center for Public Policy and Higher Education, *Measuring Up 2002: The State-by-State Report Card for Higher Education* (San Jose, Calif.: Author, 2002), 16.

12. National Center for Public Policy and Higher Education, *Measuring Up 2004: The National Report Card on Higher Education* (San Jose, Calif.: Author, 2004), 6.

13. National Center for Public Policy and Higher Education, *Measuring Up 2006: The National Report Card on Higher Education* (San Jose, Calif.: Author, 2006), 8.

14. Ibid., 22.

15. John Merrow, executive producer, *Declining by Degrees: Higher Education at Risk* (Cleveland, Ohio: Learning Matters, Inc., 2005), PBS documentary, transcript.

16. Ibid.

17. Robert Zemsky, Gregory R. Wegner, and William F. Massy, *Remaking the American University: Market-Smart and Mission-Centered* (New Brunswick, N.J.: Rutgers University Press, 2005), 29.

18. National Commission on Educational Excellence, *A Nation at Risk: The Imperative for Educational Reform*, April 2003, http://www.ed.gov/pubs/NatAtRisk/index.html.

19. "The College Issue," *New York Times Sunday Magazine*, September 30, 2007, 25–26.

20. Ibid., 32.

21. Ibid., 34.

22. Ibid., 43.
23. Hersh and Merrow, eds., *Declining by Degrees*, 9.

CHAPTER 3. COMMODIFICATION AND OTHER SINS

1. "The College Issue," *New York Times Sunday Magazine*, September 30, 2007, 25.
2. Audrey Williams June, "Why Presidents Are Paid So Much More than Professors," *Chronicle of Higher Education*, November 16, 2007, B3.
3. Elizabeth Greene, "A Sociologist Urges Colleges to Forget Careers and Foster Intellectual Growth," *Chronicle of Higher Education*, March 17, 2000, A20.
4. Richard K. Vedder, *Going Broke by Degree: Why College Costs Too Much* (Washington, D.C.: American Enterprise Institute, 2004), xv.
5. Ibid., 27.
6. Zemsky, Wegner, and Massy, *Remaking the American University*, 52.
7. Derek Bok, *Universities in the Marketplace: The Commercialization of Higher Education* (Princeton, N.J.: Princeton University Press, 2003), x.
8. Ibid., 6, 5.
9. Ibid., 6.
10. Ibid., 113.
11. Ibid., 200.
12. Ibid., 156.
13. Ibid., 104.
14. David L. Kirp, *Shakespeare, Einstein, and the Bottom Line: The Marketing of Higher Education* (Cambridge, Mass.: Harvard University Press, 2003), 3–4.
15. Ibid., 4.
16. Ibid., 16.
17. Ibid., 18.
18. Ibid., 33.
19. Ibid., 41.
20. Ibid., 45.
21. Ibid., 45.
22. Ibid., 41–42.
23. Ibid., 51.
24. Bok, *Universities in the Marketplace*, 97.

CHAPTER 4. THE WAY WE ARE

1. National Center for Postsecondary Improvement, *Change*, September/October 2001, 23.
2. John Immerwahr and Tony Foleno, *Great Expectations: How the Public and Parents—White, African-American and Hispanic—View Higher Education* (San Jose, Calif.: National Center for Public Policy and Higher Education, May 2002), 33–34.
3. John Immerwahr, *Public Attitudes on Higher Education: A Trend Analysis, 1993 to 2003* (San Jose, Calif.: National Center for Public Policy and Higher Education, February 2004), 1.
4. Ibid., 2.
5. Ibid., 3, 11.
6. John Immerwahr and Jean Johnson, *Squeeze Play: How Parents and the Public Look at Higher Education Today* (San Jose, Calif.: National Center for Public Policy and Higher Education, May 2007), section 1, pp. 11, 17.

7. Ibid., section 1, p. 2.
8. Ibid., section 1, pp. 29–37.
9. "Special Report," *Chronicle of Higher Education*, May 7, 2004.
10. Immerwahr and Johnson, *Squeeze Play*, section 1, p. 22.
11. Ibid., section 1, p. 23.

CHAPTER 5. THE RAIN MAN COMETH—AGAIN

1. Robert Zemsky and William F. Massy, "The Rain Man Cometh," *AGB Reports*, January/February, 22.
2. Ibid.
3. Colin Diver, "Is There Life after Rankings?" *Atlantic Monthly*, November 2005, volume 296, number 4, http://www.theatlantic.com/doc/200511/shunning-college-rankings.
4. Educational Conservancy, "Beyond Ranking: Responding to the Call for Useful Information," Conference Planning Paper, September 25, 2007.
5. "Cover Story," *BusinessWeek*, October 23, 2006.
6. National Survey of Student Engagement, "The College Student Report—Sample," 2007.
7. National Survey of Student Engagement, "NSSE-USA TODAY Initiative: Frequently Asked Questions," http://www.nsse.iub.edu/html/USAT_initiative.cfm.

CHAPTER 6. SCANDALS WAITING TO HAPPEN

1. Karin Fischer, "New York Asks 60 Colleges to Explain Ties to Lenders," *Chronicle of Higher Education*, February 16, 2007, A32.
2. Kelly Field and Josh Keller, "New York Attorney General Accuses Colleges of Deceiving Students on Their Loans," *Chronicle of Higher Education*, March 30, 2007, A22.
3. Kelly Field and David Glenn, "House Panel Interrogates Spellings on Student Loans and Reading Program," *Chronicle of Higher Education*, May 18, 2007, A21.
4. Jonathan D. Glater, "College Loans by States Face Fresh Scrutiny," *New York Times*, December 9, 2007.
5. Ibid.
6. Ibid.
7. Brad Bumsted, "Pigging Out at PHEAA," *Pittsburgh Tribune-Review*, September 2, 2007.
8. Pennsylvania, Department of the State Auditor, "Auditor General Jack Wagner Finds PHEAA Gave $7.5 Million in Bonuses to Hundreds of Employees," News Release, October 4, 2007.
9. "The Million-Dollar President, Soon to Be Commonplace?" *Chronicle of Higher Education*, December 24, 2006, B3.
10. Audrey Williams June, "College Presidents Break into the Million-Dollar Club," *Chronicle of Higher Education*, November 18, 2005, B12.
11. Paul Fain, "University of California President Will Keep His Job," *Chronicle of Higher Education*, June 2, 2006, A25.
12. Ibid.
13. Eleanor Yang, "UCSD Chancellor Gets Extra $248,000," *San Diego Union-Tribune*, January 19, 2006.
14. Eleanor Yang Su, "Fox Quits One of 10 Board Positions," *San Diego Union-Tribune*, December 21, 2007.

15. Karen W. Arenson, "Columbia to Pay $1.1 Million to State Fund in Loan Scandal," *New York Times*, June 1, 2007.
16. Paul Basken and Kelly Field, "Investigation of Lenders' Ties to Colleges Expands," *Chronicle of Higher Education*, April 13, 2007, A1.
17. Jonathan D. Glater and Sam Dillon, "Student Lender Planned to Woo Officials," *New York Times*, April 10, 2007.
18. Karen W. Arenson, "Columbia Fires Its Director of Student Aid," *New York Times*, May 22, 2007.
19. Karen W. Arenson and Diana Jean Schemo, "Report Details Deals in Student Loan Industry," *New York Times*, June 15, 2007.
20. Scott Jaschik, "Admissions Official and Consultant—at the Same Time," *Inside Higher Education*, February 1, 2008.
21. Alan Finder, "Event for Education Officials Sets One-on-One Sales Meetings," *New York Times*, July 10, 2007.
22. Ibid.
23. Ibid.
24. Robert Zemsky, "Into the Wind," http://www.chronicle.com/review/brainstorm/zemsky/into-the-wind.

CHAPTER 7. THE FOUR HORSEMEN OF ACADEMIC REFORM

1. Kelly Field, "Federal Commission Holds First Meeting," *Chronicle of Higher Education*, October 28, 2005, A32.
2. Special Report, "Thirty & Broke," *Business Week*, November 14, 2005.
3. National Center for Public Policy and Higher Education, *Measuring Up 2004: The National Report Card on Higher Education* (San Jose, Calif.: Author, 2004), 8.
4. Floyd Institute for Public Policy Analysis, Franklin and Marshall College, *Pennsylvania's Higher Education Participation Survey* (Lancaster, Pa.: Author, 2005), 8.

CHAPTER 8. FLAT-WORLD CONTRARIANS

1. Karen Hughes, e-mail message to interested parties, US/TAG to ISO/TC 232 Educational Services, March 1, 2007.
2. University of Phoenix Web site, "About Us," http://www.phoenix.edu/about%5Fus/about_us.aspx.
3. Noam Cohen, "M.I.T. Education in Taiwan, Minus the Degree," *New York Times*, April 2, 2007.
4. Tamar Lewin, "U.S. Universities Rush to Set Up Outposts Abroad," *New York Times*, February 10, 2008.

CHAPTER 9. THE WRONG-WAY WEB

1. Robert Zemsky and William F. Massy, *Thwarted Innovation: What Happened to e-learning and Why* (West Chester, Pa.: The Learning Alliance, 2004), 8–9.
2. Larry Cuban, *Oversold and Underused—Computers in the Classroom* (Cambridge, Mass.: Harvard University Press, 2001), 13.
3. Ibid., 18.
4. Ibid., 66.
5. Ibid., 133.
6. Ibid., 170–173.
7. Ibid., 175.

8. Laura Isensee, "Relying on Technology Hinders Learning—Opinions," *Daily Texan,* January 29, 2003.

9. Facebook Web site, http://www.facebook.com.

CHAPTER 10. WERE LEARNING TO MATTER

1. Derek Bok, *Our Underachieving Colleges: A Candid Look at How Much Students Learn and Why They Should Be Learning More* (Princeton, N.J.: Princeton University Press, 2006), 8.

2. Ibid., 66.

3. Ibid., 319.

4. Ibid., 48.

5. Ibid., 116–117.

6. John D. Bransford, Ann L. Brown, and Rodney R. Cocking, eds., *How People Learn: Brain, Mind, Experience, and School* (Washington, D.C.: Committee on Developments in the Science of Learning, National Research Council, 1999), intro.

7. James Elwood Zull, *The Art of Changing the Brain: Enriching Teaching by Exploring the Biology of Learning* (Sterling, Va.: Stylus Publishing, 2002), 5.

8. Ibid., 13.

9. Ibid., 14.

10. Ibid., 93–94.

11. Ibid., 62–63.

12. Ibid., 63.

13. Ibid., 232.

14. Ibid., 129.

15. Ibid., 161.

16. Ibid., 184.

17. Ibid., 228.

18. Ibid., 245.

19. Carnegie Mellon University, Eberly Center for Teaching Excellence Web site, "Learning Principles," http://www.cmu.edu/teaching/principles/learning.html.

20. Ibid.

21. Carnegie Mellon University, Eberly Center for Teaching Excellence Web site, "What We Do," http://www.cmu.edu/teaching/eberly/WhatWeDo/index.html.

22. (Neuhauser, Presentation Materials, February 29, 2008).

23. Zull, *The Art of Changing the Brain,* 19.

24. Ibid., 43.

CHAPTER 11. BUILDING BLOCKS

1. William C. Friday and Rev. Theodore Hesburgh, *A Call to Action: Reconnecting College Sports and Higher Education,* Knight Foundation Commission on Intercollegiate Athletics, June 2001, http://www.knightfoundation.org/research_publications/detail.dot?id=178173.

2. Australian Universities Quality Agency Web site, http://www.auqa.edu.au/qualityaudit/qa/.

3. National Academy of Sciences Committee on Science, Engineering, and Public Policy (COSEPUP), *Rising Above the Gathering Storm: Energizing and Employing America for a Brighter Economic Future* (Washington, D.C.: National Academies Press, 2007), 25.

4. Robert Zemsky, Gregory R. Wegner, and William F. Massy, *Remaking the American University: Market-Smart and Mission-Centered* (New Brunswick, N.J.: Rutgers University Press, 2005), 49.

5. Doug Lederman, "The Harvard Trickle-Down Effect," *Inside Higher Education*, January 7, 2008.

CHAPTER 12. CHANGING STRATEGIES

1. European Higher Education Area, *Joint Declaration of the European Ministers of Education* (Bologna, Italy: June 19, 1999), 1.

2. Pew Higher Education Roundtable, *Policy Perspectives*, volume 1, number 1, 7.

Index

About the Author

In the *Chronicle for Higher Education* Robert Zemsky recently described himself as someone "old and round enough to be mistaken for a pooh-bah." In a forty-year career he has pioneered the use of market analyses for higher education, served as the University of Pennsylvania's chief planning officer, the founding director of Penn's Institute for Research on Higher Education, the convener of the Pew Higher Education Roundtable, chair of The Learning Alliance, and a member of the U.S. Secretary of Education's Commission on the Future of Higher Education (better known as the Spellings Commission). More recently he has focused on what globalism might mean for higher education, on what technology has not accomplished, and on how to make learning more important in the higher education marketplace.